mix it up

Recent Sociology Titles from W. W. Norton

Code of the Street by Elijah Anderson

In the Trenches: Teaching and Learning Sociology by Maxine P. Atkinson and Kathleen S. Lowney

Social Problems, Third Edition, by Joel Best

The Family: Diversity, Inequality, and Social Change by Philip N. Cohen

You May Ask Yourself: An Introduction to Thinking like a Sociologist, Fifth Edition, by Dalton Conley

Race in America by Matthew Desmond and Mustafa Emirbayer

The Real World: An Introduction to Sociology, Fifth Edition, by Kerry Ferris and Jill Stein

Introduction to Sociology, Tenth Edition, by Anthony Giddens, Mitchell Duneier, Richard P. Appelbaum, and Deborah Carr

Essentials of Sociology, Sixth Edition, by Anthony Giddens, Mitchell Duneier, Richard P. Appelbaum, and Deborah Carr

The Contexts Reader, Second Edition, edited by Douglas Hartmann and Christopher Uggen

Thinking Through Theory by John Levi Martin

Readings for Sociology, Eighth Edition, edited by Garth Massey

American Society: How It Really Works, Second Edition, by Erik Olin Wright and Joel Rogers

Families as They Really Are, Second Edition, edited by Barbara J. Risman and Virginia E. Rutter

Sex Matters: The Sexuality and Society Reader, Fourth Edition, by Mindy Stombler, Dawn M. Baunach, Wendy Simonds, Elroi J. Windsor, and Elisabeth O. Burgess

Gender: Ideas, Interactions, Institutions by Lisa Wade and Myra Marx Ferree

More than Just Race by William Julius Wilson

Cultural Sociology: An Introductory Reader by Matt Wray

For more information on Norton Sociology, please visit wwnorton.com/soc

mix it up

popular culture, mass media, and society

david grazian

University of Pennsylvania

W. W. Norton   New York   London

NORTON

W. W. Norton & Company has been independent since its founding in 1923, when William Warder Norton and Mary D. Herter Norton first published lectures delivered at the People's Institute, the adult education division of New York City's Cooper Union. The Nortons soon expanded their program beyond the Institute, publishing books by celebrated academics from America and abroad. By mid-century, the two major pillars of Norton's publishing program—trade books and college texts—were firmly established. In the 1950s, the Norton family transferred control of the company to its employees, and today—with a staff of four hundred and a comparable number of trade, college, and professional titles published each year—W. W. Norton & Company stands as the largest and oldest publishing house owned wholly by its employees.

Editor: Sasha Levitt
Managing editor, College: Marian Johnson
Project editor: Caitlin Moran
Editorial assistant: Miranda Schonbrun
Copyeditor: Theresa Kay
Production Supervisor: Liz Marotta
Design Director: Rubina Yeh
Book Designer: Brian Sisco
Photo Editor: Travis Carr
Layout by Carole Desnoes
Composition by Jouve North America
Manufacturing by LSC Communications

2009049573

W. W. Norton & Company, Inc., 500 Fifth Avenue, New York, NY 10110
www.wwnorton.com

W. W. Norton & Company, Ltd., Castle House, 75/76 Wells Street, London W1T3QT

1 2 3 4 5 6 7 8 9 0

For my family

Contents

Preface to the Second Edition

SOME ARGUE THAT POP CULTURE IS DISPOSABLE; OTHERS FIND IT despicable. No matter: In one form or another, it is here to stay. As a sociologist, one of the fun aspects of my job is deciphering what it all means, in part by exploring what different kinds of popular culture—mystery novels, dance music, animated films, reality television shows, video games, social media—may have in common. What makes popular culture *popular*, exactly? How do its numerous creators bring popular culture into existence? How do media companies like Spotify, Amazon, Sony, and Viacom decide which products to promote? Why do people seem to enjoy some genres of entertainment more than others?

Since you are reading this preface, perhaps these kinds of questions have occurred to you from time to time. The purpose of this book is to begin a sincere intellectual conversation about popular culture, admittedly a topic often mocked for being trivial, ephemeral, tacky, and lacking in scholarly and academic merit. To those naysayers who think pop culture is unworthy of study, I would offer the reminder that the Disney Corporation took in revenues of over $55 billion in 2016. The previous year, *Star Wars: The Force Awakens* grossed over $2 billion worldwide at the box office, and the song "See You Again" by Wiz Khalifa featuring Charlie Puth from the *Furious 7* soundtrack received more than two billion views on YouTube. In 2016, an average of nearly 112 million TV viewers tuned in to watch the Denver Broncos defeat the Carolina Panthers in Super Bowl 50. Regardless of whether *Dancing with the Stars* shares the artistic integrity of the New York City Ballet, popular culture matters deeply, to its countless fans, its creative producers and champions, and especially to the global economy. As scholars and students of society and social life, it certainly ought to matter to us, so let's get to it. Let's mix it up.

Like all popular culture, this edition benefited greatly from the contributions of many collaborators, and I thank them here. First and foremost, an enthusiastic round of applause for my editor, Sasha Levitt, and the entire Norton staff for the professionalism they brought to this project. In particular, I would like to thank Liz Marotta and Caitlin Moran for managing the book as it moved through production. Travis Carr deserves credit for his brilliant photo research, as does Theresa Kay for her copyediting prowess, and Miranda Schonbrun for her editorial assistance. I am also grateful to a number of editorial reviewers who commented on earlier chapter drafts: Jill Bakehorn, Rick Baldoz, Charles Brown, Carolyn Chernoff, Jessie Finch, Allison Foley, Todd Nicholas Fuist, Karen Honeycutt, Emily J. Kennedy, Jesse Klein, Susan McDonic, Amara Miller, Lakshmi Srinivas, and Oliver Wang. Finally, a note of thanks to Karl Bakeman for his continued support.

Mix It Up developed out of a course I have taught at Penn in various iterations since my arrival there in 2001, and I thank the many sociology graduate students who helped to shape its curriculum by heroically serving as my teaching assistants in the lead-up to this Second Edition: Rachel Ellis, Betsie Garner, Lindsay Wood Glassman, Pete Harvey, Alex Hoppe, Radha Modi, Bridget Nolan, Frank Prior, Patricia Tevington, Chelsea Wahl, Junhow Wei, and Sarah Zelner. I also thank my colleagues at Penn for their encouragement and good cheer throughout the duration of this project, and Eric Klinenberg, Gordon Douglas, and the entire crew at the Institute for Public Knowledge at NYU for hosting me as a Visiting Scholar since 2015. My pop culture—savvy colleagues and friends, including Mike Cimicata, Sean Davis, John Doyle, Dave Gerridge, Scott Hanson, Jerome Hodos, Jason Schnittker, Bryant Simon, and Matt Wray, always supply much lively discussion.

Finally, I must thank my patient and caring wife, Meredith Broussard, and our precocious son, who schooled me on topics ranging from Harry Potter to *Minecraft* to pop music recorded during this century. There are no two people with whom I'd rather watch *Looney Tunes* and *Shark Tank*. This book is dedicated to them.

David Grazian
New York City

Popular culture is produced, consumed, and experienced collectively within a context of overlapping sets of social relationships.

everything counts

THE SOCIAL ORGANIZATION
OF POPULAR CULTURE

LIKE GREAT WORKS OF ART OR SCIENTIFIC PROGRESS, EVEN THE MOST imaginative popular culture owes its reality to the hard-earned achievements of the past. On May 13, 2006, Barbados-born singer Rihanna scored her first No. 1 single on the Billboard U.S. pop chart with the catchy dance hit "SOS (Rescue Me)." Rihanna completed the song for Def Jam Recordings after being signed by its then-president and CEO, rapper Jay Z. The lead single off her sophomore effort *A Girl Like Me* (2006), "SOS" was produced by Jonathan "J. R." Rotem, and its lyrics and music were written by Rotem and Evan "Kidd" Bogart.

Actually, that is not entirely accurate, since one other songwriter is also credited with composing the music for the single, specifically its irresistible bass line and drum beat. That songwriter is Ed Cobb, who wrote "Tainted Love," a song released in the 1980s by the British new wave duo Soft Cell, from which Rotem and Bogart liberally sample as background rhythm for their recording of "SOS." A one-hit wonder, Soft Cell's "Tainted Love" slowly climbed the Billboard U.S. Hot 100 singles chart in 1981 to No. 8, and before the duo exited into oblivion, the song managed to spend what was at the time a record-breaking 43 weeks on the pop charts. Like other 1980s British invasion artists (Depeche Mode, the Human League, Joe Jackson, the Cure), Soft Cell incorporated depressing song lyrics of unrequited love with postpunk improvisation and synthesized sound effects. In their dance remix of "Tainted Love," Soft Cell accomplished all three by integrating the signature track with a second song, "Where Did Our Love Go?" with vocals accompanied only by a sparse synth-pop bass line and beat.

Rihanna pays homage to "Tainted Love" when she sings, "You got me tossin' and turnin' and I can't sleep at night," the one "SOS" lyric borrowed from the 1980s classic. But Soft Cell can't really take credit for the line, either, since the northern soul and rhythm-and-blues singer Gloria Jones actually performed the original version of Ed Cobb's "Tainted Love" in 1964 and later rerecorded it in the mid-1970s with her husband Marc Bolan of the English rock band T. Rex. In fact, "Where Did Our Love Go?" is also a cover, also recorded in 1964, by the all-female Motown group the Supremes. With its lead vocals sung by Diana Ross, "Where Did Our Love Go?" was the first of 12 No. 1 songs recorded by the Supremes; their other top-charting hits include "Baby Love," "You Can't Hurry Love," "Stop! In the Name of Love," and "You Keep Me Hanging On," the last of which Rihanna also pays homage to in "SOS": "I'm out with you / Ya got me head over heels / Boy you keep me hanging on / By the way you make me feel."

What does this discography tell us about popular culture? Perhaps the clearest lesson to be gleaned is that pop music, like Greek tragedy and Elizabethan drama, can transcend its historical moment to enjoy endless cycles of rediscovery and reinvention (Griswold 1986), just as "Tainted Love" began as a 1960s northern

FIGURE 1.1:
The Origins of "SOS (Rescue Me)"

2006

SOS (Rescue Me)

Performed by Rihanna
Produced by Jonathan "J. R." Rotem
Written by Rotem, Evan "Kidd" Bogart, and Ed Cobb

1981

**Tainted Love/
Where Did Our Love Go?**

Performed by Soft Cell
Produced by Mike Thorne
Written by Ed Cobb

1976

Tainted Love

Performed by Gloria Jones and Marc Bolan
Produced by Marc Bolan
Written by Ed Cobb

1964

Tainted Love

Performed by Gloria Jones
Written by Ed Cobb

1964

Where Did Our Love Go?

Performed by the Supremes
Written by Lamont Dozier, Brian Holland, and Edward Holland Jr.

soul song and found new life as a 1980s synth-pop classic, which two decades later would be sampled for inclusion on a 2006 dance hit. The creators of popular culture rely on an endless repository of past work to inform their development of new and future projects, from pop singles to animated cartoons to feature films. In such cases, the first step to achieving success as a cultural *producer* is to be a savvy *consumer* of mass media and popular culture.

Moreover, the half-century history of "Tainted Love" spotlights a number of cultural producers whose combined efforts carried this song through its numerous incarnations (see fig. 1.1). Popular culture is never the product of a solitary artist but always emerges from the *collective activity* generated by interlocking networks of cultural creators. This is not to suggest that Rihanna would not have recorded "SOS" at all, if not for these many participants—only that without their cumulative input and influence, her song would have sounded different (Becker 1982).

All this highlights the major argument of this book: *Popular culture is produced, consumed, and experienced within a context of overlapping sets of social relationships*. Some of those relationships are forged out of a spirit of musicianship and camaraderie, as illustrated by the two members of Soft Cell. Many more are contractual relationships between artists and business firms built out of economic convenience, such as the relationship between Rihanna and Def Jam Recordings, or between Def Jam and its parent company Universal Music Group. Still others represent the close bonds between cultural creators and their audiences, or among the members of a social group who maintain a shared sense of identity, whether on the basis of class, race, nationality, religiosity, gender, or sexuality. This opens up a range of interesting questions: How are pop music genres such as rap, rhythm and blues, country, and heavy metal organized by industry personnel and audiences on the basis of social status? How are global pop cultural styles such as Afro-Cuban jazz, Turkish hip-hop, Bhangra dance music, and Bollywood film shaped by the local and regional settings in which they are transplanted? These questions all point to the centrality of social relationships in the creation, consumption, and experience of popular culture.

What Makes Pop Culture Popular?

In common parlance, *popular culture* refers to the aesthetic products created and sold by profit-seeking firms operating in the global entertainment market—horror movies, reality television, dance music, fashion magazines, graphic novels, literary fiction, remote-controlled toys, fast-food hamburgers, online video games. But understanding popular culture sociologically first requires that we define exactly what we mean by these two words of subtle complexity, *popular* and *culture*. Let us begin at the beginning: What does it mean for pop culture to be *popular*? It sounds simple, but in fact the word *popular* carries several distinct (and at times contradictory) connotations. First, and perhaps most obviously, (1) culture that is "popular" is *well liked*, and in a market economy that popularity is often best demonstrated through *commercial success* as measured by Nielsen ratings, iTunes downloads, ticket sales, or box-office revenue. In 2015, the top-grossing films included *Star Wars: The Force Awakens*, *Jurassic World*, *Inside Out*, and *Avengers: Age of Ultron*. That last film took in more than $1.4 billion in global box-office receipts and starred the highest-paid film actor in the world, Robert Downey Jr., who earned $80 million in 2015. He has starred in recurring roles as Sherlock Holmes and Tony Stark/Iron Man in some of the biggest film franchises of all time, and his movies have grossed nearly $4 billion worldwide. Other popular A-list actors who today earn $20 million or more per film include Leonardo DiCaprio, Tom Cruise, Will Smith, Matt Damon, Johnny Depp, Sandra Bullock, and Denzel Washington.

In the digital age, we can measure popularity according to noncommercial criteria as well. In 2016 the celebrity with the most Twitter followers worldwide was Katy Perry, with more than 95 million users; she bested Justin Bieber (91 million), Taylor Swift (83 million), and President Barack Obama (80 million). On Facebook, Portuguese soccer pro Cristiano Ronaldo has the most fans (117 million), fol-

According to one definition, popular culture is well liked and commercially successful, as exemplified by global blockbusters such as *Star Wars: The Force Awakens*.

lowed closely behind by Colombian pop star Shakira. If you think that is a lot, bear in mind that the most viewed YouTube video of all time has been streamed more than 2.7 *billion* times—the music video for "Gangnam Style" by Korean one-hit-wonder Psy.

Unfortunately, audiences hardly look favorably upon all popular culture, and some of it isn't particularly well liked by anyone, especially annoyingly repetitive TV advertisements or well-known celebrities who seem to be famous for, well, simply *being famous* despite an obvious lack of talent or achievement. In this sense, (2) popular culture refers to icons or media products that are globally *ubiquitous* and easily *recognized* (if perhaps disliked or mocked) the world over (Gamson 1994; Gabler 2000). The most clarifying examples come from the diamond-encrusted world of high society, and in our contemporary culture, Exhibit A is reality television star Kim Kardashian West and her overexposed sisters. While Kim, Khloé, Kourtney, Kylie, and Kendall's fame may seem quite strange, their celebrity is actually modeled after similarly ostentatious wealthy men and women from earlier generations, including serial divorcée Zsa Zsa Gabor, whose nine husbands included Conrad Hilton Sr., the founder of Hilton Hotels. (He was also the great-grandfather of a far more recent celebrity socialite, Paris Hilton.) There are certainly more universally liked exemplars, as illustrated by the waves of loss felt worldwide after the widely reported deaths of John F. Kennedy Jr., born just after his father won the American presidency in November 1960, and Princess Diana, the former wife of Prince Charles of Wales. Today, Diana's eldest son, Prince William, and his wife, Kate Middleton, similarly enjoy this kind of larger-than-life celebrity.

However, despite the differences between the Kardashians and members of the British royal family, many critics see these icons as two sides of the same coin of mainstream mass culture. According to their worldview, (3) popular culture refers to commercial media thought to be trivial, tacky, and pitched to the lowest common denominator as *mass culture* intended for general consumption, like canned soup or chewing gum (MacDonald 1957). In this context, popular culture—Justin Bieber, Big Macs, *Dancing with the Stars*—is unfavorably compared to the fine arts as represented by Italian opera, French nouvelle cuisine, and *cinéma vérité*. In these instances, the *populations* implicated by the use of *pop* culture as a pejorative label tend to be socially marginalized by class, race, and often age—hence the critical panning of melodramatic "pop" stars who target preadolescent and teenage audiences, such as boy bands like One Direction, contestants on NBC's *The Voice*, and former Disney starlets like Selena Gomez and Miley Cyrus.

TABLE 1.1
Definitions of Popular Culture

Definition	Examples
Popular culture is often *well liked*, as best demonstrated in a market economy through *commercial success*. (In the digital age, the extent to which pop culture is well liked can also be measured with alternative metrics such as webpage views, Twitter followers, or Facebook likes.)	Films such as *Star Wars: The Force Awakens* or *Jurassic World*; beloved celebrities such as pop star Katy Perry or soccer star Cristiano Ronaldo
Popular culture refers to icons, celebrities, or media products that are *well known* the world over.	Kate Middleton or Kim Kardashian West
Popular culture refers to commercial media considered *mass culture*—trivial, tacky, and pitched to the lowest common denominator for general consumption.	Commercial pop stars who target teen audiences, such as One Direction, Justin Bieber, or Miley Cyrus
Popular culture refers to culture considered to *belong to the people*, given its association with democratic populism and authenticity.	Recording artists whose music speaks to the experiences of ordinary working-class people, such as Bob Marley or Bruce Springsteen
Popular culture refers to media events simultaneously experienced by mass audiences in real time.	The Super Bowl, Olympic Games, Academy Awards, U.S. presidential debates

Mass culture also has its many defenders, including those who argue for its intellectual complexity and depth, increasing innovativeness and social relevance, kitschy fun and contemporary cool, and similarities to past cultural touchstones now canonized as great art (Simon 1999; Johnson 2006). According to the American Film Institute, mass culture movies aimed at young people—*Snow White and the Seven Dwarfs*, *Star Wars*, *Toy Story*, *The Lord of the Rings: The Fellowship of the Ring*—represent some of the greatest cinematic accomplishments in U.S. history.

Yet for another set of artists and audiences, (4) popular culture is associated with songs, dances, and other artistic expressions *belonging to the people*, given its association with democratic populism and authenticity. This characterization of popular culture refers to songwriters and recording artists who create roots-oriented music (such as blues, folk, reggae, and certain strains of American rock, R&B, country, and rap) said to channel the traditional hopes and dreams of ordinary working-class people. They include legends such as Muddy Waters, Woody Guthrie, Johnny Cash, Bob Dylan, Nina Simone, Bob Marley, and Bruce Springsteen. In more recent years, contemporary hip-hop and R&B artists such as John Legend, Common, Alicia Keys, Lauryn Hill, D'Angelo, and J. Cole have continued in this fashion by writing and recording protest songs that resonate with the Black Lives Matter civil rights campaign (Tillet 2015).

Finally, (5) popular culture can refer to media events that national and even global mass audiences experience simultaneously, in real time, whether on television or online. These events include professional sports events such as the Super Bowl and the World Series, international competitions like the Olympic Games, and staged political events such as U.S. presidential debates and State of the Union addresses to Congress. They also include the ever-proliferating number of televised awards shows populating the airwaves: the Academy Awards, Grammy Awards, Emmy Awards, Tony Awards, Golden Globe Awards, People's Choice Awards; the list goes on (English 2005).

Defining Culture

As if the multiple and contradictory connotations of the word *popular* were not confusing enough, defining *culture* can be equally frustrating, particularly since this complex term has finely differentiated meanings in a variety of dispersed intellectual traditions and academic disciplines. For example, in the humanities, culture represents what Raymond Williams (1983, p. 90) identifies as "the works and practices of intellectual and especially artistic activity," particularly those that lead toward "a general process of intellectual, spiritual and aesthetic development." The first part of this definition suggests the rarefied forms that culture manifests in the humanities: great novels and concertos, classical architecture and painting, Wagnerian opera and contemporary experimental poetry. In the fields of literature, music, philosophy, and art history, culture represents the most revered expressions of the human condition—Shakespeare's *King Lear* and *Hamlet*, Dostoyevsky's *Crime and Punishment* and Melville's *Moby-Dick*, Beethoven's Fifth Symphony and Bach's Toccata and Fugue in D Minor. As for culture's purpose, it is not merely one of entertainment but "intellectual, spiritual and aesthetic development," nothing less than the cultivation of the mind toward greater enlightenment and epicurean pleasure. It is only through the fine arts that an individual—and by extension, an entire human society—can truly come to be thought of as civilized or, as they say, "cultured."

This humanist vision of culture suggests a high-minded and perhaps inaccessible world of challenging ideas communicated through complicated texts and compositions. In contrast, in the social sciences, culture refers to "a particular way of life, whether of a people, a period, a group, or humanity in general" (Williams 1983, p. 90). To the sociologist (or anthropologist, psychologist, economist, political scientist, or communications scholar, for that matter), culture refers to a mode of living in the world as a social being, as represented by the shared practices, rituals, behaviors, activities, and artifacts that make up the experience of everyday life. For example, culture can refer to the styles of cooking and eating enjoyed by a people—their cuisines, recipes, ingredients, spices, kitchen tools, and table manners. We can appreciate this fact even though it is hard to imagine our *own* modern culinary folkways—say, slurping down Froot Loops cereal for breakfast—as particularly cultural. After all, it would not be unusual to find the serving vessels and utensils of an ancient society (such as their clay pitchers, metal spoons, or drinking goblets) exhibited in an art museum or in an archaeology textbook. The improvised games children play—Double Dutch, kickball, hopscotch, freeze tag, dodgeball—are also cultural, as are our dirty jokes, obscene gestures, and other locker-room antics.

To this end, sociologists of culture are interested in a wide spectrum of everyday rituals and social activities associated with public life, including sports participation and spectatorship, dating and courtship, retail shopping, beauty and cosmetic enhancement, dining and coffee drinking. However, for some this anthropological conception of culture may seem to suggest an impossibly broad inventory of possible topics for analysis, as vast as human civilization itself. A helpful way to cut culture down to a manageable size is to focus on three properties common to both the humanist and social scientific understandings of culture. Culture is richly *symbolic*, invested with meaning and significance. The meanings attributed to culture are never simply given but are the product of human invention and *collectively shared* by a demonstrably large number of people. (It is in this sense that sociologists argue that culture and meaning are "socially constructed.") Finally, for culture to be sensibly understood, it must be *embodied* in some kind of recognizable form.

To best emphasize these three properties of culture, Wendy Griswold (1986, p. 5; 2004, p. 13), a sociologist at Northwestern University, characterizes the sociology of culture as the study of *cultural objects*, or "shared significance embodied in form." Cultural objects are social expressions of meaning that have been rendered into something tangible, like a Greek epic poem or a bronze sculpture. By the same token, cultural objects can be found in the world of popular culture as well as the fine arts—Homer's *Iliad* and Homer Simpson, Alexander Pope and *Scandal*'s Olivia Pope, Jonathan Swift and Taylor Swift, Nathaniel Hawthorne's *The House of the Seven Gables* and Netflix's *House of Cards*. While sociologists of culture investigate and analyze "the works and practices of intellectual and especially artistic activity," these creative compositions not only include classical music and nineteenth-century Russian literature but also mass media enjoyed in the contemporary world as a regular feature of everyday life: rock, rap, country music, celebrity-gossip tabloids, animated cartoons, billboard advertising, cable newscasts, comic books, reality television, food blogs, and *Minecraft*. As the British synth-pop band Depeche Mode sang back in 1983 on its *Construction Time Again* album, everything counts in large amounts.

In fact, a popular cultural object need not even be a traditional form of visual or aural media: It could be a meaningful nonverbal gesture, like a wide smile, a conspiratorial wink, an enthusiastic thumbs-up, or an aggressively pointed middle finger (Geertz 1973, pp. 6—7; Katz 1999, pp. 18—86). It could be an icon, like Abraham Lincoln (Schwartz 1996, 1998; Schwartz and Schuman 2005), or Albert Einstein, or the Statue of Liberty, or the Volkswagen or Apple logo. In this sense popular cultural objects operate at the level of language, with their articulated if complex shared meanings ready to be decoded among participants who inhabit a common social environment or context. Like language, the meanings attached to cultural objects both *endure over time* and yet are also capable of *innovation* and *change*, just as the definitions of certain words maintain stability over time even as they take on new and altered meanings. (Examples in the digital age include terms such as *tweet, text, drive, bit, hack, chip*, and *mouse*.)

Popular Culture as Collective Activity

Now that we have discussed a variety of meanings and exemplars associated with popular culture in the interests of developing as inclusive a definition as possible, the next step is to examine how popular culture can be best understood as an inherently social phenomenon. In his work on the social organization of culture and the arts, the sociologist Howard S. Becker (1982) observes that its production is first and foremost a *collective activity*. Whether a Jane Austen film adaptation or a dragon-themed video game, popular cultural objects are produced by collaborative webs of interconnected individuals working together toward a common goal and eventually consumed and experienced by audiences who attach shared meanings to them.

According to Becker (1982), media and popular culture are produced in the context of *art worlds*, or networks of participants whose combined efforts create movies, musical compositions, websites, graphic novels, advertising, and so forth. For some types of pop culture, the collective nature of creative production is readily apparent, as anyone who has scanned the thousands of names listed in the closing credits at the end of a feature film surely knows (Becker 1982, pp. 7—9). Perhaps a less obvious example of the secondary creative workers or *support personnel* who labor in relative anonymity in the culture industries are those people necessary for recording music, since even songs credited to a single artist like Beyoncé, Nicki Minaj, Taylor Swift, or Carrie Underwood rely on teams of songwriters, producers, session musicians, studio engineers, and sound mixers. In the music industry, support personnel may also include the software developers responsible for the digital technology that enables the easy transfer of performed music into binary code and back into realized sound, and the record producer who matches the appropriate set of effects pedals to each guitarist, or edits preprogrammed electronic beats and sampled bass sounds into a pulsating rhythm track (Seabrook 2015). Even the digital artwork that accompanies the delivery of online music requires the cooperative efforts of product managers, art directors, photographers, archivists, liner note writers, copy editors, and other support staff (Becker 1982).

Given the collective nature of producing popular culture, it only makes sense that in a complex society like our own, networks of creative personnel are organized according to a highly segmented *division of labor*, as the aforementioned examples from recorded music and film suggest (Becker 1982, p. 7). The world of cinema alone could fill entire textbooks, given its limitless slate of specialized jobs: visual effects gaffer, gang boss painter, best boy, focus puller. A cursory look at university degree programs in fields of cultural production further highlights the emphasis toward specialization in the creative industries. For example, at New York University's Tisch School of the Arts, students can earn graduate diplomas in dramatic writing, game design, interactive telecommunications, and moving image archiving and preservation.

But while contemporary art worlds are notable for their high degree of segmentation, they are also known for their ability to efficiently organize *cooperative links* among a wildly diverse array of contributors who depend on one another when producing the stuff of pop culture and entertainment media (Becker 1982, pp. 24–28). Sometimes these participants collaborate regularly, like the four musicians who make up the Irish rock band U2, or the 110 members of the Chicago Symphony Orchestra, or the permanent editorial staff of *Rolling Stone*, or the thousands of compensated workers and unpaid interns employed by Walt Disney Pictures or Sony Music Entertainment. Other cultural producers work jointly with one another on a more ad-hoc basis. Television postproduction teams incorporate a range of creative workers (including video editors, sound engineers, and studio musicians) who work on clearly defined projects for a specified period of time, such as a single season (Faulkner 1971). A fashion magazine spread employs photographers, models, casting agents, lighting technicians, makeup artists, copywriters, graphic designers, and other creative personnel, some of whom may work together for only a single day (Mears 2011).

The Social Context of Popular Culture

The collaborative efforts of those who produce popular culture do not take place in a vacuum but in the context of lived social life, and that context matters in a variety of subtle and not-so-subtle ways. For instance, during the first half of the twentieth century, the invention of discrete genre categories in the music industry reflected the widespread residential and market segregation of African American audiences from white consumers (Massey and Denton 1993; Peterson 1997). For this reason, otherwise indistinguishable music styles are often differently classified and subsequently advertised and sold on the basis of race—note the musical and lyrical similarities between 1950s blues, R&B, and rock 'n' roll.

From an industry perspective, rock 'n' roll emerged as the most commercially viable of these genre categories in the 1950s, particularly among white teenagers—which is why even young readers have heard of Elvis Presley but few popular music fans remember the great African American blues performer Arthur "Big Boy" Crudup, who in 1946 wrote and recorded "That's All Right (Mama)," which Presley covered and released in 1954 as his first single. Most pop music listeners have also never heard of the blues and R&B singer Big Mama Thornton, whose original 1952 recording of "Hound Dog" is today overshadowed (rightly

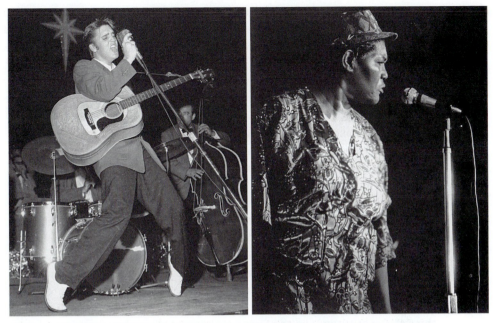

How do social contexts affect the creation and consumption of popular culture? Consider the story of Elvis Presley (left), who covered "Hound Dog," which was originally recorded in 1952 by Big Mama Thornton (right).

or wrongly) by Presley's version, which *Rolling Stone* named one of the Top 20 rock 'n' roll songs of all time.

The physical and social infrastructure of our cities and towns determines the fate of popular culture as well. For example, the development of privatized suburbs and gated communities during the 1940s and 1950s contributed to an overall decline in urban nightlife and public leisure and a simultaneous rise in the popularity of home entertainment—particularly television. In 1953 two-thirds of family households in America owned at least one television set, and by the mid-1960s that figure had grown to a whopping 94 percent (Hannigan 1998; Cohen 2003, p. 302). As for the homegrown popular culture indigenous to the city, during the 1970s the interconnectedness and accessibility of New York's underground transit system facilitated the urban development of a citywide community of subway graffiti writers and muralists (Lachmann 1988). But by the 1980s, circumstances changed when increased police surveillance, the implementation of extreme security measures in the city's train yards such as razor wire and guard dogs, and the tireless vigilance of transit cleaning crews all converged to diminish New York's subway graffiti subculture, perhaps forever (Lachmann 1988; Gladwell 2002, pp. 142–43).

This last example illustrates the highly influential role that government and the state play in the cultural production process. Through public funding agencies such as the National Endowment for the Arts, the government directly contributes to certain kinds of cultural growth through its financial support of theaters, museums, and film festivals. The Federal Communications Commission renders decisions on what sorts of socially defined "indecent" or "obscene" images or language may be permitted on the public airwaves and how many radio stations one company may own in a given regional market (Klinenberg 2007). Local and national laws also affect the context in which popular culture is manufactured and performed. In the 1920s, the early jazz music made famous by Louis Armstrong and Duke Ellington emerged during the era of Prohibition, which meant that some of the great music of that period was performed in illegal speakeasies and other clandestine haunts, its proprietors under constant threat of arrest for serving alcohol to patrons (Kenney 1993; Absher 2014). Similarly, U.S. federal laws surrounding the use of MDMA and other illegal drugs drove the hallucinogen-fueled electronic rave dance scene underground during the height of its popularity in the 1990s (Reynolds 1999). Further anti-rave legislation and enforcement in cities across the country spelled the eventual death knell for this once vibrant subculture. More recently, copyright laws and U.S. Supreme Court rulings have constrained the ability of music producers to liberally sample whole sections of previously released songs without permission.

Likewise, we should be reminded that the rule of law protects the freedoms of cultural producers as well. Thanks to the rigorous and continual defense of the U.S. Constitution and the First Amendment throughout our nation's history, U.S. popular culture flourishes in a far more liberal political environment than in other countries. In 2012 Russian authorities arrested and imprisoned members of the feminist punk-rock band Pussy Riot for staging a political media stunt in an Orthodox church in Moscow. According to the *New York Times*, the band "infiltrated the Cathedral of Christ the Savior wearing colorful balaclavas, and pranced around in front of the golden Holy Doors leading to the altar, dancing, chanting and lip-syncing for what would later become a music video of a profane song in which they beseeched the Virgin Mary to rid Russia of [its autocratic president Vladimir] Putin" (Herszenhorn 2012). Meanwhile, China earns the shameful distinction of imprisoning more of its own journalists than any other country in the world, and the Chinese government regularly censors Internet sites to prevent the free dissemination of dissident speech (Meredith 2007, p. 152). In a 2015 report measuring Internet-related civil liberties around the world, the independent watchdog organization Freedom House ranked China last out of 65 nations, behind Iran, Cuba, and Myanmar (Wong 2015).

Members of feminist punk-rock band Pussy Riot perform in a Russian Orthodox Church in Moscow in protest of President Vladimir Putin's government. Two members of the band were subsequently imprisoned for "hooliganism."

Audiences and the Consumption of Popular Culture

In Quentin Tarantino's 1994 movie *Pulp Fiction*, what's in the briefcase that Vincent Vega and Jules Winnfield retrieve for their mob boss? Did advertising genius Don Draper conceive of the famous Coca-Cola "I'd Like to Teach the World to Sing" commercial in the final episode of AMC's *Mad Men*? Is The Weeknd's 2015 No. 1 hit "Can't Feel My Face" about cocaine use? For these examples, the answer depends on who is doing the responding, because questions of meaning, interpretation, and value are not ultimately decided by the creators of media and popular culture, but by its *consumers*. (This is not to say that the intentions or objectives of cultural creators do not matter; rather, it is to emphasize that they are hardly the *only* determinants of meaning that matter. Moreover, the multiple creators of a cultural object—say, the screenwriter, director, and leading or supporting actors of a movie or television show—may disagree among *themselves* as to the meaning or value of their collaborative work.) While in the world of cultural criticism all sorts of value judgments are rendered as if they were fact—*Walt Whitman is the center of the American literary canon* (Bloom 1994), *Bruce Springsteen is the mythos of rock 'n' roll sprung to life* (Alterman 2001, p. 9), *Tom McCarthy's Oscar-winning film* Spotlight *was the best movie of 2015* (Hornaday 2015; Orr 2015; Reed 2015; Travers 2015)—sociologists recognize that these arguments are simply claims to be argued and contested by

How do social factors shape the meaning and value of popular culture? For instance, how do fans' and critics' arguments about Bruce Springsteen being "the mythos of rock 'n' roll sprung to life" reflect the multivocal status of cultural objects?

fans and detractors who attribute sometimes contradictory meanings to films, books, and music, meanings that are always up for grabs. In this sense, cultural objects are *multivocal* because they say different things to different audiences (Griswold 1987).

Of course, simply because audiences fabricate the meanings and interpretations attributed to popular culture, we should not necessarily infer that they do so randomly. When vast numbers of people invest a cultural object with shared meaning, it has the potential to hold sway in the world as if it were absolute and irrefutable, rather than socially constructed. Various listeners may enjoy or dislike Bruce Springsteen's music, but almost no one disputes that he is a *rock* musician—even though music genres like "rock" are social inventions and industry labels that are always subject to debate and change. (Remember, the stylistic differences between 1950s blues, rock 'n' roll, and R&B are negligible at best. To emphasize the contestable nature of the rock genre category, try a thought experiment: How many hip-hop fans would identify Run-D.M.C., Public Enemy, or N.W.A. as "rock 'n' roll" performers? Perhaps not many, yet all three rap acts have been inducted into the Rock and Roll Hall of Fame.)

Since audiences draw on their own social circumstances when attributing meaning and value to popular culture, these meanings are often patterned according to persistent systems of social organization structured by differences in socioeconomic status, nationality, race, ethnicity, gender, sexuality, religion, or age. For example, in her study of romance novels and their predominantly female readers, Janice Radway (1991) discovers that Midwestern housewives enjoy romances for the independence and self-reliance typically assigned to their plucky heroines; their stories thus provide a much needed if temporary escape from the exhausting labor of child rearing and household management. In an analysis of audience reception of the 1956 motion picture *The Searchers*, a Hollywood Western, JoEllen Shively (1992) discovers that despite the frequently negative portrayal of American Indians in film, Native American men are enthusiastic fans of the genre, citing the beauty of the natural landscapes where Westerns are often set, and the free and independent cowboy lifestyle commonly celebrated in such movies. Meanwhile, since the cartoonish stereotypes of American Indians as heartless kidnappers and violent scalpers often depicted in traditional Westerns do not correspond to their contemporary self-image, Native Americans simply ignore such slights, identifying more with the heroic cowboys and frontiersmen featured in Hollywood cinema and portrayed by classic movie stars such as John Wayne, Gary Cooper, and Clint Eastwood.

Audiences draw on their social identities and life experiences to make sense of media and popular culture, and those whose shared worldviews inform their understandings of culture in systematic ways are called *interpretive communities* (Radway 1991; also see Fish 1980). Yet as this last example illustrates, people's social circumstances not only influence the kinds of meanings

According to JoEllen Shively, many Native American men are fans of classic Westerns in spite of the way the films portray American Indians. Why are these fans an example of an interpretive community?

they attribute to cultural objects, events, and experiences but also the kinds of pop culture they choose to consume in the first place. Urban professionals are more likely to appreciate abstract art than working-class suburbanites (Halle 1993). In the United States, women read for leisure more than men and are more likely to join book-discussion groups (Long 2003; Griswold 2008). According to the Pew Research Center, in 2014 only 57 percent of senior citizens aged 65 and older identified as Internet users, as opposed to 97 percent of adults aged 18—29.

Many otherwise potential audiences are excluded from certain cultural pursuits due to their exorbitant costs, such as designer fashion, gourmet cuisine, nightclub bottle service, or exotic tourism. Likewise, some activities require excessive investments in time, like participating in U.S. Civil War reenactments or the annual Burning Man festival, a week-long radical arts event that takes place in the isolated Black Rock Desert, 120 miles north of Reno, Nevada. Other cultural pursuits, such as reading the postmodern fiction of Thomas Pynchon or enjoying French New Wave cinema, may require an appropriately cosmopolitan upbringing or advanced educational background to successfully navigate. With regard to computer literacy and Internet usage, there is significant evidence that a "digital divide" endures that reflects class and racial inequalities persistent in U.S. society.

Pop cultural consumer habits and experiences are not only shaped by one's specific social circumstances but also by the impact of outside social actors and structural forces. Successful touring bands and other traveling shows may not perform in small towns, preferring more populated cities and their affluent crowds. Political partisans, religious groups, and other community organizations may protest the final edit of a made-for-television movie, scaring away sponsors and thus blocking its dissemination on the airwaves. Media gatekeepers such as Oprah Winfrey may promote a book to millions of their fans, all but ensuring that consumers will follow closely behind (Griswold 2008, p. 59).

Finally, it bears remembering that audiences often consume media and popular culture together as collective activities. As noted above, many readers enjoy novels and literary nonfiction as a communal pursuit by participating in book clubs (Gladwell 2002, pp. 169–75; Long 2003), and cities like Philadelphia and Chicago have organized "One Book, One City" programs that promote the shared reading of a single book (Griswold 2008, pp. 58–59). (Since 2010, the books chosen for the "One Book, One Chicago" project have included Michael Chabon's *The Adventures of Kavalier & Clay*, Isabel Wilkerson's *The Warmth of Other Suns*, Markus Zusak's *The Book Thief*, Saul Bellow's *The Adventures of Augie March*, and Toni Morrison's *A Mercy*.) Televised events such as the Super Bowl and the Academy Awards draw together audiences who throw viewing parties to commemorate the occasion and share the experience with friends, as does the annual NCAA college basketball tournament, and guilty pleasures like *The Real Housewives of New Jersey* and *The Bachelor.* Competitive games from poker and chess to Settlers of Catan attract players to tournaments across the country. Massively multiplayer online role-playing games (MMORGs) such as *World of Warcraft* provide opportunities for millions of online gamers to expand their interpersonal networks by aligning and collaborating with fellow players in a collective if virtual environment (Castronova 2005). And lest we forget: Even in an age of touch-screen tablets and digital home theaters, many U.S. consumers still attend live theatrical and musical performances, sporting events, political rallies, and feature films in large public venues, just as they have for generations.

Gamers test out a new video game at the annual E3 gaming conference. How do massively multiplayer online role-playing games (MMORGs) like World of Warcraft *present opportunities to build social networks in the virtual world?*

Producing and Consuming Popular Culture

The last several years have marked a heyday for popular culture spoofs through mash-ups, in which creators sample, manipulate, and juxtapose together two or more media, all in the name of irony and extreme pop culture awareness. A series of YouTube videos splice together scenes from various Muppet movies into trailers for darker films like Christopher Nolan's *The Dark Knight Rises* and Martin Scorsese's *The Wolf of Wall Street*, while others feature Miss Piggy lip-synching Rihanna's profanity-laced 2015 hit "Bitch Better Have My Money," and Scooter rapping Eminem's "My Name Is," accompanied by Kermit the Frog as Dr. Dre. In a much lighter parody, YouTubers digitally incorporate the Minions from the *Despicable Me* films into action sequences from *Furious 7* to amusing effect.

The striking thing about these mash-ups is that all evidence suggests that they were designed by pop culture fans themselves—not as cookie-cutter creations of the large-scale media production process, but as a delightfully unpredictable part of the contemporary consumer experience. As much of this chapter has already illustrated, audiences often consume popular culture in highly active and creative ways. The organization of book clubs requires more than the passive absorption of a text but also its interrogation, especially as readers come together to discuss, debate, and disagree with its finer points. Digital media platforms and streaming services such as Spotify let music fans seek out hard-to-find recordings online and develop their own playlists independent of the organized listening experience provided by the traditional album format. In some ways, they transform culture in the very moment of its consumption. Moreover, thanks to advances in digital audio software such as GarageBand and Pro Tools, almost any amateur with a laptop can produce a professional-grade music recording within a few hours, just as the rise of digital cameras along with software such as Photoshop and iMovie allow consumers to create, manipulate, and distribute visual images with ease and little training. Maker spaces provide resources that allow ordinary people to collaboratively tinker with robotics, computer hardware, 3D printers, laser cutters, and cutting-edge programming languages—the arts and crafts of the digital age.

These new media technologies—as well as sixteenth-century forms of social organization, like reading groups—blur some of the distinctions between cultural consumption and production by democratizing the tools of pop culture making while freeing enterprising consumers to hack away at more traditional media and cultural creations. As NYU journalism professor Clay Shirky (2008) observes, in an environment in which digital technology is embedded in our everyday gadgets (iPhones, Fitbit trackers) and social media platforms allow us to post homemade videos and tweet opinions, everyone is a media outlet.

As for cultural producers themselves—filmmakers, photographers, musicians, novelists, screenwriters—our self-referential culture practically requires professional media makers to harness the ravenous energies of the consumer as part of the creative process. All of Quentin Tarantino's films, from *Reservoir Dogs* (1992) to *The Hateful Eight* (2015), are filled with B-movie references from spaghetti Westerns to martial-arts films, just as episodes of the Fox TV

Students at a technical college get hands-on experience with additive manufacturing, also known as 3D printing. The proliferation of inexpensive 3D printers and digital cameras along with software such as iMovie and GarageBand help users blur the lines between cultural consumption and production.

series *Family Guy* spoof long-forgotten 1980s sitcoms like *Mr. Belvedere*. As we discussed in the introduction, dance, pop, and hip-hop music producers regularly sample from obscure hits from the past, and disc jockeys mine the crates of their record collections for unusual contributions to the emergent stereo soundscape. In 2004 Brian Joseph Burton, better known as recording artist and producer Danger Mouse, released *The Grey Album* online—an unauthorized mash-up of the a cappella version of hip-hop impresario Jay Z's *The Black Album* overlaid with various sampled cuts from *The Beatles*, the self-titled 1968 LP record commonly referred to as the *White Album* (for its original white cover). By blending Jay Z's "99 Problems" with samples of the Beatles' "Helter Skelter," "Encore" with "Glass Onion" and "Savoy Truffle," and "What More Can I Say" with "While My Guitar Gently Weeps," Danger Mouse offered the music world a new way to think about the production *and* consumption of media and popular culture, even as he blurred the difference between the two.

Three Approaches to the Sociology of Media and Popular Culture

Now that we have explored the social and collective foundations of popular culture and its production and consumption, our next goal is to develop a comprehensive set of theoretical tools to help explain how pop cultural fads, fashions, trends, and phenomena succeed and decline over time, and what the social consequences of their popularity may be. To this end, in the following chapters I introduce three theoretical approaches to the sociology of media and popular culture. In the next chapter, I present the *functionalist* approach, which illustrates how culture "functions" as an engine that generates solidarity within human groups and societies. Borrowing from research on the pro-social functions of religion and culture in the earliest primitive societies, I rely on this paradigm to explore how more contemporary collective rituals from professional football games to rock music festivals similarly serve to forge emotional bonds of recognition, identity, and trust within communities and other social groups. At the same time, I show how pop culture provides the source material that allows consumers to socialize with strangers in public about relevant issues of the day. The functionalist approach helps to explain the excitement surrounding celebrity scandals and other large-scale media events among audiences who might otherwise seem to have little else in common.

In Chapter 3, I introduce the *critical* approach to media and popular culture. According to this paradigm, the ascendance of certain kinds of pop culture can be explained primarily in terms of their ability to reflect and reinforce the enormous economic and cultural power of the mass media industry. In contrast to the functionalist perspective, which suggests that pop culture is something that we as a society create for ourselves, the critical approach provides a top-down model of popular culture as a form of domination, albeit a strangely irresistible kind of domination that takes the form of sexually suggestive beer ads, addictive video games, social media profiles, and the carnival of public spectacle ironically referred to as "reality" television. In this chapter, I apply this theoretical perspective to a number of contemporary issues in media and popular culture, particularly the ubiquity and symbolic power of brands such as McDonald's, Nike, and Starbucks, and the loss of privacy and control over our personal information in the digital age.

Finally, in Chapter 4, we explore the *interaction* approach to pop culture. In contrast to the critical approach (which might explain a film's popularity on the basis of its marketing budget), the interaction approach emphasizes the power that informal processes such as word of mouth and peer influence enjoy in the cultural marketplace. According to this perspective, our consumer tastes are deeply affected by the people connected to us, and so the success of certain kinds of popular culture depends not on big-budget advertising but on micro-level interactions such as those exemplified by small-group encounters, online networking, crowdsourcing, and other informal modes of cultural diffusion. In describing this theoretical approach, I address a number of related issues, including the importance of early adopters and social media in determining the fate of new technologies and fashion styles, and the power that cultural scenes and collaborative online worlds play in fostering innovation and change, whether in local music subcultures or Internet fan fiction sites.

Denver Broncos football fans cheer on their NFL team. How does popular culture bring communities together?

we are the champions

A FUNCTIONALIST APPROACH TO POPULAR CULTURE

ON ANY GIVEN SUNDAY FROM SEPTEMBER THROUGH JANUARY, football maniacs from across the country prepare for their National Football League (NFL) home team's weekly matchup. Before game time, local fans of the Philadelphia Eagles tailgate in the parking lot of Lincoln Financial Field, quaffing down soft pretzels and Yuengling Lager beer. Although their team has never won a Super Bowl (they last won a national championship in 1960), Eagles diehards are no less passionate, and armchair quarterbacking about last week's loss seems like an official local pastime all its own. Not for nothing did *New York Times* sports reporter Jere Longman title his 2005 book about the Eagles *If Football's a Religion, Why Don't We Have a Prayer? Philadelphia, Its Faithful, and the Eternal Quest for Sports Salvation*. Indeed, as illustrated by Robert DeNiro's portrayal of a suburban Eagles fanatic and occasional gambler in David O. Russell's 2012 film *Silver Linings Playbook*, fans of "The Birds" can be a neurotic and superstitious bunch. When the Eagles actually made it to Super Bowl XXXIX back in 2004 (only to lose to the New England Patriots by a field goal), I encountered a fan covered in green and black makeup with his van painted to match, all in anticipation of a downtown pep rally and Sunday evening's big game. "EAGLES! EAGLES!" he shouted at all comers. The poor guy didn't seem to notice or care that it was only Tuesday, days away from scheduled local festivities and the main event. Heck, I've heard Eagles fans chant—"E-A-G-L-E-S—EAGLES!" on a subway ride home from a Phillies *baseball* game.

What explains the collective enthusiasm of football fans in the United States, or soccer fans in Brazil, or cricket fans in Australia (Foer 2004; Kaufman and Patterson 2005)? After all, such sports are forms of entertainment in which spectators watch complete strangers play competitive games with obscure rules, and in the case of professional team sports, the athletes are rarely from their "home" cities in any real sense. In fact, often the teams themselves are transplants from someplace else, like the Los Angeles Dodgers (from Brooklyn, New York), Oakland A's (from Philadelphia), Washington Nationals (from Montreal), Tennessee Titans (from Houston), and the Oklahoma City Thunder (from Seattle). Teams sometimes carry over their old names to new cities, often nonsensically so, as when the National Basketball Association's New Orleans Jazz moved to Salt Lake City, Utah, but retained their identity as the Jazz even though Utah enjoys decidedly less of a regional music heritage than New Orleans, the actual birthplace of jazz. (Plus, lest we forget, some professional sports teams do not even play in their *own* cities, as both the New York Giants and Jets compete in East Rutherford, New Jersey.) Given the increasing mobility of professional teams and their athletes (to say nothing of the obvious turnover of high school and college players, who eventually graduate from their schools), aren't sports fans really just rooting for the uniforms, as comedian Jerry Seinfeld once joked?

Actually, he wasn't all that far off—we do cheer on team uniforms, mascots, colors, and banners, at least as much as we do the players themselves—and in this chapter we rely on the tools of sociology to explain why. Specifically, this chapter describes the first of three sociological approaches used in this book: the *functionalist* approach. According to a functionalist approach to popular culture, our obsession with professional and intercollegiate athletics, celebrity magazines, and other forms of mass entertainment can be explained in terms of their social uses (or literally their *function*) in generating solidarity among the individual members of a larger society or community. Through the power of ritualistic spectator events such as playoff games and rock concerts, sports and other forms of popular culture and entertainment bring strangers together in a collective spirit of camaraderie, however temporarily. Moreover, these shared moments provide opportunities for fans to express their feelings and opinions about otherwise sensitive topics, such as race relations and the ethics of work. In this chapter, I draw on the functionalist perspective to explore these social phenomena as they relate to celebrity culture, national politics, and, most of all, the world of sports entertainment.

Foundations of the Functionalist Approach

In his seminal 1912 book *The Elementary Forms of Religious Life*, the French sociologist Émile Durkheim seeks to understand the social role that religion plays in the functioning of human societies. In many ways, Durkheim himself was perfectly suited for this scholarly task. As a nonobservant Jew who happened to have hailed from several generations of rabbis, he was at once both intimately familiar with the myriad symbols, rituals, and beliefs of religious thought and practice yet held few personal investments in their ultimate meaning or purpose. He embarks on his intellectual journey by beginning, well, at the beginning, by describing some of the earliest religions known to humans, particularly the ancient spiritual faiths of American Indians and Aboriginal Australians. These are societies for whom religion was notably the central organizing institution of their existence: It structured their governance, work routines, and knowledge of the natural world. (This is in contrast to present-day Americans, for whom religion is only one of many forms of cultural identification and social organization, along with nationhood and ethnicity, for example.)

Durkheim observed that these early religions relied heavily on the role of signs, images, and symbols, many of which were drawn from the natural world, as in the case of totemic religions that rely on animals (e.g., kangaroos, snakes, crows) as symbols (1912/1995, pp. 99–126). What was the purpose of these symbols? Durkheim argues that religious symbols or images represent not merely gods, or beliefs, but the religious group members themselves and what he refers to as their *collective conscience*—just as national flags may be thought to represent not only the idea of a nation, but its actual citizens. (This is one reason why some Americans view the burning of Old Glory as a deeply violent symbolic act.)

Durkheim also recognized how often these images were evoked in religious rituals and practices as a means of creating symbolic boundaries demarcating the separation of *sacred* and *profane* elements in the universe. For instance, many religions adhere to dietary codes that restrict the eating of certain foods considered dirty, filthy, dangerous, or otherwise taboo: Observant Jews abstain from eating non-kosher foods such as shellfish and pork, while Islamic dietary rules prohibit the consumption of pork as well (Douglas 1991). Likewise, the three major Western religions organize time itself into sacred occasions (Lent and Easter Sunday, the holy month of Ramadan, Yom Kippur and the Sabbath) as well as place (Jerusalem, Mecca, the Church of the Holy Sepulcher, the Western Wall, the Temple Mount). As Durkheim explains, systems of classification and boundary maintenance related to the differentiation between the sacred and the profane help societies reinforce distinctions between themselves and other groups, on the basis of insider and outsider status.

Finally, religious rituals involving large groups of people present opportunities for generating what Durkheim calls *collective effervescence*, a shared feeling of identity in which the individual members of the group (whether a tribe or a congregation) experience waves of emotion, a sense of unity and togetherness. The effervescent energy of crowds is considered so central to religious ceremonies that laws, customs, and traditions of faith all but demand that rituals be performed collectively. In Judaism, certain prayer rituals require the presence of a quorum, or *minyan*, of at least 10 participants. During the annual Islamic pilgrimage to Mecca, or the Hajj, three million adherents converge on the Saudi Arabian city to engage in collective worship and celebration, as the black civil rights leader Malcolm X (1964, p. 343) recollects in his *Autobiography*:

> We parked near the Great Mosque. We performed our ablutions and entered. Pilgrims seemed to be on top of each other, there were so many, lying, sitting, sleeping, praying, walking. . . . Then I saw the Ka'ba, a huge black stone

Muslim pilgrims (left) pray in Mecca, and a Sri Lankan woman (right) prays at a statue of the Buddha. According to Durkheim, religions use rituals to separate the sacred from the profane. What are the social functions of these distinctions?

house in the middle of the Great Mosque. It was being circumambulated by thousands upon thousands of praying pilgrims, both sexes, and every size, shape, color, and race in the world. . . . Faces were enraptured in their faith.

To sum up, Durkheim argues that it is these basic elements of religious life— shared symbols and images, imagined boundaries separating the sacred from the profane, and rituals that help participants generate collective effervescence—that provide the social glue that binds societies together through thick and thin. Of course, Durkheim recognizes that the modern world is defined not by religiosity but secularism, a belief in science over faith in an age of dynamic innovation and change. This worries him greatly because he fears that "there can be no society that does not experience the need at regular intervals to maintain and strengthen the collective feelings and ideas that provide its coherence and its distinct individuality" (1912/1995, p. 429). While religions continue to flourish throughout the world, they may not have the same hold over modern individuals that they once did among Native Americans and Aborigines, if for no other reason than that our lives are organized according to the logics of a variety of competing social institutions (e.g., nation-states and their judicial systems, the global economy, science-based medicine) rather than simply religion. This is especially the case in pluralistic societies like the United States where various faiths, denominations, and sects divide entire societies into highly differentiated mosaics of religious belief. Meanwhile, in our enlightened age of invention and discovery, it appears that "the great things of the past that excited our fathers no longer arouse the same zeal among us, either because they have passed so completely into common custom that we lose awareness of them or because they no longer suit our aspirations. Meanwhile, no replacement for them has yet been created." As Durkheim poignantly remarks, "The former gods are growing old or dying, and others have not been born" (p. 429).

And yet Durkheim concludes *The Elementary Forms of Religious Life* on an optimistic note: "A day will come when our societies once again will know hours of creative effervescence during which new ideals will again spring forth and new formulas emerge to guide humanity for a time. . . . There are no immortal gospels, and there is no reason to believe that humanity is incapable of conceiving new ones in the future" (pp. 429—30). What will those new gospels teach us? What kinds of symbols will emerge to reorient our identities, our social place in the world? What kinds of rituals will rejuvenate societies by generating the collective effervescence they need to thrive? What will serve as the social glue that will help bind societies together, through thick and thin?

Rituals of Solidarity and Social Cohesion in Popular Culture

A functionalist approach to popular culture emphasizes how the symbols, rituals, and practices surrounding its production and consumption can bring people together by generating a shared sense of social solidarity. The culture surrounding sports entertainment provides a powerful example. In the world of professional athletics, cities and regions are represented by team franchises that employ a range of symbols engineered to foster collective attachment. Like Native American and Aboriginal tribes, sports teams are typically signified by animalistic totems, whether the Chicago Bears, Atlanta Falcons, Miami Dolphins, Los Angeles Rams, Cincinnati Bengals, Detroit Lions, Indianapolis Colts, Baltimore Ravens, or the Denver Broncos. (One of the reasons many civil rights groups such as the NAACP as well as scholarly organizations like the American Sociological Association have rallied against the promotion of even reverential team mascots such as the Washington Redskins or the Cleveland Indians is that they stereotype and objectify American Indians as if they, too, were anthropomorphized animal totems.) Team nicknames, logos, and jerseys provide further means of symbolic attachment, and this is particularly emphasized during competitions that pit two teams against one another, each player's uniform emblazoned with bold colors, insignias, and other demarcating symbols used to differentiate opposing teams on the field of play, and among rival fans in the grandstands.

Just as religions create symbolic orders that distinguish among the sacred and the profane, team regalia help participants maintain the illusion of difference between opposing franchises. (I describe this difference as illusory given the manufactured nature of team identity, as emphasized by the excessive mobility of players and teams to different cities, as noted earlier, and the rapid creation of recent expansion teams.) Collective rituals surrounding the celebration of adversarial team differences further bolster the social integration of like-minded fans. These rituals of boundary maintenance include pep rallies, tailgate parties, celebratory parades, and the main sporting events themselves, in which athletes perform alongside support personnel such as cheerleaders, marching

How do sports teams create social solidarity?

Statement by the Council of the American Sociological Association on Discontinuing the Use of Native American Nicknames, Logos and Mascots in Sport

March 6, 2007

WHEREAS the American Sociological Association comprises sociologists and kindred professionals who study, among other things, culture, religion, media, sport, race and ethnicity, racism, and other forms of inequality;

WHEREAS the American Sociological Association recognizes that racial prejudice, stereotypes, individual discrimination and institutional discrimination are socially created phenomena that are harmful to Native Americans and other people of color;

WHEREAS the American Sociological Association is resolved to undertake scholarship, education, and action that helps to eradicate racism;

WHEREAS social science scholarship has demonstrated that the continued use of Native American nicknames, logos and mascots in sport reflect and reinforce misleading stereotypes of Native Americans in both past and contemporary times;

WHEREAS the stereotypes embedded in Native American nicknames, logos and mascots in sport undermine education about the lives of Native American peoples;

WHEREAS social science scholarship has demonstrated that the continued use of Native American nicknames, logos and mascots in sport harm Native American people in psychological, educational, and social ways;

WHEREAS the continued use of Native American nicknames, logos and mascots in sport shows disrespect for Native American spiritual and cultural practices;

WHEREAS many Native American individuals across the United States have found Native American nicknames, logos and mascots in sport offensive and called for their elimination;

AND, WHEREAS the continued use of Native American nicknames, logos and mascots in sport has been condemned by numerous reputable academic, educational and civil rights organizations, and the vast majority of Native American advocacy organizations, including but not limited to: American Anthropological Association, American Psychological Association, North American Society for the Sociology of Sport, Modern Language Association, United States Commission on Civil Rights, National Association for the Advancement of Colored People, Association of American Indian Affairs, National Congress of American Indians, and National Indian Education Association;

NOW, THEREFORE, BE IT RESOLVED, that the American Sociological Association calls for discontinuing the use of Native American nicknames, logos and mascots in sport.

bands, dancers, fuzzy mascots, and the most enthusiastic of fans draped in team colors and covered with face paint. Like religious ceremonies, these rituals take place within special worlds marked off in time (March Madness, Monday Night Football, Super Bowl Sunday) and space (Chicago's Wrigley Field, Boston's Fenway Park). Such events feature synchronized body movements (stadium waves) and incantations (cheers, fight songs), and all help generate a heightened sense of collective effervescence among feverish participants. One of the most frequent pop songs sung at sporting events around the world is the British band Queen's 1977 hit "We Are the Champions." As its catchy refrain assures listeners, "No time for losers, 'cause we are the champions of the world." According to lead singer Freddie Mercury, "I was thinking about football [presumably soccer] when I wrote it. I wanted a participation song, something that the fans could latch on to" (*Time Out: New York* 2012).

Rituals of solidarity among local high school and college sports teams allow small communities in places like rural Indiana and Texas to feel gigantic and mythic, greater than the sum of their parts. In his bestselling book *Friday Night Lights* (later made into a critically acclaimed film and television series), H. G. Bissinger (1990) observes how the Permian Panthers high school football team brings together its hometown citizens like nothing else. In the West Texas oil town of Odessa, magic happens on Friday nights when the Panthers take the field. Under the bright lights of a $5.2 million stadium, the school's players, coaches, cheerleaders, and marching band perform to crowds of nearly 20,000 people who shout the home team's cheer, "*MO-JO! MO-JO!*" Neighbors flood the high school's pep rallies, gab about individual players' physical strengths and on-the-field statistics, wear the team's colors of black and white, and threaten the head coach whenever the Panthers lose to a longtime rival like the Rebels, a high school team from nearby Midland, Texas, the former hometown of President George W. Bush.

Meanwhile, the professional sports entertainment culture of more populated and cosmopolitan cities like New York, Los Angeles, Houston, Atlanta, and Miami gives locals otherwise divided on the basis of national origin, socioeconomic class, race, and ethnicity a sense of commonality and even intimacy through a shared identity. This social solidarity asserted itself during the 1990s when complete strangers embraced and high-fived one another on the streets of Chicago after the Bulls won each of their six NBA championships, or in 2016 when a reported five million Cubs fans celebrated the team's World Series victory over the Cleveland Indians at a hometown parade and rally. Large cities like these often feel like anonymous, lonely worlds (Simmel 1903/1971; Wirth 1938; Lofland 1973), and professional sports teams can bring people together in a spirit of camaraderie atypical among strangers in the urban metropolis.

Moreover, it bears remembering that while U.S. intercollegiate and professional sports rivals attract fans of opposing teams, nearly all participants still identify with the national culture to a greater or lesser degree. (Exceptions perhaps include Canadian teams and individual athletes from abroad, such as the six-foot-eleven NBA small forward Giannis Antetokounmpo from Greece.)

Before kickoff, Kansas City Chiefs fans salute the American flag as the National Anthem plays. Sporting events are an opportunity to celebrate our shared patriotism and national identity.

For this reason, sporting events in the United States generally emphasize American identity and national pride through a variety of rituals. Performers sing the national anthem before solemn crowds, while after the terrorist attacks of September 11, 2001, Major League Baseball (MLB) home teams replaced the singing of the always light-hearted and sometimes partisan "Take Me Out to the Ball Game" with the more unifying "God Bless America." The attacks also occasioned commemorative ceremonies at professional football games and NASCAR races, replete with flag displays and a contingent of firefighters and police, the symbolic heroes of 9/11 (Collins 2004b, p. 68), just as sporting events present opportunities to honor military servicepersons and veterans during wartime. These rituals evoke the celebration of shared patriotism and national identity as a kind of civic religion and can generate an even greater sense of social solidarity and collective effervescence than the more playful, team-oriented cheering expected during game time. (For this reason, the Pentagon has contracted with professional sports teams for millions of dollars to hold what have become known as "paid-for-patriotism" events that honor U.S. armed-services personnel, as unearthed by a 2015 Senate investigation; see Huetteman 2015.) Other public rituals also generate this kind of spirited nationalism, including political rallies, campaigns and elections, commemorative parades, and holiday celebrations.

It is also not difficult to imagine how other kinds of popular entertainment featuring large effervescent crowds might achieve similarly social ends. Throughout rock music history, arena and stadium concerts have brought fans together in shared moments of collective solidarity and bliss, notably the live performances of superstar acts like U2 and the Rolling Stones. As a live entertainer, Bruce Springsteen has been known to give four-hour marathon concerts that energize his fans, diehards who holler along with the singer-songwriter when he performs 1970s hits like "Thunder Road" and "Born to Run." During their epic career from the late 1960s through the mid-1990s, the Grateful Dead—perhaps the most successful touring rock band of all time—regularly drew crowds of self-identified "Deadheads," dedicated fans who followed the band along their concert tour route to every show. These performances assumed the character of New Age spiritual gatherings in which audience members clad in tie-dyed and beaded clothing sang along together to surrealist tunes—"Box of Rain," "Eyes of the World," "Sugar Magnolia," "China Cat Sunflower," "Friend of the Devil," "Dark Star"—and performed free-form circle dances to improvised drum solos and guitar jams, often under the influence of psychedelic drugs such as LSD. Contemporary rock music festivals such as Lollapalooza, Coachella, and Bonnaroo continue to provide successive generations of music fans with shared collective experiences enjoyed in the presence of tens of thousands of amped-up fellow travelers. So successful are these festivals that they have become reliable generators of revenue for the music industry and their artists in a post-CD age. According to *Rolling Stone*, in 2014 a standard festival headliner like the Canadian indie rock band Arcade Fire could expect to bring in $2–$3 million per performance, while superstar and former Beatle Paul McCartney may earn up to $4 million per show (Knopper 2014).

In today's highly mediated cultural environment, live streaming and tele-vised events have the potential to generate similarly effervescent experiences among what we might call an *imagined community* of viewers who, despite their lack of physical proximity to one another, still feel as if they are members of a collective audience sharing the simultaneity of a moment (Anderson 1991). Recent events include the historic 2008 election of President Barack Obama, the 2011 Arab Spring political revolutions, the 2013 Boston Marathon bombing, the 2015 U.S. Supreme Court ruling on same-sex marriage, and the Black Lives Matter demonstrations held around the country in reaction to a series of high-profile police killings of unarmed black men, including Michael Brown in Ferguson, Missouri, and Walter Scott in North Charleston, South Carolina.

Ironically, reproduced media images of live events such as parades, marches, and rallies can often generate as much if not *greater* feelings of solidarity among audiences, while the actual events themselves can feel chaotic, disorienting, and even boring to live spectators lost among the noisy crowds they attract (Lang and Lang 1953). In the case of Obama's celebratory acceptance speech in Chicago's Grant Park on November 4, 2008, the occasion attracted so many people that even those who were present could only really see the candidate from afar on the jumbo video screens placed near the stage. Meanwhile, audiences watching at home not only enjoyed close-up camera shots of the president-elect and his family from the comfort of their living rooms, but they also likely had a much better view of the effervescent crowd than the actual participants themselves.

The excitement generated by such events has led to the institution of regu-larly scheduled live telecasts engineered to create collective effervescence on demand. Occasions such as the annual Academy Awards ceremonies and the quadrennial Democratic and Republican presidential nominating conventions

Televised events such as the Opening Ceremonies of the 2016 Summer Olympics in Rio are engineered to create collective effervescence among an imagined community of viewers.

are staged affairs promoted and televised to a worldwide audience. The historian Daniel Boorstin (1961) refers to these kinds of media rituals as *pseudo-events*, happenings held simply for "the immediate purpose of being reported or reproduced" (p. 11). Competitive reality television series such as *Survivor, Dancing with the Stars*, and *The Voice* replicate the staged features of these ritual events by filming their season finales in real time before enormous studio audiences, perhaps in the hope that the collective enthusiasm of the live spectators will rub off on home viewers. The collective solidarity generated by these live events is only bolstered when accompanied by online streams of up-to-the-minute commentary posted by bloggers and social media users on Twitter and Facebook.

To a large extent, professional sporting events are similarly enacted for the purposes of being transformed into televised entertainment for a mass audience, which is why they are so often scheduled in prime time to conform to the needs of commercial network television. For example, because of the 12-hour time difference between Beijing and New York, in 2008 NBC struck a deal with the International Olympic Committee to move key Summer Games events such as swimming and gymnastics to the morning so they could be shown live on prime-time American television (Carter 2008). Similarly, the Super Bowl is always shown in the early evening on a Sunday night, which helped it attract a peak audience of 120.8 million viewers in 2015, making it the most watched program in television history. Perhaps for this reason, the following year advertisers paid an average of $5 million to air a 30-second commercial during Super Bowl 50 (Ward 2016).

Popular Culture as a Resource for Public Reflection

Great literature, drama, and myth take abstract ideas and universal themes such as death, betrayal, love, envy, regret, ambition, and revenge and make them come alive by embodying them in fictional characters and their fantastic trials—Oedipus, Romeo and Juliet, Don Quixote, Dr. Frankenstein, Ebenezer Scrooge, Jay Gatsby. These myths gain their cultural power from their ability to express the otherwise ineffable sense of what it feels like to be human. In the last century, artists have taken advantage of the narrative possibilities of mass media technology to illuminate these same crucial literary themes in visually compelling ways. Obvious cinematic examples include the Orson Welles master-piece *Citizen Kane* (1941), the Francis Ford Coppola film *The Godfather* (1972) and its sequel *The Godfather, Part II* (1974), and the Martin Scorsese picture *Raging Bull* (1980), all of which feature extraordinarily complex and self-destructive figures from Charles Foster Kane to Michael Corleone to Jake LaMotta. (Recent examples from the world of television and streaming video include the HBO modern-day epics *The Sopranos* and *The Wire*, the Emmy Award—winning AMC series *Mad Men*, and Netflix's *House of Cards*.) These dramas provide templates for examining the human condition, warts and all; to paraphrase the anthropologist Clifford Geertz (1973, p. 448), they are stories we tell ourselves about ourselves.

While seemingly superficial by comparison, to a certain extent the culture of celebrity and entertainment performs a similar function. In contemporary culture celebrities are treated as mythical archetypes to whom we assign all sorts of extreme attributes, whether beauty and grace, or avarice and gluttony (Gabler 2000). Regardless of how little we may care for them as individual people (Gamson 1994), we obsess over their reported comedic highs and tragic lows

Dramas like House of Cards, *starring Kevin Spacey as ruthless and complicated Frank Underwood, tackle universal themes such as ambition and betrayal.*

because their spotlighted stories provide resources for reflecting on the social world and the human experience. For example, let us take a popular staple of celebrity gossip: cheating and adultery. Tales of two-timing in Hollywood are legion and tend to be highly publicized affairs. Actor Jude Law and his fiancée, actress Sienna Miller, broke off their engagement after it was revealed in 2005 that Law was sleeping with Daisy Wright, his children's nanny. (This was soon after actor Ethan Hawke and actress Uma Thurman divorced because Hawke had an affair with their nanny, who he eventually married in 2008.) When former Swedish model Elin Nordegren discovered in 2009 that her husband, golf champion Tiger Woods, had been cheating on her with multiple mistresses, the ensuing domestic argument drove the fleeing Woods to crash his Escalade into a fire hydrant and a tree at two in the morning. (Nordegren reportedly chased him out of the house with—what else?—a golf club.) By the end of 2015 pop singer Gwen Stefani and Gavin Rossdale, lead singer and rhythm guitarist for the British rock band Bush, split up amid allegations of Rossdale's infidelities with *their* nanny, as did actor and director Ben Affleck and actress Jennifer Garner. The most famous case of public adultery in recent history took place not in Hollywood but in Washington, where President Bill Clinton was discovered to have carried on an illicit affair with Monica Lewinsky, a White House intern, in the 1990s. (Their dalliances were said to have taken place in the only room in the world where the president could be guaranteed absolute privacy: the Oval Office.) He was caught during his second term, a scandal that eventually led to his impeachment by the House of Representatives in 1998 and acquittal by the U.S. Senate in 1999.

Why were these stories so publicized, and why did readers follow them so intently? In many ways, these tales of relationships gone awry serve the same function as Aesop's fables, traditional folktales, and morality plays: They give tangible form to otherwise abstract ethical dilemmas concerning the nature of human relations and social behavior. In doing so they become readily available conversation starters, or "water cooler talk" (named for the habit of white-collar workers kibitzing by water coolers, coffee machines, or other shared office amenities), whereas adulterous affairs and one-night stands among *actual* friends and acquaintances are generally not considered appropriate topics for public discussion, particularly in the workplace. Meanwhile, chatter surrounding the lives of famous celebrities offers ordinary people opportunities for reflection and debate on these and other grave matters without fear (or at least concern) of embarrassing the principal characters of such gossip. Other delicate topics regularly made available for public discourse as a result of having emanated from the world of celebrity and entertainment culture include May/December romances, cancer survival, drug addiction, rapid weight loss and gain, and the consequences of elective plastic surgery. Nor do such topics end there: Recall the endless public discussions sparked by the 2014 indictments of NFL football stars Ray Rice of the Baltimore Ravens for aggravated assault against his fiancée, and Adrian Peterson of the Minnesota Vikings for causing reckless or negligent injury to his own child; *NBC Nightly News* anchor Brian Williams's suspension in

What is the social function of celebrity gossip?

2015 for having exaggerated his journalistic exploits during the Iraq War; the avalanche of sexual assault allegations against comedian and actor Bill Cosby dating back to the 1960s; and the extraordinarily offensive public remarks Donald J. Trump made about women, Mexican immigrants, POWs, Muslims, and the disabled during his presidential campaign. In each of these instances, the celebrity status of those involved provided an excuse for the rest of us to discuss sensitive topics of conversation and pass moral judgment with ease.

We rely on celebrity gossip for much lighter food for thought as well. For instance, the enthusiasm surrounding celebrity pregnancies and parenthood reaches a fever pitch in entertainment tabloid magazines. In 2008 *People* paid a reported $14 million for the exclusive rights to publish photographs of Angelina Jolie and Brad Pitt's newborn twins. (The celebrity couple promised to donate the money to charity.) The babies were featured on the magazine's cover, just as Jennifer Lopez and then-husband Marc Anthony's newborn twins were earlier that year. (In comparison to Brangelina, the latter couple was reportedly paid a relatively paltry $6 million for their photo rights.) In March 2016 a single issue of *US Weekly* featured the following "news" items:

- Prince William and Duchess Kate Middleton "fight" to give their two-year-old son and 10-month-old daughter "a normal childhood," accompanied by photographs of the royal family on a ski vacation in the French Alps.
- *The Jersey Shore* reality TV personality Jenny "JWow" Farley snuggles her daughter, Meilani, 20 months, at a Seaside Heights, New Jersey, bash.

- Actress Anne Hathaway seen hiking while pregnant and "due in the spring."
- Actress Keri Russell seen bicycling while pregnant and "due in the spring."
- Actress Lucy Liu tags a pic of her six-month-old son #babyyoga.
- Actress Charlize Theron takes her four-year-old son to his music lesson in Los Angeles.
- Socialite Ivanka Trump on how her four- and two-year-olds were "all laughs helping me finish some emails" while playing with her computer.
- Reality TV personality Kim Kardashian West posts a cute photo of her three-month-old son on Twitter.
- *Teen Mom 2* reality TV personality Jenelle Evans and her year-long custody battle over her 20-month-old son.
- Victoria's Secret model Behati Prinsloo on her four-month pregnancy with her husband Adam Levine, Maroon 5 frontman and celebrity judge for *The Voice*.

What is with this obsession over the children spawned by celebrities? One answer has to do with the production of entertainment news. Celebrities crave free publicity, but only if it promises to reflect them in a positive light. But while celebrities encourage the publication of laudatory, puffed-up profiles and other *fluff* pieces, journalists seek to uncover *dirt*, whether professional or personal—not necessarily because it tends toward the negative and tawdry (i.e., the tales of adultery discussed earlier), but because it is regarded as scarce information and therefore more likely to sell to inquiring readers on the basis of its news value (Gamson 1994). In negotiations between celebrity publicists and magazine editors, baby stories are then seen as the ultimate compromise in which everyone wins: The celebrity is shown doting on her (or his) newborn children, selfless as can be, while the editors get access to the most intimate sanctuary of a famous person, the home or hospital bed, during a potentially once-in-a-lifetime event (for that particular celebrity, at least).

While this explains why magazines run such stories, it does not shed much light on why readers might care about celebrity pregnancies or births in the first place, outside of the obvious pleasure we receive from seeing cute pictures of happy babies and toddlers. Here, a functionalist perspective can help provide an answer. First, bear in mind the universality of pregnancy, childbirth, and parenthood in people's lives—after all, we all came from

Why do celebrities and media outlets love to feature stories about celebrity children? Why do consumers like to read them?

someone's belly. Second, while childbirth obviously represents a celebrated milestone for parents, such experiences are fraught with anxieties, especially for women. Will my baby be healthy? What if she turns out to have a crippling peanut allergy? Will I ever get my body back into trim shape? Will I have to put my career on hold? Is the father around, and if so, is he up to the challenge of hands-on parenting? Widespread media coverage of childbearing and child-rearing celebrities allows for a public airing and intense discussion of these anxieties without devastating social repercussions for gossipmongers or their targets. They also permit cultural consumers to make judgments on the parenting styles of others without necessarily appearing judgmental (and without ostracizing their friends and neighbors). This explains the popularity of MTV reality shows like *16 and Pregnant* and *Teen Mom* that shame young working-class mothers as unprepared and irresponsible parents. Of course, public judgments about parents need not be negative or abusive, as illustrated by the large numbers of fluffy news items praising celebrity fathers for simply being involved in their children's lives at all. (Notably, celebrity mothers are rarely congratulated for their parenting efforts to the same extent as fathers, thus naturalizing the differences in gender expectations that society commonly assigns to men and women.)

Bringing the discussion full circle, we can see how the world of professional sports also provides us with opportunities to reflect on the human condition. Certainly, as evidenced through magazines like *Sports Illustrated* and televised entertainment such as ESPN's *SportsCenter* and *Monday Night Football*, media surrounding professional athletics relies on the proliferation of biographical narratives, tales of career triumph and loss, grace and virtue, heartache and victory. These stories are a staple of the sports entertainment industry, and a number of perennial narratives, or *evergreens* (Grindstaff 2002, p. 84), emerge with remarkable regularity. One set of narratives chronicles the frustrations of hard-luck franchises that success always seems to elude—Exhibit A might be baseball's Cleveland Indians, who have not won a World Series since 1948. A related set of narratives feature standardized stories about long-suffering teams who break their losing streaks after years of patience, as when the Boston Red Sox broke their 86-year drought and their famed "Curse of the Bambino" by winning the 2004 World Series. (Local superstition has it that the losing streak had been caused by trading the batting legend Babe Ruth to the New York Yankees on January 5, 1920; see Borer 2008). Other narratives similarly attach moral significance to the athletic achievements of underdogs and long shots, like the 1980 U.S. Olympic Hockey team, a collection of college and amateur players who eventually won the gold medal after beating the odds-on favorite, the Soviet Union. Athletic accomplishments based on longevity, as when Baltimore Oriole Cal Ripken Jr. broke Lou Gehrig's record in 1995 for most consecutive baseball games played, are often framed as moral fables, as life lessons that emphasize the ethics of work and perseverance.

Another set of narratives concerns the nature of the human body and its limits. In recent years the NFL has come under attack for promoting the on-the-field violence that increases players' exposure to repetitive concussions, head injuries that over time can cause loss of memory and cognitive functioning, depression, Alzheimer's, and chronic traumatic encephalopathy (CTE), a degenerative brain disease that has led to dementia and suicide in numerous high-profile cases. In many ways, scandals surrounding the illegal use of steroids and other performance-enhancing drugs in professional and Olympic sports by once-celebrated athletes—Lance Armstrong, Alex Rodriguez, Mark McGwire, Marion Jones, Manny Ramirez, Maria Sharapova—similarly provide resources for reflecting on the limits of the human body, raising questions surrounding the blurry distinction between "natural" and "enhanced" athletic abilities, the criminality of drugs and the ethics concerning the use of biomedical technology, and, ultimately, the meaning of accomplishment itself.

Finally, professional sports have long provided a dynamic context for public discussions about social inequality in America. On April 15, 1947, Jackie Robinson suited up as No. 42 and took the field for the Brooklyn Dodgers, becoming the first African American ballplayer permitted to play for a major league team since 1889. (Prior to the postwar era, black players had been segregated into a number of baseball organizations collectively called the "Negro leagues.") Robinson was arguably one of the greatest players of the game—he played in six World Series and six All-Star games, won the National League MVP, and ended his career with a .311 batting average and eventually an induction into the Major League Baseball Hall of Fame—yet at the time his invitation to join the Dodgers was so controversial that in his first months of play he braved death threats from sports fans and racial animus from some of his own teammates. But like other African American athletes whose talents and determination allowed them to break through the color barrier to achieve greatness, such as heavyweight boxing champion Jack Johnson, Robinson's courage to integrate the sport added a vital spark to a galvanizing national conversation about race and equality in the United States and lent support to other vocal defenders of racial justice in the years leading up to the civil rights era of the 1950s and 1960s. Indeed, over the years Jackie Robinson has become as much a symbol of the African American struggle for civil rights and racial equality as Rosa Parks and Medgar Evers, and today his legend endures for his heroism and character as much as for his athletic achievements. More contemporary civil rights icons from the world of sports include courageous women like African American tennis legend Serena Williams, *Sports Illustrated*'s 2015 Sportsperson of the Year who is widely regarded as the best women's tennis player of all time; Becky Hammon of the NBA's San Antonio Spurs, the first female full-time

Baseball great Jackie Robinson.

assistant coach in *any* of the four major professional men's sports in U.S. history; Kathryn Smith of the Buffalo Bills, the first female full-time assistant coach in the NFL; and Mo'ne Davis, the first girl to pitch a winning game in a Little League World Series. One must also not forget Olympic decathlon gold medalist Bruce Jenner, who earned the Arthur Ashe Courage Award at the 2015 ESPYs for coming out as transgender role model Caitlyn Marie Jenner.

Rituals of Rebellion in Popular Culture

In his research on southeast Africa, the British anthropologist Max Gluckman (1963) discovered a variety of tribal rituals in which participants temporarily exchange status positions related to gender roles. On a set of rites in Zululand, he reports:

> The most important of these rites among the Zulu required obscene behavior by the women and girls. The girls donned men's garments, and herded and milked the cattle, which were normally taboo to them. . . . At various stages of the ceremonies women and girls went naked, and sang lewd songs. Men and boys hid and might not go near. (p. 113)

Among the Swazi tribes of Africa, another ritual emphasizes the public denigration of the king. In this ceremony, priests assemble in the royal cattle pen, and amid the mooing cows they chant:

> You hate the child king,
> You hate the child king.
> I would depart with my Father (the king),
> I fear we would be recalled.
> They put him on the stone:
> —sleeps with his sister:
> —sleeps with Lozithupa ([the] Princess):
> You hate the child king.
>
> King, alas for your fate,
> King, they reject thee,
> King, they hate thee. (pp. 120—21)

Despite the seemingly transgressive character of both these displays, which Gluckman calls *rituals of rebellion*, their ultimate purpose is actually to restore and solidify the tribal social order. These rituals represent a kind of institutionalized protest that allows subordinate group members to momentarily let off steam without actually granting them real power for any significant period of time. (Note that among the Swazi tribes, only the king himself is permitted to organize the aforementioned ritual.) By temporarily inverting the hierarchical structure of the social order as a form of play, such rituals remind participants of the dominant status norms that organize and regulate society on a more daily basis.

Rituals of rebellion are similarly a staple of Western popular culture, and have been for centuries. In the European age of monarchs, court jesters were permitted to tease and provoke kings and queens, just as masks of former and current U.S. presidents and other political figures offer citizens the fun of ridiculing powerful people without negative consequence, albeit in a ritual that reminds us of their prestige. (After all, masquerade shops rarely sell masks resembling the faces of *ordinary* people.) These and other rituals of masquerade mark instances in which people announce their everyday identities by temporarily subverting them through the use of costumes, masks, and cross-dressing. In Philadelphia, the annual New Year's Day Mummers Parade brings out thousands of working-class men who march up Broad Street in sequined dresses, gowns, and face paint. During U.S. celebrations of Halloween, children (and increasingly adults) dress in a kind of drag as well. Costumes representing criminality or evil (pirates, chain gang inmates, gunslingers, witches, vampires, devils) are popular, as are outfits resembling uniforms worn in backbreaking occupations involving undesirable "dirty" work (French maids, construction workers, cowboys).

Rituals of rebellion are similarly embedded in popular entertainment and mass culture. Satirical television shows like NBC's *Saturday Night Live*, Comedy Central's *The Daily Show*, and HBO's *Veep* have created a cottage industry built around poking fun at politicians and other authority figures. Comedians Chevy Chase and Dan Aykroyd began this tradition on *Saturday Night Live* in the 1970s with imitative performances that emphasized the quirky foibles of presidents Gerald Ford and Jimmy Carter, just as Will Ferrell hilariously poked fun at George W. Bush's malapropisms in the run-up to the 2000 presidential election. In one sketch that aired October 7 of that year, Ferrell (as Bush) refers to his overall presidential campaign message as one of "strategery," while in the same sketch Ferrell's costar Darrell Hammond ruthlessly mocks Bush's Democratic opponent Vice President Al Gore by exaggerating his southern drawl and dismissive eye-rolling exhibited during one of the debates. In the run-up to the 2016 U.S. presidential election, Farrell reprised his role as Bush, while both Hammond and Alec Baldwin imitated Donald Trump, former *SNL* writer Larry David played Bernie Sanders, and Kate McKinnon spoofed Hillary Clinton, joining a cast of comedic actresses who have imitated Clinton since the 1990s, including Jan Hooks, Janeane Garofalo, Ana Gasteyer, and Amy Poehler. (In 2015 McKinnon parodied Clinton's intense preparations for the public stage: "I think you're really going to like the Hillary Clinton my team and I have created for this debate. She's warm but strong; flawed yet perfect; relaxed but *racing full speed toward the White House like the T-1000 from* The Terminator.")

How "rebellious" are these rituals? In many ways the ritualized character of these spoofs mitigates their potential bite—after all, if *all* famous politicians are ceremonially ridiculed in the same fashion by late-night comedians regardless of party affiliation, ideology, popularity, or competence, the barbs hurled against them lose much of their sting. In this sense, becoming a laugh line on

Saturday Night Live *sketches that mock politicians—including those featuring Kate McKinnon's memorable turn as Hillary Clinton during the 2016 presidential campaign—constitute modern-day rituals of rebellion. In this SNL episode, the real Clinton made a cameo appearance alongside McKinnon to show off her confident sense of humor.*

Saturday Night Live or *The Tonight Show* represents little more than a flattering sign of a person's celebrity rather than a rejection of his or her governing abilities. The joking atmosphere surrounding the political swipes made by comedians in the context of mass entertainment similarly diminishes how seriously viewers will actually evaluate such criticisms.

In fact, politicians have traditionally benefitted enormously from these kinds of comedic send-ups. A stable of elected officials have personally appeared on *SNL* to mock their political stature on national television while presenting themselves publicly as good sports, including a number of U.S. presidential candidates in the midst of their campaigns: Gore, Bush, John McCain, Barack Obama, Hillary Clinton, Sanders, and Trump. (Gore, who lost the electoral college vote in the 2000 presidential contest to Bush despite winning the popular vote, performed a memorably funny bit of self-parody on *SNL* by begging cast members of the NBC series *The West Wing* to let him sit at a studio replica of the Oval Office desk so he could spend a few brief minutes pretending to be the president.) As for Gore's Republican opponent, Ferrell's imitation of Bush may have made him seem buffoonish but in doing so portrayed him as an "aw-shucks," all-around "regular" guy—not a bad outcome for the candidate, a highly privileged scion of a former U.S. president educated at Phillips Academy, Yale, and Harvard. As if to illustrate *SNL*'s ineffectiveness as a truly rebellious political force, after Bush became president his adviser Karl Rove dubbed his weekly meeting with senior White House aides the "Strategery Group" (Zengerle 2004).

The Darker Functions of Popular Culture

This last set of points addresses some of the darker or more insidious functions of popular culture. For much of this chapter we have explored pop culture's relatively benign and prosocial functions, including the building of social solidarity and group cohesion, the generation of collective effervescence, and the affordance of resources for social reflection. But as these last examples of "rituals of rebellion" illustrate, the power of popular culture can be marshaled for a variety of purposes, and they do not benefit all members of society equally. In the case of political satire, the ritualistic nature of entertainment comedy shows like *Saturday Night Live* transforms dissent into a kind of officially sanctioned mock protest that barks but rarely bites, all while increasing the celebrity status of the targeted public figures themselves. And for what it's worth, in the *ten* presidential elections from 1980 to 2016, the candidate with the best-selling Halloween mask has wound up winning the White House (Gibbs 2008; Fox 2012).

If these collective rituals of solidarity ultimately bolster the legitimacy of those in power by artfully appropriating dissent, other celebrations of popular culture reinforce norms of social inequality in far more obvious ways. Again, the world of sports provides endless examples. High school, collegiate, and professional football teams rely on scantily clad (and unpaid or poorly paid) female cheerleaders to heighten the self-esteem of male players and fans. In competitive gymnastics, young girls and adolescents suffer through marathon training sessions, painful injuries, and, often, eating disorders as they struggle to

In elite gymnastics programs, young girls and adolescents often suffer through intense training, struggle with eating disorders, and ignore injuries in the hopes of pleasing their coaches, teammates, and parents.

please their coaches, teammates, and parents while ignoring their basic health and emotional well-being (Sey 2008).

In addition to the abuse and sexual objectification of women and girls commonly celebrated on athletic fields of play, sporting events also glorify the exploits of rich celebrity athletes who earn millions of dollars a year in salaries, bonuses, and endorsement deals. In 2016, 10 Major League Baseball players collected total salaries of more than $25 million, and two players made at least $30 million, both starting pitchers: Clayton Kershaw of the Los Angeles Dodgers and David Price of the Boston Red Sox. In the 2015—16 season, nine NBA basketball players made $20 million or more, including Dwyane Wade ($20 million), Derrick Rose ($20.09 million), Kevin Durant ($20.16 million), Dwight Howard ($22.36 million), Carmelo Anthony ($22.88 million), LeBron James ($22.97 million), and top moneymaker Kobe Bryant ($25 million). Meanwhile, according to *Forbes*, the most profitable sport in the world is American football: The average NFL team is worth $2 billion—the richest team is the Dallas Cowboys, valued at $4 billion—and 17 NFL team owners are among the 400 wealthiest Americans.

Meanwhile, the collective effervescence produced by rituals of solidarity does not always produce communal bliss but often descends into a kind of mob mentality or groupthink, sometimes with violent consequences. On Sunday night, June 14, 1992, the Chicago Bulls achieved their second consecutive championship victory in the NBA finals by beating the Portland Trail Blazers in six games. The win was immediately followed by widespread celebration on the streets of Chicago, a display of revelry that eventually erupted into destructive rioting and the looting of grocery and liquor stores in the city's South and West Side black neighborhoods. By night's end, nearly 350 stores in the city had been looted, more than 1,000 people were arrested, and 90 police officers sustained injuries (Rosenfeld 1997). Riots also took place in Montreal in 1993 after the Canadiens (the city's professional National Hockey League team) won the Stanley Cup Finals, and in Vancouver, British Columbia, in 1994 after the Canucks *lost* the Stanley Cup championship to the New York Rangers. (Unsurprisingly, hockey is seriously popular in Canada, as is soccer in Italy, where rioting fans in Catania killed a police officer in 2007.)

The film **Hoop Dreams** *tells the story of two young men from Chicago who struggle to escape the inner city and become basketball stars.*

It is also worth bearing in mind that popular culture provides not only a resource for reflection but also distraction, and again, the world of professional sports provides a number of fitting examples. (In fact, the word itself derives from the French *desporter*, which means "to divert, amuse, please, play.") Too many young men from impoverished inner-city neighborhoods risk their futures on the slim hope that they will grow up to play professional basketball. (Only 0.03 percent of all high school men's basketball players make it to the NBA.) Cities desperate for the glory and visibility associated with professional athletics offer sweetheart deals (such as financing new stadium construction projects) to attract and retain sports franchises while virtually ignoring their crumbling schools and public infrastructure. Finally, the collective effervescence and inspirational narratives generated by sports entertainment can be appropriated all too easily for advertising campaigns that draw on the prestige of world-class athletes such as LeBron James, Stephen Curry, and Peyton Manning to sell Papa John's pizza, Under Armour athletic wear, Nike sneakers, Coca-Cola soft drinks, Samsung electronics, Degree deodorant, Brita water filters, Gatorade energy drinks, Nationwide insurance, DirecTV, and McDonald's.

Despite the value of the functionalist perspective, making sense of this darker side of sports and entertainment requires expanding our purview to include alternative sociological understandings of how popular culture works. In the next chapter, we will explore the efficacy and relevance of our second approach to popular culture, the *critical* approach.

WHILE THE WORLD OF BRANDING AND ADVERTISING IS HARDLY new, today it seems as though brands have penetrated every nook and cranny of our society. At universities, endowed professorships include the Taco Bell Distinguished Professor of Hotel and Restaurant Administration at Washington State, the Kmart Chair of Marketing at Wayne State, the Yahoo! Chair of Information-Systems Technology at Stanford, the LEGO Professor of Learning Research at MIT, the Anheuser-Busch Professor of Management at Penn, and the Coca-Cola Distinguished Professor of Marketing at the University of Arizona (Klein 2002, p. 101). Our professional sports stadiums and arenas have been renamed for their corporate sponsors: Houston's Minute Maid Park, Washington's FedEx Field, New England's Gillette Stadium, Los Angeles' Staples Center, Philadelphia's Citizens Bank Park, Cleveland's Quicken Loans Arena, and New Orleans' Smoothie King Center.

Thanks to McDonald's, product placement has worked its way into morning news programs: The fast-food giant has paid to have its iced coffees and other menu items featured prominently on anchors' desks in Chicago, Seattle, and Las Vegas (Clifford 2008). Around the globe, the story is the same: Pizza Hut and Kentucky Fried Chicken stand in view of the ancient pyramids of Giza in Alexandria, Egypt, while McDonald's serves Big Macs at Guantanamo Bay in Cuba, inside Windsor Castle in England, and under Prague's Museum of Communism in the Czech Republic (Smith 2015). McDonald's has also established 2,800 outlets across China, Hong Kong, and South Korea, with plans to open an additional 1,500 stores in the next five years (Zillman 2016). Meanwhile, Starbucks Coffee Company maintains 600 stores throughout the Arab world in Jordan, Kuwait, Oman, Lebanon, Saudi Arabia, Bahrain, Qatar, and the United Arab Emirates.

In contrast to the homegrown culture of Texas high school football discussed in Chapter 2, the proliferation of branding in contemporary culture suggests the need for a more top-down model to explain where much popular culture comes from and its effect on our overall sensibilities. According to a *critical* approach to popular culture, the ascendance of certain kinds of pop culture can be explained by the enormous economic and cultural power of the mass media industry. In contrast to the functionalist perspective discussed in the last chapter, the critical approach emphasizes the darker aspects of popular culture—its ubiquity and dominance in our society, its consolidated ownership among a few multinational corporations, its ability to manufacture desires, perpetuate stereotypes, and mold human minds, particularly those of children. In this chapter, I apply this theoretical perspective to shed light on the organization of the media industry,

Image on pp. 46-47: A graphic from Adbusters *magazine criticizing corporations for encouraging consumerism.*

A critical approach to pop culture can be used to explain the global dominance of brands such as McDonald's and KFC.

the reproduction of social inequality through popular culture, and the inescapable power of the brand.

Foundations of the Critical Approach

In his nineteenth-century critiques of modernity, the German social theorist Karl Marx was among the first thinkers to draw attention to the problems associated with the emergence of mass culture under capitalism. For Marx, a society's culture and its symbolic imagery reflect its economic and social structure and reproduce it over time. In his great polemic, *The German Ideology*, Marx argues that the prevailing ideologies and cultural norms of any society serve to benefit its ruling classes and perpetuate their power. As an example, he observes that the emergence of codes of chivalry and valor during the Middle Ages helped to persuade untold numbers of soldiers to proudly fight to their deaths on behalf of their leaders during the Crusades. (In the context of modern capitalism, one might similarly argue that the U.S. cult of individualism and liberty promotes entrepreneurialism, the deregulation of markets, regressive tax policies, and other social and economic programs favorable to business and wealthy elites.) As Marx writes, "The ideas of the ruling class are in every epoch the ruling ideas: i.e., the class which is the ruling *material* force of society, is at the same time its ruling *intellectual* force. The class which has the means of material production at its disposal, has control at the same time over the means of mental production, so that thereby, generally speaking, the ideas of those who lack the means of mental production are subject to it" (Tucker 1978, p. 172).

In later years, Marx's theories of culture and society, especially his indictment of abusive forms of ideology, would be reworked and updated by like-minded

An image from Leni Riefenstahl's Triumph of the Will. *How is this film of Hitler's rally at Nuremberg an example of cultural hegemony at work?*

scholars throughout the twentieth century. One such thinker, Antonio Gramsci, an Italian political philosopher imprisoned during Mussolini's reign in fascist Italy, recognized the ideological power of culture as an effective means of social control. In contrast to the coercive violence suggested by the excessive deployment of police and military force during this period, Gramsci (1971, pp. 169—70) draws on Niccolò Machiavelli's sixteenth-century political treatise *The Prince* to explain how societies may be even more seamlessly controlled through the dissemination of mass media because it disarms and immobilizes its audience by engineering popular consensus through the power of persuasion. This form of dominance, often referred to as *cultural hegemony*, is most pointedly illustrated by the use of propaganda in Nazi Germany, such as Leni Riefenstahl's *Triumph of the Will*, the glorifying documentary film of Adolf Hitler's 1934 rally at Nuremberg that helped inspire millions of ordinary German citizens to submit to Nazi rule.

During Hitler's rise to power, a number of secular Jewish intellectuals from Germany fled to the United States, where many turned their attention to the power of U.S. media and popular culture, particularly Disney cartoons, commercial radio, jazz music, and Hollywood film. Regarding commercial jazz and popular music, Theodor Adorno identifies its "factory-made" standardization as the root of its "lasting domination of the listening public and of their conditioned reflexes" (Adorno 1989, p. 202). In a 1947 essay, "The Culture Industry: Enlightenment as Mass Deception," Adorno and his frequent collaborator Max Horkheimer further assert the homogeneity and hegemonic power of commercial popular culture: "Culture now impresses the same stamp on everything. Films, radio and magazines make up a system which is uniform as a whole and in every part. . . . Under monopoly capitalism all mass culture is identical, and the lines of its artificial framework begin to show through" (Adorno and Horkheimer 1993, p. 31).

Adorno and Horkheimer propose a top-down theory of mass media, comparing U.S. popular culture to political propaganda by arguing that the irresistible films and music created by culture-producing firms under monopoly capitalism—such as the Big Five movie studios of Hollywood's Golden Age (MGM, Fox, Warner Bros., RKO, and Paramount)—help their companies solidify and maintain economic power and social dominance. (Until the collapse of the studio system, the dominance of the Big Five was due in no small part to their earlier ownership of theater chains in addition to film studios, giving them control over the distribution of not only their own movies but those of their would-be competitors as well.) As Adorno and Horkheimer observe, "Movies and radio need no longer pretend to be art. The truth that they are just business is made into an ideology in order to justify the rubbish they deliberately produce. They call themselves industries; and when their directors' incomes are published, any doubt about the social utility of the finished products is removed. . . . The result is the circle of manipulation and retroactive need in which the unity of the system grows ever stronger" (p. 32).

To this end, Adorno and Horkheimer argue that rather than satisfy preexisting desires among audiences, the media and culture industry relies on advertising, popular music, and the glamour of cinema to invent new (and largely useless) desires for consumer goods, all to be fulfilled through shopping and entertainment—thus creating endless markets for the surplus products sold by department stores, fashion houses, jewelers, cosmetics firms, tobacco and liquor companies, the automobile industry, and, of course, the film studios and record companies that helped to manufacture the desires for such things in the first place. As the progressive rock band Pink Floyd sang on their 1975 album *Wish You Were Here*, "What did you dream? / It's alright, we told you what to dream / So welcome to the machine."

Additionally, Adorno and Horkheimer argue that the formulaic amusements provided by popular culture encourage "the stunting of the mass-media consumer's powers of imagination and spontaneity," rendering working- and middle-class audiences so deluded that they overlook the source of their own exploitation as underpaid workers, deprived of autonomy and creativity on the job. As they write, "The sound film, far surpassing the theatre of illusion, leaves no room for imagination or reflection on the part of the audience. . . . All the other films and products of the entertainment industry which they have seen have taught them what to expect; they react automatically. The might of industrial society is lodged in men's minds" (p. 34).

In an essay on the "regression of listening," Adorno warns of the psychological impact that contemporary popular music has on its fans:

It is contemporary listening which has regressed, arrested at the infantile stage. Not only do the listening subjects lose, along with freedom of choice and responsibility, the capacity for conscious perception of music, which was from time immemorial confined to a narrow group, but they stubbornly reject the possibility of such perception. . . . They are not childlike, as might be expected on the basis of an interpretation of the new type of listener in terms of the introduction to musical life of groups previously unacquainted with music. But they are childish; their primitivism is not that of the undeveloped, but that of the forcibly retarded. . . . There is actually a neurotic mechanism of stupidity in listening, too; the arrogantly ignorant rejection of everything unfamiliar is its sure sign. Regressive listeners behave like children. Again and again with stubborn malice, they demand the one dish they have once been served. (Adorno 1997, pp. 286, 290)

These kinds of criticisms of U.S. popular culture would be echoed throughout the second half of the twentieth century and into our present digital age by a vast array of scholars, public intellectuals, journalists, and artists troubled by the ever-increasing hegemony and consolidated economic power of the culture industries, the global proliferation of their market-tested products, and what some regard as an overall lowering of cultural standards along the way. In his book *Amusing Ourselves to Death*, Neil Postman (1984) warns American readers that our collective reliance on television for our news as well as entertainment has transformed our national public discourse into "dangerous nonsense . . . shriveled and absurd" (p. 16). In a series of penetrating and incisive essays for the edgy journal the *Baffler*, cultural critic Thomas Frank (1997) pokes fun at

In 1927, Warner Bros. released The Jazz Singer, *which became the first feature-length film with dialogue, though it had only 350 words. Why did Adorno criticize the Hollywood film industry and the glamour of cinema?*

how contemporary advertisers attempt to tap into the lucrative youth market by appropriating images of countercultural style to repackage mundane products from diet colas to sugarless chewing gum as rebellious, radical, hip, and on the bleeding edge of extreme cool, sometimes to ridiculous effect. Note how recent ad slogans include laughably "subversive" mantras: "The cleaner you are, the dirtier you get" (Axe Body Spray); "It's gonna get messy" and "Eat like you mean it" (Carl's Jr.); and "Think outside the bun" and "Live Más" (Taco Bell). In *Fast Food Nation*, a shocking exposé and indictment of McDonald's, Burger King, and the entire industrial food system, journalist Eric Schlosser (2002) uncovers a

A young labor activist protests working conditions in South Asian factories contracted by the retailer H&M.

gold mine of industry secrets: the subpar quality of most fast-food burger meat, the chemical additives that give McDonald's French fries their delicious flavor, the poor treatment of adolescent fast-food workers, and the ad campaigns that target small children and public school districts.

Meanwhile, in the last few decades a variety of exciting social movements—many led by young people—have mobilized activists against some of the culture industry's biggest offenses. They include the widespread abuse of sweatshop labor employed to produce brand-name fashion and toys in China, Vietnam, Thailand, and other developing countries; the lack of diversity in Hollywood casting and the negative representation of women and racial and ethnic minorities in television and film; the warrantless access to private online communications, Internet browsing histories, and mobile phone records granted to the U.S. National Security Agency (NSA) by digital service providers; and the consolidation of newspaper, radio, television, and cable ownership in monopolized media markets controlled by a mere handful of companies (Klein 2002; Klinenberg 2007; Vega 2014; Ansari 2015; Thorp 2016).

The Power of the Media and Culture Industry

What American child cannot recognize the blue-and-white lettering of Nabisco's Oreo logo, or the smiling leprechaun who adorns every box of General Mills' Lucky Charms breakfast cereal? The global dominance of the culture industries is illustrated by the ubiquity of the world's most recognizable brands—Starbucks, Lego, Prada, IBM, Samsung, American Express, BMW, L'Oreal, Gucci, Ikea, Adidas, FedEx, Pepsi, Intel, eBay, Nestle, Mercedes, Visa, Honda. In 2016 Interbrand undertook a survey of the 100 Best Global Brands, as measured by financial analysts on the basis of customer demand, consumer loyalty, and forecasts of current and future revenues attributable to the brand, among other valuation strategies. Interbrand's rankings should surprise few readers: Its top five brands were Apple (#1), Google (#2), Coca-Cola (#3), Microsoft (#4), and Toyota (#5). Other pop culture brand leaders included Amazon (#8), McDonald's (#12), Disney (#13), Facebook (#15), Nike (#18), Louis Vuitton (#19), and H&M (#20). The cultural dominance of these brands is reflected in their economic power. Interbrand estimates Coke's brand value at more than $73 billion; meanwhile, the Coca-Cola Company employs more than 120,000 workers, enjoys distribution in more than 200 countries, markets 700+ different beverages, and sells 1.9 billion consumer servings of liquid refreshment *per day.*

The seemingly limitless variety of Coke products—Coca-Cola Classic, Diet Coke, Sprite, Fanta, Dr. Pepper, Barq's, Honest Tea, Schweppes, Dasani, Minute Maid, Fruitopia, Evian, Fresca, Odwalla, Powerade, Hi-C, FUZE Iced Tea, Mello Yello—suggests a vast and sticky landscape of consumer choices at the same time that it reminds us of the singular dominance of Coca-Cola as a beverage monopoly. (For its own part, Coca-Cola's longtime rival Pepsi is the label behind Gatorade, Mountain Dew, 7 Up, Sierra Mist, Mug Root Beer, SoBe, Tropicana, Lipton Iced Tea, Naked, IZZE Sparkling Juice, Aquafina Water, Tazo, Brisk Iced Tea, and Starbucks Frappuccino.) As goes the concentration of the soft-drink industry, so goes the pop culture field as a whole. While the total output of the media, culture, and entertainment industries (movies, books, music, television shows, DVDs, comics, video games) seems infinite, it represents the effort of only a small handful of highly profitable multinational corporations. Most readers know that only four major broadcast networks (CBS, NBC, ABC, and Fox) control primetime television programming on free U.S. TV. But it may surprise some to learn that nearly all popular music sold in the United States today is released on a record label controlled by one of only three major media companies: Sony Music Entertainment, Warner Music Group, and the biggest, Universal Music Group. Similarly, the English-language trade-book publishing industry is dominated by just five firms: HarperCollins, Hachette, Macmillan, Penguin Random House, and Simon & Schuster. There are only six major Hollywood film studios: 20th Century Fox, Columbia, Disney, Paramount, Universal, and Warner Bros. The few parent companies that produce and distribute most of the planet's mass-marketed music, films, books, and television are the portrait of consolidated media and cultural power.

Sony Corporation. Sony employs a workforce of more than 130,000 people, and in fiscal year 2015 enjoyed $68 billion in revenue worldwide. Their holdings include Sony Music Entertainment, one of the three major record companies in the world. The corporate power behind Pitbull, Jennifer Lopez, Carrie Underwood, Kesha, Bob Dylan, and late pop legends Elvis Presley and Michael Jackson, its subsidiary labels include Columbia Records, Day 1, Epic Records, Essential Records, Kemosabe Records, Legacy Recordings, Provident Label Group, RCA, Sony Masterworks, Sony Music Latin, Arista Nashville, Polo Grounds Music, Volcano, and Beach Street/Reunion Records. Its motion picture arm, Sony Pictures Motion Picture Group, includes Columbia Pictures, TriStar Pictures,

Screen Gems, Sony Pictures, and Sony Pictures Animation and has distribution deals with MGM and its subsidiary, United Artists. Its art-house division, Sony Pictures Classics, has released critically acclaimed films by auteur directors such as Woody Allen, Pedro Almodovar, Hal Hartley, Ang Lee, Todd Solondz, John Sayles, and Mike Leigh. Sony Pictures Television includes daytime soaps like *The Young and the Restless* and *Days of Our Lives*, dramas like *The Black-list* and *Masters of Sex*, and game shows like *Wheel of Fortune* and *Jeopardy!*, which air on Sony's Game Show Network (GSN). The company's DVDs are released through Sony Pictures Home Entertainment, and they can be enjoyed on the wide-screen televisions, Blu-ray players, and surround-sound theater systems made by the Sony Corporation. Meanwhile, consumers more into video games can play the latest version of *Grand Theft Auto, Fallout, Call of Duty*, and *Street Fighter* on the Sony PlayStation console developed by Sony Interactive Entertainment.

Time Warner. The company that owns the Batman franchise is no joker. Time Warner includes Warner Bros. Entertainment, Home Box Office (HBO), and Turner Broadcasting System (TBS), and used to own Time Warner Cable (now Spectrum), the second-largest cable operator in the United States, on which viewers can watch the news on CNN and enjoy their favorite programs on HBO, Cinemax, TNT, Cartoon Network, Adult Swim, and truTV, all of which are also owned by Time Warner (as is the CW, a joint venture with CBS Corporation). Meanwhile, as its TV production wing, Warner Bros. Television's successful series include *The Big Bang Theory, 2 Broke Girls, The Flash, Person of Interest, The Vampire Diaries, Shameless*, and *Mike & Molly.* The company releases its movies (which include the *Sherlock Holmes* franchise, the *Hobbit* trilogy, *The Lego Movie*, and all the *Harry Potter* films) through Warner Bros. Pictures, New Line Cinema, and Castle Rock Entertainment, and it owns the entire DC Comics empire from Superman to Wonder Woman.

Walt Disney Company. Mickey Mouse is one rich rodent. In addition to Disney's many theme parks and family resorts, Disney owns ABC Studios and the ABC Television Network (including ABC News and ABC Sports), as well as ESPN, Life-time, A&E, and the Disney Channel. The company creates and distributes movies under Walt Disney Pictures and its Pixar Animation Studios, Touchstone Pictures, and Marvel Entertainment; DVDs are distributed through Walt Disney Studios Home Entertainment. They also license their global brand through Disney Toys and Disney Apparel, all sold at Disney Stores throughout North America, Europe, and, in recent years, Asia. (At 9,257 square feet, the Disney Store in Shanghai is the largest in the world.) In addition to Donald Duck and Goofy, Disney owns the Muppets, and in 2012 they bought *Star Wars* creator George Lucas's special-effects studio Industrial Light & Magic (along with Lucasfilm, his movie and television production company) for more than $4 billion. Disney's classic films (*Snow White and the Seven Dwarfs, Pinocchio, Bambi, The Jungle Book*) are legendary, while its more recent moneymakers may be even bigger: *Frozen* and *Inside Out*; all the *Iron Man, Captain America*, and *Avengers* films; and the biggest U.S. box-office hit of all time, *Star Wars: The Force Awakens*.

In 2015, the Walt Disney Company opened its first Disney Store in China. At 54,000 square feet, the Shanghai flagship is the largest Disney Store in the world.

Viacom. The centerpiece of this conglomerate is Viacom Media Networks, which includes some of the hippest real estate on cable television for teens—MTV, Comedy Central, VH1, Spike TV, Nickelodeon and Nick Jr., TV Land, CMT, Logo, and Black Entertainment Television (BET) Networks, which targets African American audiences and other consumers of black popular culture. Viacom's motion picture arm is the Paramount Pictures Corporation, which includes Paramount Pictures, Paramount Animation, its art-house division Paramount Vantage, MTV Films, Nickelodeon Movies, and Paramount Home Entertainment. Its film library includes *The Godfather* and *Indiana Jones* films, *Forrest Gump, Titanic*, and the *Transformers* franchise.

CBS Corporation. Formerly part of the Viacom family, the CBS Corporation owns the CBS Television Network, CBS Radio, Showtime (SHO), The Movie Channel (TMC), and the CW (owned jointly with Warner Bros.). CBS Television Studios coproduces hit programs, including the entire *NCIS* franchise, *Jane the Virgin, Crazy Ex-Girlfriend, Elementary, Hawaii 5-0*, and *The Late Show with Stephen Colbert*. Meanwhile, CBS also owns Simon & Schuster, one of the five largest English-language trade-book publishers in the world: Its imprints include Scribner, Free Press, and Pocket Books.

Comcast Corporation. Headquartered in downtown Philadelphia, Comcast is the largest broadcasting and cable company in the world, the largest Internet service provider in the United States, and the third-largest home telephone service provider in the country. Moreover, as the owner of NBC Universal, it is the parent company of the NBC Television Network, as well as MSNBC, CNBC, USA,

Bravo, E! Entertainment Television, Sprout, Oxygen, Syfy (formerly known as the SCI FI Channel), and Telemundo, the Spanish-language television network. Its Universal Television produces Fox's *Brooklyn Nine-Nine*, Hulu's *The Mindy Project*, and Netflix's *Unbreakable Kimmy Schmidt*. NBC Universal's movie wing includes Universal Pictures, its art-house division Focus Features, Working Title Films, Illumination Entertainment, and Universal Studios Home Entertainment. Its motion-picture franchises include *The Fast and the Furious, Pitch Perfect, Despicable Me*, and *Jurassic Park*. As aggressive as a *Tyrannosaurus rex*, Comcast also holds investments in the Weather Channel, Fandango, and Hulu, and owns the Philadelphia Flyers, the city's National Hockey League team.

21st Century Fox. Formerly the media and broadcasting wing of News Corporation (which owns the *Wall Street Journal, New York Post, National Geographic*, and HarperCollins, another one of the five largest English-language trade-book publishers in the world), 21st Century Fox's motion picture arm includes 20th Century Fox, its art-house division Fox Searchlight Pictures, and Blue Sky Studios. (Besides the original *Star Wars*, Fox's films include *Avatar, The Martian*, the *Fantastic Four* films, and all of the *X-Men* movies.) It owns the Fox Broadcasting Company and the cable channels FX, FXX, Fox Sports Networks, and Fox News. It produces and distributes TV programming through 20th Century Fox Television and Fox 21 Television Studios, including Showtime's *Homeland*, ABC's *Modern Family*, and Fox's *Empire, New Girl*, and TV's longest-running American scripted prime-time series, *The Simpsons*. Fox also owns and operates 18 local television stations and has nearly 220 affiliate stations around the country.

Along with the five most powerful digital media companies in the world—Amazon, Apple, Facebook, Google, and Microsoft—these seven mega-firms wield enormous power. They control billions of dollars of assets, hundreds of thousands of jobs, and untold political influence in Washington, particularly with regard to media policy. In part because of their lobbying efforts, in the mid-1990s Congress passed the Telecommunications Act of 1996, which eliminated many of the caps on media ownership that formerly limited the number of newspapers and radio and television stations a single firm could control. As a result of this landmark legislation, monopolies like Cumulus Media are able to own and operate 454 radio stations in 90 U.S. media markets. Sinclair Broadcast Group owns and operates, programs,

The cartoon character Bart Simpson was created for the Fox Television Network, which is owned by 21st Century Fox. Over the years, Bart has been used to market many products including candy bars, fast food, toys, and magazines.

or provides sales services to 172 television stations (and 482 channels) in 81 U.S. markets. The largest U.S. newspaper publishing chain, the Gannett Company owns 80 newspapers, including the *Arizona Republic*, *Des Moines Register*, *Detroit Free Press*, *Indianapolis Star*, *Milwaukee Journal Sentinel*, and Gannett's flagship paper, *USA Today*, which has both the highest print circulation in the country and the most digital traffic of any newspaper website. But the biggest winner of the Telecommunications Act may be iHeartMedia, the largest radio station owner in the country with a whopping 858 broadcast radio stations in 150 markets—they reach a quarter of a *billion* U.S. listeners monthly.

In addition, note that for all the talk about the diversity of news and entertainment offered on the Internet, the most popular sites are owned by the globe's wealthiest media giants. According to the Project for Excellence in Journalism's 2015 report on *The State of the News Media*, the 10 most visited news sites on the web include (in descending order) Yahoo-ABC News (Disney), CNN Network (Time Warner), NBC News Digital (Comcast), Huffington Post, CBS News (CBS Corp.), *USA Today* (Gannett), BuzzFeed, the *New York Times*, Fox News (21st Century Fox), and the UK's *Mail* Online/*Daily Mail*. According to the Alexa U.S. Traffic Rankings for May 2016, the 10 most visited U.S. websites overall include (again, in descending order) Google, Facebook, YouTube (owned by Google), Amazon, Yahoo, Wikipedia, eBay, Twitter, Reddit, and LinkedIn (owned by Microsoft). Other commercial powerhouses in the Top 20 include Netflix (#11), Craigslist (#12), Pinterest (#13), Microsoft's Live (#14) and Bing (#15), and Instagram (#18).

When we recognize popular culture's relationship to these media giants, it tends to lose some of its glamour and cool. After all, it is hard to identify with your favorite rebel-yelling bands and fabulous rappers after you realize that their music videos are little more than commercials for one of the three major record labels, and that our rock and hip-hop heroes have been packaged and sold like soft drinks and potato chips by multinational corporations. Bart Simpson doesn't seem so subversive when revealed as a marketing icon employed to boost the power of 21st Century Fox and its billionaire chairman Rupert Murdoch.

Amid an illusionary paradise of endless cable channels, Top 40 radio stations, pop music groups, and beverages laden with high-fructose corn syrup, we discover that all are owned by the same minuscule number of elite parent companies beholden to shareholders concerned with profits, above all. Perhaps it is no wonder that the cookie-cutter products of this consolidated media industry sometimes seem so boringly similar, offering the same tired sounds and identically bland tastes, even if their coatings are as deceptively differentiated as the iridescent-colored marshmallows in a bowl of frosted Lucky Charms.

Reproducing Social Inequality

The critical approach to popular culture emphasizes how the popularity of commercial movies, cable TV, cartoons, video game consoles, and country music serves to increase the profits of giant corporations such as Sony, Comcast, Disney,

Inexpensive "fast fashion" retailers rely on cheap labor at clothing factories such as this one in Bangladesh, where workers often toil for long hours for pitiful wages in unsafe conditions.

and Microsoft. As our everyday purchases bolster their economic power to even greater heights, they simultaneously widen the gulf between these enormous companies and their would-be competitors: independent filmmakers, online music labels, open-source software developers, and hyperlocal bloggers. The inequality between local startups and global multinationals plays itself out on the world's stage as well, as the international dominance of U.S. products from fast-food hamburgers to celebrity-endorsed sneakers snuffs out local traditions in faraway places like China, where the rise of global capitalism represents its own kind of cultural revolution. The social inequality existing between wealthy nations like the United States and developing countries in the Global South is best exemplified by the conditions of export processing zones in Mexico, Vietnam, Thailand, Indonesia, Sri Lanka, Bangladesh, and the Philippines, where millions of sweatshop factory workers stitch brand-name clothes and shoes for Nike, Reebok, Champion, Liz Claiborne, Old Navy, and the Gap for no more than a few dollars per day (Klein 2002).

While not as severe as the exploitation of low-wage labor abroad, the culture industries treat their U.S. workforce with a similar lack of dignity and care. McDonald's and Starbucks have been accused of relying on intimidation tactics to prevent their underpaid workers from unionizing. Fast-food restaurants like McDonald's typically hire unskilled adolescent workers because they are thought to be docile employees willing to work for low pay without complaint (Schlosser 2002, p. 68). Meanwhile, since the 1990s media outlets from VH1 to *Men's Journal* have driven down industry wages by relying on unpaid interns as a surplus pool of free labor (Frederick 2003), and in recent years many companies have been successfully sued in court by former interns seeking lost wages. In 2014 the magazine publisher Condé Nast settled a class-action lawsuit for $5.85 million to compensate its unpaid interns who worked for the *New Yorker, Vanity Fair*, and *Vogue* without pay. The following year Viacom agreed to pay its former MTV and BET interns a $7.2 million settlement (Stempel 2014; James 2015). NBC Universal and Warner Music Group have similarly settled class-action lawsuits brought on behalf of unpaid interns (Miller 2014; Gardner 2015).

If their worker-unfriendly policies heighten the inequality between labor and capital (to use Marx's language), the media industries have also been accused of exacerbating the social inequality often experienced by women in the workplace. In 2015, plaintiffs filed a class-action lawsuit against Microsoft for gender bias, arguing that for years "women were unfairly discriminated against on the basis of their gender, passed over for raises and promotions, and ranked below their male counterparts during bi-annual performance reviews" (Lapowsky 2015). In recent years, Twitter and Facebook have both been sued for gender discrimination (O'Brien 2015). Although Facebook's chief operating officer Sheryl Sandberg urges professional women to seek empowerment at work in her bestselling book *Lean In*, here are the sad facts: Globally, only 31 percent of Facebook employees are women, while men make up 85 percent of Facebook's technical workforce and 77 percent of all senior-level management positions (Goel 2014).

Is the seemingly more glamourous world of Hollywood entertainment any different? According to the *New York Times Magazine*, in 2014 the six major film studios combined (excluding their art-house divisions) released only *three* movies directed by women. Meanwhile, in that year men made up 95 percent of cinematographers, 89 percent of screenwriters, 82 percent of film editors, 81 percent of executive producers, and 77 percent of producers (Dowd 2015). As a response to Hollywood sexism behind the camera, in May 2015, the American Civil Liberties Union filed a grievance with the U.S. Equal Employment Opportunity Commission demanding investigations into "the systemic failure to hire women directors at all levels of the film and television industry" (Miller 2015).

Meanwhile, in front of the camera, Hollywood reproduces social inequality by reinforcing degrading stereotypes of women, minorities, and the poor in countless images produced for the mass market. Hollywood films have historically portrayed their male villains as ethnic caricatures, whether Native American (*The Searchers*), Japanese (*The Bridge on the River Kwai*), African American (*Live and Let Die*), Vietnamese (*The Deer Hunter*), Mexican (*Despicable Me 2*), Russian (*Iron Man 2*), or Arab (*American Sniper*). Meanwhile, female villains in film are often portrayed as psychotic and emotionally unstable—Alex Forrest (played by Glenn Close) in *Fatal Attraction*, Annie Wilkes (Kathy Bates) in *Misery*, Hedy Carlson (Jennifer Jason Lee) in *Single White Female*, Amy Dunne (Rosamund Pike) in *Gone Girl*.

The poor depiction and treatment of African Americans in film deserves particular attention. The Academy of Motion Picture Arts and Sciences has

Films such as American Sniper *(left)* and TV shows such as Homeland *(right)* perpetuate damaging stereotypes of Arabs as terrorists.

historically ignored the achievements of black actors and actresses, and public outrage surrounding this long-running slight reached a fever pitch in 2016 when not a single black male or female performer was nominated for an Academy Award, prompting the #OscarsSoWhite protests in which a number of high-profile celebrities spoke out against racism in Hollywood. In fact, the kinds of performances by African Americans that *do* draw praise in the film industry are quite telling. In the entire history of the Oscars, only 10 performances have ever earned an African American woman the Best Actress nomination—and in *all* of these cases the actress performed a poor or low-income character. (In nine of those cases, the character was actually *homeless*, or at least on the verge of being so.) Meanwhile, of the 20 performances by black men that have ever garnered a Best Actor nomination, 13 portrayed a character being arrested or incarcerated, and 15 involved violent or criminal behavior. (These figures were all complied by Thorp 2016.)

On the small screen, these and other stereotypes prevail. Political thrillers like Showtime's *Homeland* portray Arab men as untrustworthy at best and terrorists at worst (Durkay 2014). Reality TV shows portray young working-class women as trashy, alcoholic, sexually promiscuous, and dumb (particularly on MTV drunk-fests such as *Real World*, *The Challenge*, and *Jersey Shore* or the channel's shaming circuses like *16 and Pregnant* and its follow-up series *Teen Mom*), while family sitcoms depict proletarian men from Archie Bunker to Homer Simpson as overweight, insensitive louts. The history of television is full of caricatures of backwards country-bumpkins from *The Beverly Hillbillies* to *Duck Dynasty*. Hip-hop videos typically portray African American men as street thugs and black women as barely dressed objects of sexual desire. In both television and film, black comedians from Eddie Murphy to Martin Lawrence to Tyler Perry dress in drag to caricature black women as ugly and overbearing (Collins 2005, p. 125). During commercial breaks, women of all racial backgrounds appear in advertisements for Coors Light, Miller Lite, Bud Light, and other American beers as ditzy brunettes, mud-wrestling vixens, and buxom party girls.

These pop cultural conventions lead to typecasting in the television and film industries that prevents female and minority actors from finding substantive roles. According to the Ralph J. Bunche Center for African American Studies at UCLA, in 2014 only 12.9 percent of lead film roles went to minorities, even though they account for nearly 40 percent of the U.S. population. On broadcast television, minorities performed in only 8.1 percent of lead roles during the 2013–14 season. (On cable TV the figure was 16.6 percent, down 3 percent from the previous year.) As Indian American actor Aziz Ansari pointed out in the *New York Times* in 2015, "When Hollywood wants an 'everyman,' what it really wants is a straight white guy. But a straight white guy is not every man. The 'everyman' is everybody." When they *do* get cast in Hollywood roles, racial and ethnic minorities are often pigeonholed into a small number of parts limited to stock characterizations and ludicrous stereotypes. As Ansari observes, "Even though I've sold out Madison Square Garden as a standup comedian and have appeared in several films and a TV series, when my phone rings, the roles I'm offered are often defined by ethnicity and often require accents."

Ansari's frustrations are not uncommon. Sociologist Nancy Wang Yuen (2008) finds that Asian American performers routinely find themselves auditioning for roles that seem little more than a conflation of ethnic stereotypes. According to one of her male informants, an Asian American actor in his late 50s:

> It's just that people who write these characters, most of the time they don't know very much about us. They get a very mixed image, because they don't know. They throw everything together. I mean, every Asian culture is mixed in. The name, place, culture, age, generation. It's amazing, you read, sometimes you read a character that you kind of, okay, this character's name is Vin, which is Vietnamese, right. And that he originated from Cambodia, which is another country altogether. But he's being pursued by the Tongs, which happen to be a Chinese criminal element. And that he [performs] a particular culturally specific behavior as bowing, which is Japanese. (p. 34)

Another one of Yuen's informants, a South Asian American actress, complained that casting directors consistently passed her over because her skin tone was considered too dark, or alternatively, too light (p. 41). According to African American actress Viola Davis, star of ABC's *How to Get Away with Murder*:

> When it comes to women of color, especially women of darker hue, there's a limit. . . . It's historical. Hold up a paper bag to your face. If your skin is

lighter than that, you're all the good things: smarter, prettier, more successful. If you're darker, you're ugly. That's been working its way through our race for hundreds of years. I'm dark-skinned. You can't compare me to Taraji [P. Henson], Kerry Washington or Halle Berry, the other black women on TV. I wanted to play a fully realized, dark-skinned woman, and just doing that alone could be revolutionary. (Quoted in Galanes 2015)

At the same time, all women of color lack opportunities in Hollywood casting, whether for film or television. Again, as Davis eloquently put it in her 2015 acceptance speech after becoming the first black woman to ever win an Emmy Award for best actress in a drama:

"In my mind, I see a line. And over that line, I see green fields and lovely flowers and beautiful white women with their arms stretched out to me, over that line. But I can't seem to get there no how. I can't seem to get over that line."

That was Harriet Tubman in the 1800s. And let me tell you something: The only thing that separates women of color from anyone else is opportunity. You cannot win an Emmy for roles that are simply not there.

Meanwhile, all women experience sexism in the film and television industries. Even Hollywood's top-paid celebrity actresses—Jennifer Lawrence, Scarlett Johansson, Charlize Theron, Sandra Bullock, Julia Roberts, Reese Witherspoon, Cameron Diaz, Angelina Jolie—generally make considerably less than their male A-list counterparts. In a high-profile case of corporate espionage in 2014, hacked emails sent among Sony Pictures executives revealed that Academy Award—winner and global box-office draw Jennifer Lawrence was paid significantly less than her male costars for appearing in David O. Russell's 2013 film *American Hustle* (Kohn 2014). Older actresses additionally face the indignities of ageism in the culture industries.

Popular Culture as Social Control

When assessing the critical approach to popular culture, it is easy to see how the media and culture industries reinforce dominant stereotypes in society, and few would deny that movie studios, television networks, and record companies are profit-making enterprises beholden to the desires of stockholders and billionaire CEOs. (In the business world of media and pop culture, 21st Century Fox's Rupert Murdoch is worth $10.6 billion; Nike's Philip Knight, $24.4 billion; Google's Sergey Brin and Larry Page, $34.4 and $35.2 billion, respectively; Facebook's Mark Zuckerberg, $44.6 billion; Amazon's Jeffrey Bezos, $45.2 billion; and Microsoft co-founder Bill Gates, $75 billion.) But arguments about the hegemonic power of pop culture as a means of social control are always the most difficult to swallow. How many readers would admit that they are easily manipulated by television commercials or magazine advertisements? Perhaps that might have been the case generations ago, but not

Orson Welles (center) explains to reporters that his dramatization of H. G. Wells's The War of the Worlds *was in fact just a dramatization.*

today, not in the twenty-first century. In October 1938 Orson Welles directed and narrated a radio adaptation of H. G. Wells's science fiction novel *The War of the Worlds*, and during the broadcast, warnings of a Martian invasion in New Jersey proved so realistic to some listeners that it caused widespread hysteria. Surely, most readers would insist, contemporary audiences would never be that gullible.

It is probably true that in these media-savvy times it would take a lot more than a radio program to generate the kind of panic experienced during the 1930s. And yet evidence suggests that we may not be as immune to pop culture's sirens as we would like to believe. It is worth noting that one of the most popular books of the 1950s was Vance Packard's classic *The Hidden Persuaders*, a biting critique of media manipulation and consumerism published in an age of anxiety surrounding the influence of mass culture. The book sold more than a million copies, and yet advertising is still with us and shows no signs of disappearing anytime soon. If anything, our society is even more brand conscious today than during Packard's era.

Of course, to suggest that advertising "works" is not quite the same as arguing that male viewers of beer commercials are gullible enough to believe that all that stands between them and a rollicking threesome with a set of blonde twins is a six-pack of Coors Light. (It is just as unlikely that anyone could be *that* cuckoo for Cocoa Puffs.) Rather, cultural hegemony operates at the level of common sense—it is a soft power that quietly engineers consensus around a set of myths that we have come to take for granted, even if the Cola Wars between Coke and Pepsi still remain contested. What sorts of ideas? For now, let us consider just a handful.

Last season's fashions are *so* last season. Why do the makers of automobiles, designer handbags, shoes, and jeans introduce new models every year, regardless of whether their products have been substantially altered? Clearly, it is an easy way for a company to synthetically rejuvenate excitement around its brand. More important, the introduction of new products generates sales by devaluing the recently purchased styles and fashions in which consumers have already invested. Economists refer to this practice as *planned obsolescence* because it makes last season's must-have items seem obsolete and worthlessly out-of-date. Although based on completely fabricated desires, many consumers insist on replacing their perfectly fine (and sometimes hardly worn) boots and handbags with newer iterations every year because they believe that the shelf lives of such goods are determined by the artificial cycles of the fashion industry rather than their durability and aesthetic beauty. (While smartphones, tablets, laptops, and gaming systems are also manufactured according to a logic of planned obsolescence, rapid changes in digital technology, particularly with regard to data storage capacity, make such differences in successive models at least somewhat substantive.)

Shopping completes us. Americans have grown used to thinking of their wardrobes and other collections of consumer items and experiences as incomplete, forever requiring new purchases to fill the emptiness—even though we accumulate more today than at any time in world history. The average adult buys 48 new pieces of clothing apparel annually, while the typical child collects an average of 70 new toys per year (Schor 2005, pp. 9, 19). Even self-styled hipsters, bohemians, and other "anti-consumerists" find ways to accumulate obscure vinyl records, expensive stereo components, snarky T-shirts, and secondhand clothing (or at least duds that *look* secondhand). Every unattended feature-film release, concert, and sporting event can easily represent what feels like a missed opportunity for fulfillment, while every purchase brings with it a kind of relief, however ephemeral.

We can all live like celebrities. Consumerism has always had a competitive edge to it in the United States, as families have tried to keep up with the Joneses living on their block. But while we have grown accustomed to comparing our lifestyles to those of our next-door neighbors, in recent years we have aimed much higher, evaluating our consumption relative to reference groups that live financially beyond our own means. As middle-class shoppers have increasingly borrowed on their credit cards to spend more and more on upper-class trappings—luxury automobiles, expensive vacations, designer apparel, and handbags—their consumer debt has skyrocketed. According to the Federal Reserve Board, Americans collectively carry $3.57 trillion in consumer debt, while the typical U.S. household owes $15,355 in credit card debt (Tepper 2015). And yet this spending has not necessarily made consumers any happier—in fact, their excessive purchasing may have only served to highlight existing disparities between the middle classes and the superrich. As Boston College sociologist and economist Juliet Schor (1998, p. 5) observes in *The Overspent American: Why We Want What We Don't Need*, "Advertising and the media have played an important part in stretching our reference groups. When twenty-somethings can't afford much more than a utilitarian studio but think they should have a New York apartment to match the ones they see on [television], they are setting unattainable consumption goals for themselves, with dissatisfaction as a predictable result. When the children of affluent suburban and impoverished inner-city households both want the same Tommy Hilfiger logo emblazoned on their chests and the top-of-the-line Swoosh on their feet, it's a potential disaster."

Our self-worth is determined by our looks and cultural norms of sexual attractiveness. Advertisers and fashion magazines—particularly those that rely on gorgeous actresses and models to sell products—simultaneously promote ideals of beauty and sexual desirability. Over time, the proliferation of airbrushed images of perfected bodies with toned muscles, rock-hard abs, and flawless skin normalizes otherwise unattainable expectations of body definition, physical fitness, and sexual allure. Perhaps as a result, college campuses have recently witnessed an epidemic of eating disorders among women. According to one study, between 60 and 80 percent of female college students engage in regular binge eating and other unhealthy behaviors, including those associated with anorexia nervosa and bulimia. Moreover, "many college women who are at normal weights continue to express a strong desire to be thinner and to hold

As illustrated by this H&M billboard along London's Oxford Street, airbrushed images of beautiful models (both female and male) greet us wherever we go, promoting unrealistic expectations of sexual attractiveness.

beliefs about food and body image that are similar to those of women who have actual eating disorders" (Hesse-Biber, Marino, and Watts-Roy 1999, pp. 385–86). These anxieties affect college men as well as women. Psychologists observe that contemporary "advertisements celebrate the young, lean, muscular male body, and men's fashions have undergone significant changes in style both to accommodate and to accentuate changes in men's physiques toward a more muscular and trim body" (Mishkind, Rodin, Silberstein, and Striegel-Moore 1986, p. 545). Correspondingly, 95 percent of college-age men report dissatisfaction with specific aspects of their bodies, particularly their chest, weight, and waist, as well as their arms, hips, stomach, shoulders, and height (p. 546).

Increased anxieties over physical appearance can be most easily observed in the recent numbers of patients receiving elective plastic surgery. According to the American Society of Plastic Surgeons, doctors performed 15.9 million cosmetic procedures in 2015, at a total cost of $13.3 billion. Of these procedures, 226,000 were performed on patients 13 to 19 years of age.

Diamonds are forever. Today we commonly think of diamonds as an eternal symbol of love and romance, marriage and commitment, and many U.S. women expect any credible marriage proposal to be accompanied by the proffering of an engagement ring featuring a solitaire diamond. But where did such an expectation come from? In fact, it was invented by the advertising agency of N. W. Ayer, where in 1947 a copywriter coined the phrase, "A diamond is forever," for a marketing campaign for De Beers, one of the largest diamond mining and trading companies in the world (Mead 2007, p. 57). This campaign has been so influential in changing the culture of American romance that in 2000, *Advertising Age* named "A diamond is forever" the best advertising slogan of the twentieth century. (The magazine's runner-up was Nike's "Just do it.")

Brands matter. Rationally speaking, branding should not factor into our purchasing decisions, certainly not as much as pricing, quality, or convenience. Yet as we demonstrate by choosing name-brand medications over their practically identical generic or store-brand counterparts (Advil or Motrin IB over CVS's ibuprofen, Tylenol over Target's acetaminophen), we respond quite favorably to branding and associate brands with quality and reliability. Brands connote status, which is why Starbucks

Celebrity-inspired fragrances such as Rihanna's Riri are proof positive of the power of the brand in contemporary society.

succeeds at selling its caffeinated beverages at expensive prices, even though according to *Consumer Reports* McDonald's coffee beats the upscale chain in its unbiased taste tests. Is it any wonder that Apple's celebrated iPhone is the world's top-selling smartphone, even though many other brands offer comparable features for less money (Rooney 2015)? Even more to the point, only the symbolic power of the brand can explain the sales of "celebrity-inspired" fragrances like Kim Kardashian's (ironically named) scent True Reflection. The number of pop singers with their own perfume lines is simply staggering: Beyoncé's Rise, Taylor Swift's Wonderstruck, Rihanna's RiRi, Katy Perry's Purr, Lady Gaga's Fame, Shakira's Elixir, Ariana Grande's Ari.

Brands are especially powerful symbols among small children. According to a 2001 Nickelodeon study, "The average ten-year-old has memorized 300 to 400 brands. Among eight- to fourteen-year-olds, 92 percent of requests are brand-specific, and 89 percent of kids agree that 'when I find a brand I like, I tend to stick with it'" (Schor 2005, p. 25). Meanwhile, another study revealed "nearly two-thirds of mothers thought their children were brand aware by age three, and one-third said it happened at age two" (p. 25). No wonder that in 2015 the most popular Kellogg's breakfast cereal was Tony the Tiger's Frosted Flakes, and the top-selling breakfast cereal overall was kid-friendly Honey Nut Cheerios, which is owned by General Mills, the brand empire that also owns Wheaties, Cinnamon Toast Crunch, Trix, Lucky Charms, Chex, Count Chocula, Franken Berry, and Kix cereals, as well as comfort brands such as Betty Crocker,

How do corporations make their products more appealing to children?

Pillsbury, Bisquick, Progresso, Green Giant, Old El Paso, Hamburger Helper, Fruit Roll-Ups, and Häagen-Dazs.

When Popular Culture Attacks

According to the critical approach to popular culture, the primary motivation for designing and programming media and popular culture is money—not creativity, not free expression, not pleasure, and certainly not fun, but the unabashed pursuit of profit. According to such a perspective, the celebration of a film as a work of art, the cheerful adoration of a professional football team, and the joy of a cartoon as experienced by a young child all serve to reinforce the power and hegemony of the culture industries. This power represents the economic dominance of the corporation (through its control of capital, intellectual property, and jobs) as well as a widening of the social gulf between the industrialized and developing world, multinationals and their nonunionized workers, men and women, whites and racial and ethnic minorities, and the affluent and less well-off classes in the United States. The hegemony of the culture industries represents a softer kind of power as well, a means of manipulating consumers through clever advertising, brand exposure, and the habituation of fashion cycles. The end result is a world that feeds on style over substance, superficiality over gravitas, and myth over reality.

Yet in recent decades the strategies of the culture industries have grown even more insidious. In 2015 Coca-Cola was publicly shamed for having funded "scientific" research that tried to argue that diet sodas were healthier than drinking water, and that exercise was a more preferable method of obesity control than calorie reduction (*New York Times* 2015; Rainey 2016). Facebook collects private data on its users by tracking them across devices and sells that information to third-party advertisers (Goel 2014). Many e-commerce retailers engage in price discrimination by offering consumers differential pricing based on their user profiles, including Amazon, Home Depot, Sears, Expedia, Orbitz, Priceline, Staples, and Travelocity (Wilson 2014). Even more disturbingly, the big-box discount chain Target mines data on consumers' purchasing patterns to build algorithms that predict whether someone in their household is pregnant, and then forwards them coupons and other directed promotions without revealing that they have been "targeted" in this manner. As one Target executive revealed to Charles Duhigg (2012) from the *New York Times Magazine*:

> We have the capacity to send every customer an ad booklet, specifically designed for them, that says, "Here's everything you bought last week and a coupon for it," one Target executive told me. "We do that for grocery products all the time." But for pregnant women, Target's goal was selling them baby items they didn't even know they needed yet.
>
> "With the pregnancy products, though, we learned that some women react badly," the executive said. "Then we started mixing in all these ads for things we knew pregnant women would never buy, so the baby ads

looked random. We'd put an ad for a lawn mower next to diapers. We'd put a coupon for wineglasses next to infant clothes. That way, it looked like all the products were chosen by chance.

"And we found out that as long as a pregnant woman thinks she hasn't been spied on, she'll use the coupons. She just assumes that everyone else on her block got the same mailer for diapers and cribs. As long as we don't spook her, it works."

Many of these corporate strategies specifically target young people. In their attempts to expand their market base, alcohol and tobacco companies have historically advertised to children and adolescents on Comedy Central, ESPN, and BET, and in magazines such as *Rolling Stone* and *Sports Illustrated* through the use of kid-friendly ad mascots that have included R. J. Reynolds's Joe Camel and Budweiser's longstanding menagerie of Clydesdale horses, frogs, lizards, and a bull terrier named Spuds MacKenzie (Schor 2005, pp. 132–36). Companies advertise inside public high schools and universities through their sponsorship of athletic teams (Nike, Adidas, Under Armour), exclusive soft drink and fast-food vending contracts (Coca-Cola, Pepsi, Pizza Hut, Taco Bell, McDonald's, Subway, Burger King), bookstore management (Barnes & Noble), and Channel One, a video-based teaching aid that requires students to sit through commercials wedged into pseudo-educational current-events programming (Klein 2002). Meanwhile, corporations recruit young people to become *cool hunters*—that is, to research the underground trends of fashion-forward youth to appropriate them for mass consumption (Gladwell 1997, 2002; Klein 2002).

But while the critical approach to understanding media and pop culture provides us with a useful window into the machinations of the culture industries, it cannot answer all of the questions that interest social scientists and other scholars. For example, while the culture industries are deeply influential tastemakers, are we not equally subject to the oppositional messages delivered by competing institutions of social control?

SURGEON GENERAL'S WARNING: Smoking By Pregnant Women May Result in Fetal Injury, Premature Birth, And Low Birth Weight.

Until 1997 the tobacco company R. J. Reynolds advertised its Camel cigarettes directly to children with the help of Joe Camel, its corporate cartoon mascot.

(In fact, while cigarettes may be advertised to children in magazines, young people are also constantly warned about the harms of smoking in their schools and by an extraordinarily well-funded medical establishment.) Moreover, given the brute dominance of the culture industries, how is it that media firms regularly fail their shareholders by losing valuable profits and market share? If they are indeed tone-deaf to the real needs and desires of consumers, where do creative innovation and cultural dynamism come from? And since big-budget marketing campaigns do not always succeed in spite of the best intentions of advertisers, how do we adequately explain how less-well-promoted fads and fashions often *do* become popular over time? Despite the critical perspective's utility, answering these questions will require an additional approach—what sociologists call an *interaction* approach, to be examined in the next chapter.

Our cultural tastes are profoundly influenced by our peers, acquaintances, and all the other people who surround us in our everyday lives.

come together

AN INTERACTION APPROACH
TO POPULAR CULTURE

ACCORDING TO THE SOCIAL SECURITY ADMINISTRATION, THE MOST popular name for baby girls born in the United States in 2015 was Emma. This should not be terribly surprising: Emma is a lovely name. Yet only 40 years earlier, in 1975, it was ranked 421st in popularity among girls. (The top five most popular female names that year were, in descending order, Jennifer, Amy, Heather, Melissa, and Angela.) How did that happen? What can explain the meteoric rise of Emma, or any name, for that matter? After all, it is not as if there are publicists out there mounting multimillion-dollar advertising campaigns urging parents to name their children Elizabeth, or Chloe, or Meredith; nor do fashion magazines push names like Olivia or Abigail as this year's Sophia (the No. 1 name for girls in 2013), or claim that Samantha is *so* 1998, when it was ranked third in the United States. (By 2015 it had dropped to No. 40.)

A Harvard sociologist, Stanley Lieberson (2000) has done extensive research on the history of naming practices in the United States, and he offers an interesting explanation for why names change over time. He reminds us that "unlike many other cultural fashions, no commercial efforts are made to influence our naming choices" compared to "the organizational impact on tastes in such diverse areas as soft drinks, clothing, popular entertainment, automobiles, watches, rugs, lamps, vacations, food, perfumes, soaps, books, and medications" (p. xiii). However, he also observes that parents rarely name their children in a cultural vacuum, especially since they usually react to the choices made by other parents. In doing so, they are often pulled in opposing directions. On the one hand, they want their children to have distinctive names that signal their individuality, but at the same time they rarely choose names *so* unique that they are not recognized as legitimate. (Fans were flabbergasted in 2004 when actress Gwyneth Paltrow and her then-husband Chris Martin of the band Coldplay named their daughter Apple, just as they were in 2012 when Beyoncé and Jay Z named their baby girl Blue Ivy, and the following year when Kim Kardashian and Kanye West named their newborn daughter North.) As a result, the popularity of names is almost always subject to constant but incremental change based on existing tastes.

Therefore, understanding the meteoric rise of Emma requires knowing something about the surrounding context of taste inhabited by soon-to-be parents. In 1975, Emma was not a popular name, but *Emily* was: It was the 48th most popular name in the country. By 1982 it had jumped to No. 24, broke into the top 10 in 1991, the top five two years later, and by 1996 Emily was the most popular girl's name in America, and remained so for 10 years. (It has remained in the top 10 ever since.) Over time, the popularity of Emily increased the attractiveness of Emma as a kind of spinoff, a distinctive if slight variation on a more popular theme. The frequency of parents naming their baby girls Emma trailed Emily gradually, slowly inching its way up in popularity from No. 421 in 1975 to

No. 211 in 1986, No. 104 in 1992, No. 22 in 1998, No. 2 in 2003, and finally landing at No. 1 in 2008. It has remained in the top three ever since.

In Chapter 2 we explored the functionalist approach, which examines how societies rely on the stuff of popular culture—its shared symbols, stories, and collective rituals—as a kind of social adhesive that binds people together. In the next chapter we considered the critical approach, which characterizes pop culture as a dominating force, as the product of powerful profit-seeking media firms such as Disney, Time Warner, Sony, Comcast, Viacom, Apple, and Microsoft. In contrast to both functionalist and critical perspectives, an *interaction* approach emphasizes how popular culture spreads throughout a society as an outcome of interpersonal encounters experienced among groups of individuals within particular social settings and interactive contexts—whether a local music scene like New York's Lower East Side, or the virtual world of online dating apps like Tinder and Match. While the critical approach investigates the hegemony and power of behemoth corporations, the interaction approach considers the influence of one's friends, neighbors, and online networks on the diffusion of pop cultural tastes in clothing styles, movies, video games, and, of course, baby names. Instead of highlighting the impact of advertising and mass marketing on public opinion, the interaction approach considers micro-level processes such as word-of-mouth communication, social encounters within local art scenes and urban subcultures, and digital postings on websites and apps from Pinterest to Instagram. In this chapter, I apply this theoretical perspective to explore the diffusion of pop culture, the power of personal influence, and the importance of social networks on the popularity of fads and fashions in everyday life.

Foundations of the Interaction Approach

Sociologists have long emphasized the dynamics of social interaction that commonly occur within peer groups made up of individuals of relatively equal status. In *Street Corner Society*, a classic community study of Italian Americans in working-class Boston, William Foote Whyte (1943) depicts the world of "corner boys," small groups of young men who hang out on neighborhood sidewalks and street corners, barbershops, eateries, and bowling alleys, spending most of their time telling jokes, roughhousing, playing cards and dice, and defending their turf against rival gangs. In his aptly named book *The Urban Villagers*, Columbia sociologist Herbert J. Gans (1962) refers to these kinds of working-class communities as *peer group societies* in which socializing occurs several times a week not only among teenage gangs but also among close-knit groups of adult siblings, cousins, in-laws, work colleagues, church parishioners, and other neighborhood residents.

These groups obviously provide their members with camaraderie and companionship, but they also provide a space where participants develop what sociologists refer to as a *social self*. The venerated turn-of-the-century sociological theorist Charles Horton Cooley observed how individuals build their self-image from the judgments of others, or at least from what they imagine such evaluations to be (1902/1998, p. 164). In many ways, our identity

In this movie still from Richard Linklater's 1993 film Dazed and Confused, *incoming high school freshman Mitch Kramer (center) has to perform multiple presentations of self as he interacts outside a pool hall with both his classmate Sabrina (right) and his older sister Jodi (left).*

as people requires acknowledgment from society to become truly meaningful, or even to exist at all. (Even our most obviously personal identities—our first and last names—are given to us by someone else, and we rely on others to use them when addressing us.) Likewise, it is only in the context of social life among others where people can truly express their personality and distinctiveness as individuals. In developing and re-creating our social selves, we rely on our peer groups in myriad ways: We compete against our friends and acquaintances for status and prestige; internalize group-generated cultural attitudes, orientations, and tastes; and allow our comfort among our most intimate allies to inform our sense of well-being.

More contemporary sociologists have drawn on Cooley's notion of the social self to explain a variety of observable phenomena. Studies of childhood socialization illustrate how parents and teachers treat affluent kids in ways that elevate their sense of entitlement and privilege in school and other institutional settings (Lareau 2003; Calarco 2011, 2014). Such studies also reveal how norms about gender are learned, negotiated, and naturalized in everyday life, rather than biologically determined (Garner and Grazian 2016). From infancy, parents dress boys and girls in gender-specific colors and expect them to behave differently, and throughout childhood parents continue to encourage their participation in gendered activities (Witt 1997). Michigan sociologist Karin Martin (1998, pp. 495–96) argues that outside the home the gendering of children's bodies is part of the "hidden curriculum" of preschool that "controls children's bodily practices [and] serves also to turn kids who are similar in bodily comportment, movement, and practice into boys and girls, children whose bodily practices are different." In her book *Gender Play*, UC Berkeley sociologist Barrie Thorne (1993) observes how schoolteachers often use gender labels when interacting with children, particularly when dividing classrooms into opposing teams of boys and girls for in-class competitions. By reading and interpreting such socialization messages in situations supervised by grownups, young children are able, in the words of another early sociological theorist, George Herbert Mead (1934), to "take the role of the other" and eventually acquire a concept of selfhood, a self-identity embedded in social relations.

Yet one's experience of socialization is hardly limited to childhood, as we are always dependent on group dynamics to inform our interpretations of particular kinds of cultural experiences. In a seminal essay on marijuana use, Howard S. Becker (1963) observes how novice cannabis smokers must rely on more experienced users to teach them to identify the physical effects of the drug and interpret those effects as specifically pleasurable, rather than as harmful, uncomfortable, or strange. (This is analogous to how humans rely on social conditioning to recognize certain foods as delicious or even edible, such as pig's blood in Hungary, fried scorpions in China, or Spam in the United States.) Similarly, retired Penn sociologist Randall Collins (2004a) reveals how various tobacco smoking rituals performed in sacred Native American ceremonies, rowdy English taverns, sedate Turkish coffeehouses, and elegant dinner parties produce radically different emotional moods, even though each involves ingesting identical substances that otherwise provide the same physiological effect.

Our evaluative judgments may also be influenced by the people who surround us. In experiments on conformity conducted by social psychologist Solomon Asch in the 1950s, research subjects bowed to peer pressure when confronted with group consensus around answers to test questions that were clearly false. In one set of classic experiments, Asch formed "groups" made up of a lone subject surrounded by actors collaborating in cahoots with the experimenter. When asked to compare lines of varying lengths, the collaborators would purposely give obviously incorrect answers, and found that subjects would often agree with them, despite their better judgment. In the 1960s Asch's most famous student, the social psychologist Stanley Milgram (1974), found that test subjects were even willing to commit acts of torture—in this case, electrocuting strangers—in response to social pressure applied by experimenters. (As in Asch's experiments, the "strangers" in this case were also actors—no one was ever actually electrocuted in Milgram's lab.) More recently (and far less controversially), in experiments inviting subjects to participate in an online music market in which researchers arbitrarily assigned popularity rankings to songs, subjects were more likely to sample songs they merely *thought* were most popular, regardless of their actual quality or popularity (Salganik, Dodd, and Watts 2006; Salganik and Watts 2008). These social dynamics play out in the real world as well. To take but one example, statistics show that professional sports teams perform better on average during home games than away games—especially in soccer and basketball—because the emotional energy of the noisy crowd can involuntarily nudge referees to make calls that favor the home team. (Strangely, crowd behavior seems not to have the same measurable impact on *player* performance.)

How else do our social surroundings affect us? Erving Goffman (1959) characterizes personhood as a multiplicity of roles or *presentations of self* that we strategically embody when participating in different social worlds, as illustrated by how our interpersonal demeanor shifts as we move among varied settings: college residence halls, doctors' offices, first dates, yoga classes, family dinners, baseball games, weddings. Goffman relies on the metaphor of the theater, comparing the social roles we play to dramatic performances enacted on a set of public stages. For example, while female undergraduate students at Penn, where I teach, typically wear androgynous athletic clothing to class, when they attend parties held in Philadelphia's nightclubs and cocktail lounges they dress according to hegemonic norms of femininity, costumed in high-heeled shoes, designer jeans, revealing tops, and heavy makeup. According to a 20-year-old sophomore preparing for an evening out at a hip restaurant and lounge, "I knew this place was really trendy, so I wanted to dress the part. That includes 7 jeans, a James Perse off-the-shoulder black shirt, and of course stilettos. I knew it was going to be an older crowd, and I didn't want to look like a college student" (Grazian 2008, p. 96). (For the record, during such outings male undergrads similarly wear expensive brand-name attire along with cologne and complicated hair products.) Our constantly changing situational contexts—and the people we expect to find there—ultimately determine the specific selves we choose to publicly present to the world at any given moment in time.

These observations contribute to the major argument of this chapter, that our knowledge and experience of popular culture is often conditioned by the social contexts in which we interact with other people. First, our consumer and cultural tastes—the music we like, the food we eat, the clothes we wear—are deeply influenced by our peers, acquaintances, and all the other people who surround us in our everyday lives. This does not mean that we slavishly adore the same rock bands praised by our classmates or that we necessarily choose our best friends based on a shared love of rap, or reggae, or Russian folk music—all it means is that the people around us *matter* in some significant way. In fact, we often violently react *against* those closest to us, as when well-off American youth broke with the Victorian prudishness of their parents in the 1920s to embrace the red-hot blues and swing of the Jazz Age (and again during the rock 'n' roll era of the 1950s), or when today's youth reject the classic rock and punk music enjoyed by their parents for more dance-oriented pop songs (see Seabrook 2015). Social media platforms such as Facebook and Instagram have exponentially increased the size of our social networks and the efficiency and speed with which we can communicate to their far corners and back.

Second, while the production of popular culture may be centralized among a handful of music labels, film studios, television networks, streaming content providers, and media conglomerates, the eventual *success* of their efforts may depend just as much on the micro-level interactions among individuals within small groups, social scenes, and online networks in the context of everyday life. The social media technologies of the digital age have completely upended and reconfigured yesterday's cultural production and network distribution channels, particularly given the vast resources that web platforms such as YouTube, Twitter, Facebook, Instagram, and Blogger offer to independent and amateur creators, digital celebrities, and even ordinary people like you and me. (In fact, top YouTubers like Daniel Middleton—or DanTDM—whose *Minecraft* videos are watched by 11.5 million subscribers, and LGBT activist Tyler Oakley, whose 8 million subscribers follow his personal obsessions with Lady Gaga and Taco Bell, may enjoy more fame and adoration among American teenagers than more traditional celebrities like movie stars.) To understand how fads and fashions succeed and go viral, we must first examine how human groups work—how they are structured, facilitate the passage of knowledge and taste, use social media, and ultimately influence the diffusion of popular culture.

Social Networks and the Spread of Fashions and Fads

Social networks consist of individuals connected to one another through a variety of relationships, whether based on kinship, authority, friendship, romance, or work. The most primary kind of social network is a *dyad*, or a pair of individuals linked together, such as a married couple like Hillary and Bill Clinton. In a dyadic relationship, individuals can be equals, as they are among college roommates, team co-captains, or twin siblings. They can also have an asymmetrical or hierarchical relationship, as suggested by master-servant or boss-employee relations. (In *Star Wars: The Force Awakens*, the relationship between Supreme Leader Snoke and Kylo Ren exemplifies both of these hierarchical dyadic relationships.) Network ties between individuals can also be characterized according to their relative strength or weakness, which sociologists evaluate on the basis of the amount of time individuals spend together and the emotional intensity and intimacy of their relationship (Granovetter 1973, p. 1361). For instance, marriage ties are likely to be stronger than those between coworkers or friendly acquaintances, while relations between service professionals and their clients are likely to be weaker than those among friends, even though professionals such as hairstylists, attorneys, accountants, physicians, and plastic surgeons are entrusted with access to extremely private information about their customers. In networks consisting of three individuals, or *triads*, things get complicated quickly, since the interpersonal ties existing between some individuals may be stronger or weaker than those between others, as in the case of love triangles or romantic dates burdened by an acquaintance who insists on tagging along as a third wheel.

When we refer to people as "well-connected," we acknowledge that they enjoy a large number of network ties—these are the people who have more than 2,500 friends on Facebook. The strength of such connections may be questionable since some people befriend as many classmates, distant relatives, and unfamiliar acquaintances as possible, all in an attempt to appear more genuinely popular than they otherwise would. Even though it is easy to see through this kind of ploy, such a strategy actually can have several beneficial (if unintended) consequences, because these seemingly superficial or vacuous connections, or *weak ties*, have immense practical value. When Stanford sociologist Mark Granovetter (1973) studied how people go about finding a job, he (perhaps unsurprisingly) discovered the importance of personal connections in learning about employment opportunities. But the shocking discovery he made was what *kinds* of connections matter the most in job hunting—not intimate relations and close friendships, as one might imagine, but people to whom we are *weakly* connected, even those acquaintances that one barely knows.

Why is that? The answer lies in how relationships are embedded within social networks, and the relative distance separating those networks from one another. Let's say that one day I decide to quit my job as a sociology professor and writer, and given my interests in popular culture I pledge to take up a new career in advertising. Who in my social network could I turn to about possible jobs in the ad world? My closest confidant is my wife—but she is a professor and writer like myself, and therefore knows few people in advertising. My closest colleagues at Penn would be my next bet—but guess what? They are mostly sociologists, or at least professors like me. The problem is clear: The people with whom I have the strongest personal ties have access to the same kinds of information that I do—just like me, they lack firsthand knowledge of professions located outside their immediate social world. (When my undergraduate students seek out internships, they have the same problem—their best friends are all college students like themselves, rather than professionals working in the occupational fields to which they are most attracted.) Our personal networks and peer groups tend to be somewhat insular and homogeneous on the basis of occupation and age (as well as socioeconomic status, educational background, religion, ethnicity, and race, among other social categories), and often at a remove from more distinctly different social worlds.

But what if I bypass my closest friends and colleagues and instead turn to those barely known acquaintances of mine with whom I have significantly *less* in common? Then things get more promising: I have a former student from years ago whose brother works at an advertising agency in Miami. I have the business cards of a few advertising copywriters and account planners who used to work at a New York agency where I once did a day's worth of consulting. One of my friends from high school is a management consultant, and I'll bet he knows people in advertising, or at least people who know people in advertising. You get the point—the further I move from my center of intimacy (reaching out to friends of friends of friends) the more likely I am to find someone at the far edges of my social circle who is more tightly embedded in a different professional network from my own. When searching for a job, weak social connections may ultimately prove more valuable than strong intimate ties because, although tenuous, such connections serve as *bridges* spanning otherwise separate social worlds (Granovetter 1973).

What does any of this have to do with popular culture? Quite a lot, in fact, since the kinds of knowledge that circulate within friendship networks include cultural tastes as well—tastes for particular kinds of music, movies, fashion, and fun—and birds of a feather flock together, as they say. (It is unclear whether we are simply attracted to those who share our cultural tastes, or if we naturally absorb the styles of our peers. It is likely that both processes are at play.) It also means that for most people, the secret to developing new tastes in classical opera, experimental theater, underground hip-hop, postmodern art, avant-garde jazz, or other esoteric cultural styles lies in tapping persons located outside one's immediate social network, just as an elderly person desiring to learn about current pop music, video games, blogging, or other kinds of contemporary consumer culture would be best off seeking the guidance of a grandchild or a young neighbor. (Whenever my aging parents ask for assistance using new gadgets, such as the cell phones my wife and I recently bought them, we always tell them to go to the lobby of their high-rise apartment building and grab any 12-year-old, who will surely know more about it than any of us.)

Moreover, social networks provide the key to understanding how everyday pop cultural trends, fads, and fashions—ripped skinny jeans, oversized sunglasses, yoga pants, bomber jackets, crop tops, designer sneakers—become popular. The conduits for change in fashion and taste are those persons who exist at the edges of two or more cultural worlds and are therefore best positioned to bridge the wide social gaps separating them from one another.

For example, in the world of popular music, artists who sit at the intersection of multiple genres often succeed at translating specialized musical styles for more general audiences. For instance, the contemporary popularity of blues music among mainstream audiences both in the United States and abroad owes much to the influence of U.S. and British rock musicians who steeped themselves in this early musical tradition and revived it on their own records: Bob Dylan, Jimi Hendrix, Eric Clapton, the Rolling Stones, Stevie Ray Vaughan, and Led Zeppelin (Grazian 2003). (In fact, Chicago blues legend Muddy Waters first gained international fame when he went on tour with the Stones.) George Harrison of the Beatles is probably more responsible for the introduction of Indian music to Western audiences during the 1960s than any other musician, given that he studied with Bengali sitar performer Ravi Shankar while simultaneously playing lead guitar for the most famous rock band in the entire world. More recently, Lin-Manuel Miranda was born to Puerto Rican parents in the racially diverse neighborhood of Washington Heights in New York and fed a steady diet of the city's musical theater, Latin music, and rap before he attended Wesleyan University in New England. From this unique vantage point

Beatles' lead guitarist George Harrison learns to play the sitar from a Sikh teacher in New Delhi, India, as his bandmates look on.

he was able to create the Tony award—winning musical *Hamilton*, an eclectic hip-hop homage to the life of Founding Father and first Treasury Secretary Alexander Hamilton.

Among these kinds of cultural emissaries are special people that *New Yorker* writer Malcolm Gladwell designates in his best-selling book *The Tipping Point* (2002) as *connectors* who bridge a particularly large number of discrete and insular networks. In doing so, connectors efficiently spread popular cultural fads, trends, and fashions across a variety of distinctly unique groups that would otherwise never interact. According to Gladwell, connectors are the sorts of people who truly know *everyone*—yet their cultural influence lies not only in how many *total* people they know but also how many *different kinds* of people they know. Gladwell suggests another Founding Father—Paul Revere—as an example. Drawing on the work of David Hackett Fischer (1994), a professor of history at Brandeis University, Gladwell attributes the American Revolutionary War hero's success in warning the local communities surrounding Boston of imminent British attack during his famous ride in April 1775 to his widespread social connections. In addition to being a silversmith, Revere served as a health officer of Boston and coroner of Suffolk County, founder of the Massachusetts Mutual Fire Insurance Company, and the president of Massachusetts Charitable Mechanic Association. He was also a noted fisherman and hunter, card player and theater lover, businessman, pub enthusiast, and Masonic Lodge member (Gladwell 2002, p. 56).

In other words, Revere's ability to spread his warning so effectively during his fateful ride stemmed not merely from the size or strength of his personal network but also from its almost abnormal diversity and openness. This also explains his special role as a linchpin of the revolutionary movement (Fischer 1994, pp. 301–2). In the annals of American films set in suburban high schools, his contemporary fictional counterpart would be the title character from the 1986 John Hughes film *Ferris Bueller's Day Off*, or perhaps Randall "Pink" Floyd, the central figure from Richard Linklater's 1993 movie *Dazed and Confused*, as both maintain friendships among an absurdly heterogeneous assortment of football jocks and stoners, underclassmen and mean girls, cheerleaders and dropouts, nerds and prom queens, freaks and geeks. (Given the diversity of his social networks, it is no wonder that Ferris Bueller's activities during his epic day off from school display so much cultural variety: He visits the stately Art Institute of Chicago, takes in a Cubs baseball game at Wrigley Field, lunches at a downtown gourmet restaurant, and lip-synchs Wayne Newton's "Danke Schoen" and the Beatles' "Twist and Shout" during a German American parade.) It is through connectors like Ferris or Pink—or, rather, their real-life versions like Paul Revere—that fads and fashions are likely to spread among social networks whose members would never otherwise interact with one another.

Cultural Diffusion and Word of Mouth

If social networks and their connectors provide the structural machinery for the spread of popular fads and fashions, then what are the specific processes of human interaction that facilitate pop cultural diffusion through such social circles? Market researchers emphasize the impact of *word-of-mouth* communication among consumers, especially since, unlike advertisers and public relations personnel, they have no obvious material interest in the success or failure of any particular product, brand, or lifestyle (Dichter 1966, p. 148). (Consumers also differ from professional critics, who have a vested interest in adhering to industry expectations and standards, beholden to their publishers more than their readers.) A study by the consulting firm McKinsey & Company concluded that as much as 67 percent of U.S. sales of consumer goods are based on word of mouth among friends, family, and even strangers (Taylor 2003, p. 26), while another report shows that young people rely on recommendations gleaned from word of mouth to purchase popular media such as music, movies, and games (Godes and Mayzlin 2004).

Word of mouth is also thought to have been responsible for the box-office success of many "sleeper" hit films, including *There's Something About Mary* (1998), *My Big Fat Greek Wedding* (2002), *Napoleon Dynamite* (2004), *Saw* (2004), *Little Miss Sunshine* (2006), *Juno* (2007), *Superbad* (2007), *The Help* (2011), *Boyhood* (2014), and *Mad Max: Fury Road* (2015). Over time, word of mouth has also gradually turned box-office losers like *Blade Runner* (1982), *The Shawshank Redemption* (1994), *The Big Lebowski* (1998), *Office Space* (1999), *Fight Club* (1999), and *Donnie Darko* (2001) into popular streaming favorites and DVD rentals and bestsellers. Stranger still are box-office bombs that over time

The Big Lebowski *and* The Shawshank Redemption *both bombed at the theatrical box office only to become cult classics after their release on home video.*

have come to be considered cinematic classics of the highest order: *The Wizard of Oz* (1939), *Citizen Kane* (1941), *It's a Wonderful Life* (1946), *Vertigo* (1958), and the original *Willy Wonka & the Chocolate Factory* (1971).

While word of mouth has traditionally been conceptualized as face-to-face communication among peers and acquaintances, in the digital age consumers obviously share their opinions of books, films, hotels, restaurants, and everything else on Amazon, Netflix, TripAdvisor, Yelp, and other online aggregators of customer reviews. While lacking some of the legitimacy traditionally associated with word-of-mouth communication among trusted friends and acquaintances, Internet aggregators do have the undeniable advantage of drawing on the collective intelligence of a much wider and diverse pool of consumers than any single individual could ever personally tap for advice. The advantages of crowd-sourcing also explain the surprising reliability (relative to their more traditional counterparts) of open-source software such as Linux and the online encyclopedia Wikipedia (Surowiecki 2005; Giles 2005; Ball 2007).

We tend to think of word of mouth as little more than informal chitchat, but in fact talk, texts, and tweets can be quantified, measured, and judged in a number of ways, especially given the tracking abilities of data-driven social media sites. For instance, online chatter surrounding a new movie can be evaluated according to its *volume*, or the total number of threads or postings in which it is discussed; the *intensity* or enthusiasm expressed in those discussions; the *valence*, or evaluative content (whether positive or negative) of such communication; its *dispersal* among numerous social networks or communities; and finally, its *duration* over time. Likewise, word of mouth tends to be socially patterned in consistent ways. One study suggests that conversations among consumers about retail stores are more likely to emphasize special sales events, rather than the variety or quality of available merchandise, return policies, the friendliness (or not) of employees, or everyday prices (Higie, Feick, and Price 1987). This may be due to the newsworthiness of "ONE-TIME-ONLY!" sales events that may therefore be more likely to generate talk and text, especially when compared to more routine standards and policies associated with shopping outlets.

As a general rule, while people are far more likely to talk about brands and products in a favorable manner, negative word of mouth tends to have a stronger influence and effect on consumer behavior. An early experimental study conducted at Harvard in the 1960s found that respondents were eight times as likely to receive favorable word of mouth about a certain new product; however, receivers of positive word of mouth were only 12 percent more likely to actually *buy* the product (compared to a control group), while those receiving negative word of mouth were 24 percent *less* likely to make a purchase (Arndt 1967). According to a much more recent study by two economists at the Yale School of Management (Chevalier and Mayzlin 2003), online book reviews posted on Goodreads and Barnes & Noble tend to be overwhelmingly positive, and increases in favorable reviews lead to upticks in relative sales on their respective sites. However, extremely negative one-star reviews have a bigger impact on sales than do superlative five-star raves, which may have to do with the rarity (and thus noteworthy quality) of one-star reviews.

Meanwhile, online word of mouth surrounding new Hollywood films tends to be strongest during a movie's prerelease and opening week, with a precipitous drop in volume during the second week, followed by a continuing decline (Liu 2006). Interestingly, a film's box-office success is correlated with overall word-of-mouth volume but not valence. In other words, movies that generate lots of word of mouth, or *buzz*, tend to do well *regardless of what the actual content of that buzz happens to be.* This suggests that word of mouth may function more effectively as a source of information rather than as a tool of persuasion—at the very least, it illustrates the (not necessarily true) maxim that all publicity is good publicity (or as the saying, attributed to, among others, P. T. Barnum, Mark Twain, Oscar Wilde, George M. Cohan, Will Rogers, W. C. Fields, and Mae West, goes, "I don't care what they say about me, as long as they spell my name right.").

Are there people whose word of mouth matters more than others? We have already discussed the influence of connectors who bridge diverse social networks and communities, thus facilitating the diffusion of fads and fashions among otherwise isolated groups of people. While connectors owe their influence to their structural position within and among varied groups of people, others are valued for their expertise and knowledge of popular consumer culture. For example, *opinion leaders* draw on their deep familiarity and involvement with specific kinds of cultural products, categories, or genres to make informed recommendations to their peers—what kinds of ambient or exercise music to download, which teen comedies to stream, which mystery novels to read. Opinion leaders tend to be experts in a particular field, often related to their occupation or full-time hobby.

Other people of influence lead by example, drawing on their experience not as experts to persuade those around them but as consumers themselves. They include the *early adopters* of new products—the first person in their social network to purchase the latest electric car, iPhone iteration, or most recent computer software upgrade (complete with bugs that they can troubleshoot, just for the fun of it). Early adopters exert *passive* influence when they conspicuously consume products in public, turning onlookers and bystanders on to new fads and fashions, which is how the adoption of Hush Puppies shoes by cool kids and hip designers in New York's East Village and SoHo during the mid-1990s led to a total resuscitation of the once-moribund brand (Gladwell 2002). Similarly, the adoption of Timberland leather work boots by African American men traversing the inner city, its crumbling asphalt streets strewn with broken glass and barbed wire, helped to popularize the tough shoe among hip-hop artists and eventually the wider urban youth market, catapulting the brand into a $1.6 billion success story (Walker 2008a, pp. 82−84).

Early adopters also exert *active* influence when they demonstrate to friends and acquaintances (and anyone else who will listen to them) the exciting features of their new tablet, smartwatch, headphones, or fitness tracker, often by posting reviews on their own technology blog or YouTube channel. Their motives for engaging in word-of-mouth promotion may emerge out of an altruistic desire to lend their hard-earned advice to the masses—especially given the paralysis many experience when confronted with a dizzying array of seemingly unlimited choices in the marketplace, especially for digital gadgets. (Swarthmore psychologist Barry Schwartz [2004] refers to this paralysis and indecision as "the paradox of choice.") Others might be motivated by a more self-serving need to confirm the wisdom of their purchases while showing off their status as consumer pioneers (Feick and Price 1987, p. 84).

The influence of opinion leaders and early adopters tends to be product-specific, whether their expertise concerns electronic devices, handcrafted beers, Italian motor scooters, or salsa music recordings. In contrast, *market mavens* maintain a vast wealth of knowledge about many different kinds of products and thus perhaps even greater influence over the consumer decisions and cultural tastes of their peers. (The word *maven* comes from the Yiddish word *mayvn*, meaning expert, connoisseur, authority, or one who accumulates knowledge—often sarcastically, as in "What, you wrote a textbook and now you're supposed to be some kind of pop cultural *mayvn*?") Market mavens collect information from a seemingly endless variety of sources. They tend to devour more product-oriented media than ordinary people, paying unusually close attention to consumer blogs such as Gizmodo and CNET. Market mavens are the kinds of people who actually read the fine print included in warranties that come with electric appliances and the labels of every item in their refrigerator and medicine cabinet, often in their entirety. (They are also the people who send questions and comments to the email addresses printed on packages of toothpaste, tampons, soap, and other common household goods; see Gladwell 2002, p. 276).

Yet the hallmark of mavens is not merely their obsessive quest for knowledge about brands, consumer culture, and the marketplace, but their overwhelming desire to share their widely held expertise with friends, with complete strangers, with *you*. Unlike most of us, mavens do not necessarily seek out knowledge to inform their *own* purchases as much as they anticipate using such information in social interactions and encounters *with others*. According to market researchers, when surveyed, mavens tend to agree with the following statements (Feick and Price 1987):

1. I like introducing new brands and products to my friends.
2. I like helping people by providing them with information about many kinds of products.
3. People ask me for information about products, places to shop, or sales.
4. If someone asked where to get the best buy on several types of products, I could tell him or her where to shop.
5. My friends think of me as a good source of information when it comes to new products or sales.
6. Think about a person who has information about a variety of products and likes to share this information with others. This person knows about new products, sales, stores, and so on, but does not necessarily feel he or she is an expert on one particular product. How well would you say that this description fits you?

And so, market mavens are valued not only for their expertise about brands and consumer culture but also for their desire to connect with others, sharing their meticulously collected knowledge with those with whom they interact in their everyday lives. Along with connectors, opinion leaders, and early adopters, it is their word of mouth that helps fads and fashions spread like wildfire and eventually become popular.

Collective Consumption in Subcultures, Scenes, and Social Organizations

The interaction approach to popular culture emphasizes not only the relations of cultural influence among individuals within peer networks and social circles but also the dynamics of consuming pop culture collectively in socially interactive settings. In the most informal contexts, classic party games like *Pictionary* and *Trivial Pursuit* bring people together, as do more contemporary games like *Apples to Apples, Magic: The Gathering, The Settlers of Catan*, and *Cards Against*

Humanity. While the best-selling video games of all-time—*Tetris, Minecraft, Wii Sports, Grand Theft Auto*, and *Super Mario Bros.* have all sold more than 40 million units—can obviously be played in solitude, many are enjoyed collectively in peer-group social settings in living rooms (or, in the case of *Minecraft*, virtually on shared servers). Erving Goffman (1963) would refer to these activities as *focused gatherings*, in which co-present participants are entrained on a shared objective (winning the game) as well as each other.

While focused gatherings are occasions temporarily bounded in time and space, longer-lasting social settings of collective participation in cultural consumption include *subcultures, scenes,* and *social organizations.* Among most sociologists, a *subculture* refers to a social world that stands apart from the larger society in some distinctively patterned way, often because its members invest in alternative identities and systems of belief and practice. Examples include Amish and Mennonite communities, Black Hebrew Israelite groups, and other religious sects. But for the purposes of the present discussion, we are most interested in those subcultures in which participants appropriate the raw materials of *popular culture*—including clothes, music, dance, sports, and brands—to distinguish themselves from other consumers through the creative invention of symbolic identity and style (Hebdige 1979; Gelder and Thornton 1997).

Since World War II, American subcultures, including greasers, beats, folkies, hippies, surfers, punks, skinheads, b-boys, skateboarders, riot grrls, rave kids, and indie hipsters, have stood at the forefront of pop cultural reinvention, forging colorfully expressive selves through their collective consumption of both mass-produced and alternative entertainment media, advertising, and celebrity myth. During the late 1960s, countercultural hippies celebrated the prosocial communal values of the time through psychedelic and protest rock—hits of the decade included the Turtles' "Happy Together," the Youngbloods' "Get Together," and the Beatles' "All Together Now" and "Come Together"—while the notorious Hells Angels motorcycle gang incorporated the Harley-Davidson brand into their decidedly less warm-and-fuzzy outlaw image (Thompson 1967; Gitlin 1987).

More recently, during the 1990s, rave kids collectively constructed a neo-hippie aesthetic identity by borrowing liberally from a range of pop cultural sources, creating a synthesis of gay urban disco music, preadolescence fashion and accessories (pajamas, stuffed animals, pacifiers, lollipops, backpacks), and Day-Glo psychedelic style. Meanwhile, the world of "wizard rock" represents one of the more unusual music subcultures to emerge in the new millennium. Consisting of hundreds of bands with names like Gryffindor Common Room Rejects, the Quidditch Pitch Incident, the Dudley Dursleys, and Voldemort and the Death Eaters, musicians and their fans within this subculture perform songs based on the characters and stories surrounding the *Harry Potter* franchise at public libraries around the country. If the idea of rock bands appropriating lyrics from fantasy literature sounds off-the-wall, it bears noting that the classic rock band Led Zeppelin recorded a number of songs that borrowed from J. R. R. Tolkien's *The Lord of the Rings* series, including "The Battle of Evermore" and "Ramble On." (According to the latter song's lyrics, "T'was in the darkest depths of

Mordor / I met a girl so fair / But Gollum and the evil one / Crept up and slipped away with her.")

If subcultures refer to informal groups of consumers who use the stuff of pop culture to manufacture collective identity and style, then *scenes* represent the actual places where subcultural participants experience their shared identity through social interaction (Bennett and Peterson 2004). Scenes are organized according to their spatial configurations. *Local scenes* are centralized within single venues such as folk coffeehouses, honky-tonks, juke joints, and punk rock clubs, or else are spread throughout urban neighborhoods or entertainment zones like Brooklyn's Williamsburg, Chicago's Wicker Park, or Philadelphia's Northern Liberties. In nightclubs as well as on sidewalks and street corners, local scenes provide a theatrical backdrop for public performances conducted among cultural consumers who show off their radical hairstyles and piercings, cutting-edge brands of designer jeans, or newly invented dance moves. These displays introduce fellow participants to the most current cultural fads and trends, and through prolonged exposure and evaluation these fashions will eventually be adopted or discarded, depending on the influence of local style makers and the vagaries of popular taste. Famous local scenes include the 1920s Harlem jazz scene, 1980s L.A. Sunset Strip glam-metal scene, 1990s Seattle grunge rock scene, and Nashville's longstanding country music scene.

In an age of global media, cultural scenes can easily reproduce versions of themselves in locales across the planet. These are *translocal scenes* that circulate fashions and lifestyles in patterns of cross-national diffusion (Bennett and Peterson 2004). The international rave scene is a prime example, which during its heyday in the 1990s deployed party circuit outposts in Ibiza, Goa, Tel Aviv, Cape Town, Tokyo, and other global cultural capitals. (Given the cosmopolitan nature of the foundations of electronic dance music, a creative hybrid of German techno and Chicago house music, the global character of these scenes should not be particularly surprising.) The worldwide dispersion of the rave scene encouraged devoted fans, or at least those among the young and wealthy, to make pilgrimages to these exotic hotspots, with each trip providing opportunities for transnational encounters and the exchange of cultural currency (such as up-to-the-minute knowledge about the latest artists and DJs, dance techniques, and fashion styles) among fellow jet-setters.

Inevitably, the hyperactive mingling of local and international cultures encourages cross-fertilization and genomic mutation. At Even Furthur, an outdoor electronic music festival held annually in rural Wisconsin during the 1990s, Midwestern audiences blended the dance music of the global underground with death metal to produce an interbred "darkside" scene (Reynolds 1999). The hybrid nature of this heavy metal-rave crossover revealed itself among dancing youth head-banging to techno music peppered with Black Sabbath covers, mixing Ecstasy with other synthetic drugs, and merging the rave-based symbolism of PLUR (Peace, Love, Unity, Respect) with the skull-and-bones aesthetics of the occult (Champion 1997; Reynolds 1999; Grazian 2004). Other globally circulating music scenes have produced similarly innovative cultural permutations, including Britain-based Bhangra-pop fusion and Japanese jazz music (Atkins 2000; Bennett 2000, 2001).

In the digital age, global encounters surrounding the consumption of popular culture need not take place in face-to-face settings, as web-based scenes—or *virtual scenes*—bring together fans from all over the world (Bennett and Peterson 2004). Virtual music scenes covering genres from Afro-Cuban jazz to alternative country to New Jersey—based rock rely on websites with streaming recordings and videos, concert listings, blogs, forums, and discussion boards to generate interactive discussion and lively debate among consumers and creators alike (Lee and Peterson 2004). Viewers of the HBO show *Game of Thrones* deliberate over its dramatic plot twists and controversial scenes on fan sites such as Winter Is Coming, Watchers on the Wall, A Wiki of Fire and Ice, and The Inn at the Crossroads: The Official *Game of Thrones* Food Blog.

In addition to providing opportunities for online conversation, commentary, roundtables, and recaps (with and without spoilers), these kinds of virtual scenes also provide distribution nodes for fan-produced content and opportunities for role-playing. Fan fiction websites invite participants to contribute their own stories based on the characters, settings, and themes from practically any pop cultural touchstone one can imagine, from film franchises (*The Avengers* series) to children's fantasy literature (*Percy Jackson*) to video games (*Pokémon*) to boy bands (One Direction). These sites—Fanfiction.net, Wattpad, Archive of Our Own—also invite consumers to compose crossover fan fiction that mixes and matches characters, plots, and themes from different branded cultural universes. Mashups include *Captain America* and *Frozen, X-Men* and *Glee, Transformers* and *My Little Pony*, and *Thor* and *Twilight*. Stephenie Meyer's *Twilight* series was also the basis for the most successful fan-fiction enterprise of all time, when British writer E. L. James turned her erotic take on the *Twilight* characters into the *Fifty Shades of Grey* book and film series. The three books in the *Fifty Shades* trilogy have sold more than 125 million copies.

As the proliferation of fan websites suggests, subcultures and scenes are often formalized into *social organizations* that provide more-or-less stable arenas for human interaction surrounding the collective consumption of popular culture. On the more administratively casual end of the spectrum, the number of American college-educated women participating in local book clubs has escalated since the 1980s (Long 2003, p. 19). Book clubs typically select works of literature or nonfiction to be discussed in depth at meetings held once a month in members' homes or in libraries, bookstores, or cafés. By personally reflecting on these books in one another's presence, group participants develop new and enriched ways of understanding not only literature but society itself and their place within it, a sensibility that the sociologist Elizabeth Long refers to as "a potentially transformative way of being in the world" (pp. 110—13). As for the texts themselves, the buzz generated by two-hour book-club discussions often carries over into the conversations and reading recommendations that participants make outside the context of the group, on- or offline. This word of mouth can dramatically affect the sales and overall popularity of book-club favorites (Gladwell 2002, pp. 173–74).

Like book reading, informal game playing also tends to revolve around semi-organized social groups. The Harvard political scientist Robert D. Putnam (2000, p. 103) has written on the enormous popularity of group-based card playing in the United States during the twentieth century. In 1940, 87 percent of U.S. households owned a deck of playing cards, more than owned radios or telephones. In 1958 the United States boasted 35 *million* bridge players, or almost one-third of all U.S. adults. In 1961, 20 percent of adults belonged to a regular card-playing club, and in the mid-1970s nearly 40 percent of all adults played cards at least once a month, or *four times* the number of moviegoers (pp. 103–4).

U.S. adults still play about 500 million card games a year, and while contract bridge is mostly played nowadays by senior citizens, poker playing among groups of younger people—particularly betting games such as No-Limit Texas Hold 'Em—has grown tremendously in the last 20 years. Poker playing also competes with fantasy sports leagues, in which participants draft and manage imaginary teams of real-life professional athletes with the help of gaming software and digital data analytics provided online in real time. Based on their most recent performances on the field, players' individual and team statistics determine the winners and losers of pretend matchups between league participants. According to the Fantasy Sports Trade Association, in 2015 more than 57 million fans participated in fantasy leagues in the United States and Canada. One-third of all participants were women, and the most popular sport was fantasy football.

In contrast to small-bore, informal organizations such as peer-led poker games and fantasy-sports leagues, other competitive gaming communities commonly rely on the efforts of more institutionalized social entities such as locally controlled sporting associations like Little League baseball, youth soccer, and bowling leagues. Larger and more formal social organizations coordinate national and international contests that corral thousands of fanatic cultural consumers into hotels and convention halls for concentrated interaction lasting days on end. The United States Chess Federation claims more than 85,000 members and 2,000 affiliated chess clubs and organizations, and it sanctions and rates more than 10,000 tournaments year-round, including the U.S. Chess Championship, which dates back to 1845. (For more on the social world of competitive chess, see Fine 2015.) The World Series of Poker, owned and operated by Harrah's Entertainment, hosts events around the country, including Atlantic City, Lake Tahoe, New Orleans, and an annual tournament in Las Vegas that in 2016 attracted a record 107,833 entrants from 107 different countries, and awarded more than $220 million in total prize money (Associated Press 2016). Las Vegas also hosts the annual Classic Gaming Expo, where fans break records playing 1980s arcade games from Ms. Pac-Man and Donkey Kong to Burger Time and Centipede. As *Harper's* writer Joshua Bearman (2008, p. 65) observes, the Expo represents "an important moment of social interaction for a crowd that, by all available visual evidence, spends a considerable amount of time alone."

Meanwhile, the North American Scrabble Players Association oversees active tournament players, local clubs, regional tournaments, and national championships in the United States and Canada. According to Stefan Fatsis's book *Word Freak* (2001), Scrabble clubs and tournaments are intense meeting grounds where die-hards who share an obsession with the game discuss strategy, gossip about their fellow competitors, and pore over notebooks full of arcane vocabulary lists. Some enthusiasts literally wear their gaming obsessions on their sleeves, showing off T-shirts that read "SCRABBLE PLAYERS DO IT ON THE TILES" and "DOES ANAL RETENTIVE HAVE A HYPHEN?" The game's devoted community of competitive players is homegrown, having developed organically among fans participating in local game-playing clubs, just as other kinds of fan groups, tournaments, and events surrounding pop culture mania often emerge out of the interpersonal networks of eager consumers. Perhaps the most infamous of these events are the *Star Trek* conventions first organized in 1972—three years *after* the science-fiction TV show went off the air (Walker 2008b, p. 14). At these gatherings, thousands of "Trekkies" or "Trekkers" (as fans of the show are known) walk the convention floor dressed in Vulcan regalia and kibitz over esoteric trivia about otherwise obscure episodes.

Today these fan-oriented sci-fi events have been dwarfed by comic-book conventions such as San Diego's Comic-Con International, New York Comic Con, and Wizard World, which holds conventions in more than 10 U.S. cities,

Players at the Phoenix Scrabble Tournament in Arizona. More than 150 competitors from across the United States and Canada participated in the four-day tournament to win $8,800 in prize money.

including Chicago, Philadelphia, Nashville, Portland, New Orleans, Cleveland, St. Louis, and Austin. These conventions are hugely popular: In 2015, NY Comic Con counted nearly 170,000 attendees. These events attract thousands of autograph-seeking fans of comic books, graphic novels, movie franchises, and video games as well as fantasy card-game players who compete at tables spread throughout the convention floor. In addition, participants often don homemade (or expensive, professional-quality) superhero outfits and animated-character costumes. At Wizard World, such participants include *Star Wars* fans who voluntarily provide make-believe security for convention organizers while dressed as Imperial Storm Troopers. Some of these fans are members of the Fighting 501st Legion, a group of costume enthusiasts who dress as *Star Wars* villains for charity events held by organizations such as the American Cancer Society, March of Dimes, Make-a-Wish Foundation, and the Special Olympics.

One of the tens of thousands of comic book fans attending New York Comic Con. Originally showcasing comic books and science fiction, the convention has expanded over the years to include a wider range of pop culture, such as anime, manga, animation, toys, collectible card games, video games, and comics.

The Blurry Boundary between Marketing and Reality

Given the intense relationships people form when consuming pop culture collectively in socially interactive settings, it is no wonder that brands have incorporated such activities into their standard advertising and promotional efforts. In his *Atlantic* article "Turning Customers Into Cultists," Derek Thompson (2014) observes how companies involved in the sharing or peer economy such as Uber and Airbnb attempt to unite their consumers as collaborative warriors in ideological opposition to more professionalized transit and lodging business arrangements. The review site Yelp brings together its most involved users—its Yelp Elite Squad—for exclusive invitation-only events. Given its countercultural history against technological powerhouses like IBM and Microsoft, Apple has generated a quasi-religious following of its own, with throngs of consumers crowding downtowns in anticipation of each newly released iPhone. According

Long lines are a staple of Apple iPhone launches. Brands like Apple stage their product releases as pop cultural events to be experienced collectively and in public.

to Thompson (2014), "Apple isn't just another phone manufacturer. It's a brand with a cult following, whose new products inspire sane people to squat for hours outside the nearest Apple store like Wiccans worshipping before Stonehenge." While the fanaticism surrounding Apple may be homegrown, the company has leveraged this popularity by turning its product releases into subcultural events all their own.

The cultural diffusion strategies outlined earlier in the chapter have similarly been absorbed by the public relations industry. For example, publicists actively seek out connectors, opinion leaders, early adopters, and other fashion-forward people of influence as special guests for their promotional events when hyping new urban nightclubs, restaurants, cafés, or cocktail lounges (Grazian 2008b). They recognize that connectors not only make desirable customers themselves but may also have influence over multiple and diverse friendship networks of potential consumers. To this end, theAudience, a social-media management company, promotes sponsored branded content through its 6,500 Influencers— young and hip Internet stars, or "micro-celebrities," with hundreds of thousands of followers on YouTube, Instagram, and Twitter (Brodessor-Anker 2014).

Indeed, the marketing of pop culture from independent cinema to brand-name beverages relies ever more heavily on the value of word of mouth transmitted via subcultural networks and social media. The low-budget 2007 horror flick *Paranormal Activity* (made for about $10,000) was first shown at a variety of film festivals, and then it was acquired by Paramount Pictures for about $350,000 and introduced at special midnight screenings held in select college towns across the country from Ann Arbor to Boulder to Baton Rouge. Producers invited consumers to vote on the website Eventful to bring the creepy picture to their city. To gin up interest, online viewers were shown an inexpensively produced trailer featuring terrified audience members reacting to the movie during darkened screenings in Los Angeles and Toronto (Cieply 2009). As a result of this web-based guerilla-marketing campaign, *Paranormal Activity* went on to gross $193 million worldwide, making it possibly the most profitable movie ever made.

Meanwhile, the revival of the Pabst Blue Ribbon beer brand owes its success to the clandestine or *stealth marketing* of the Pabst Brewery Company, which quietly underwrites indie events thrown by bike messengers, skateboarders, art gallery owners, independent publishers, and other bohemian denizens of the urban underground. Similarly, the Austrian company responsible for the energy drink Red Bull stages and promotes extreme sporting events—including a kiteboarding race from Miami to Cuba—as publicity stunts designed to tap into the hip networks of subcultural youth and other cool kids (Walker 2008a). These promotional strategies meet their match when compared to the efforts of *reality marketing* firms such as BzzAgent, which sends its volunteer army of ordinary people out into the world to promote such brands as Ralph Lauren Blue perfume, Lee jeans, and Al Fresco chicken sausage in their everyday lives, simply by casually chatting up the friends and acquaintances in their social networks (pp. 165–88; on reality marketing, also see Grazian 2008b, pp. 86–90). This strategy works because the kinds of people who sign on with BzzAgent take pleasure in talking about brands and popular culture, just as market mavens do. But the genius (or tragedy, depending on your point of view) of reality marketing is that it has taken the advertising industry's appropriation of word-of-mouth communication to its logical conclusion, effectively confusing the difference between marketing and reality, buying in and selling out. As the next chapter illustrates, the boundary separating the two has perhaps never been more blurred than it is today.

Pop culture is always produced as collective activity among creative collaborators working together, like the 1960s British rock n' roll band the Beatles.

we can work it out

CREATING POPULAR CULTURE

MUSICIANS ARE CAPABLE OF CREATING TRULY SHOCKING cultural moments. At the 1965 Newport Folk Festival, Bob Dylan angered many audience members by trading in his acoustic guitar for a plugged-in Fender Stratocaster and an electrified rock band when he performed "Maggie's Farm" and "Like a Rolling Stone." In 1969, Jimi Hendrix played an acid-rock version of "The Star Spangled Banner" at the Woodstock Festival in upstate New York. Yet the decisions made by even the most revolutionary musicians are governed by the physics of sound embedded in the spaces where they perform. Given its West African tropical climate, social life in Senegal has traditionally been conducted in outdoor public places. Consequentially, musicians in this region have historically emphasized polyrhythmic drumming and percussion, since it carries well outdoors acoustically. Yet if this music were performed in, say, a Gothic medieval cathedral, its rhythms would be "sonically mashed together" in an echo chamber of muddy reverberation, according to the lead singer of the Talking Heads, David Byrne (2012, p. 18). Such a space would be far more suitable for playing non-percussive music that emphasizes the chanting of long notes that overlap one another, producing simple vocal melodies that gradually evolve over time. In fact, that is exactly the kind of Western music that developed in such medieval churches—the Gregorian chants and choral music of the Middle Ages (pp. 18–19).

If we jump ahead to the 1970s and 1980s, when concerts moved into sports arenas and stadiums, we find that the music performed in such acoustically poor spaces could only sound decent if it was consistently loud, with simple rhythms accompanying straightforward chord progressions—in other words, the anthemic classic rock and heavy metal of the era (p. 27). In fact, it is no coincidence that the bands most associated with these giant music venues—Led Zeppelin, Aerosmith, AC/DC, Boston, Journey, Styx, Kiss, Bon Jovi—are considered the headliners of what became known as "arena rock." Meanwhile, although it originated on the streets of New York, hip-hop producers today emphasize a heavy bass sound specifically designed to be enjoyed where contemporary consumers listen to music: in the interiors of their cars, and on expensive audio headphones (p. 28).

In this chapter, we explore how the creation of media and popular culture is constrained by its social context. While in Chapter 3 we looked at the role that large mass media firms play in the production of pop culture (a topic we will revisit in Chapter 6), we now focus our attention on the actual artists and support personnel who make up the art worlds that create and disseminate the stuff of popular culture, including music of all genres, from classical to blues, jazz, rock, and rap. We will use the tools of sociology to examine exactly *how* context matters by taking into account not only the actual places and moments in which creators make popular culture but the significance of less obvious social realities as well, including occupational and organizational routines, aesthetic and social conventions, technological change, and the law.

Cultural Creativity as Collaborative Activity

Despite our society's cult of the creative artist as a solitary genius—Ludwig von Beethoven, Emily Dickinson, Vincent van Vogh, Miles Davis, Steve Jobs, Mark Zuckerberg—no one creates culture all on their own. In *The Sociology of Philosophies*, Randall Collins (1998) observes that the great philosophical ideas of the ages from ancient Chinese Confucianism to German Idealism and French Existentialism emerged not from the minds of individual geniuses as much as from their interactions within small communities of teachers and mentors, pupils and disciples, colleagues and rivals. Their meetings, discussions, debates, and arguments provided a fertile context for the development of refined thought, just as artists working and kibitzing together inevitably share techniques and styles, evaluate each other's work, and push each other to excel.

Sociologist Michael P. Farrell (2001) refers to collective worlds of creativity formed among friends as *collaborative circles*. According to Farrell, collaborative circles provide a kind of dynamism that drives innovation and rebelliousness in the arts. This observation explains how an intimate group of artists who studied and socialized together in Paris helped give birth to the most important art movement of the nineteenth century. Today, many of their names—Édouard Manet, Pierre-Auguste Renoir, Camille Pissarro, Paul Cézanne, Edgar Degas, and Claude Monet—are as famous as their paintings of landscapes, water lilies, fruit bowls, and ballet dancers. In many ways their French Impressionist style was invented not only in their art studios but also at Café Guerbois on the rue des Batignolles in Paris, where these painters began gathering together in the late 1860s for weekly Thursday night meetings filled with noisy conversation and impassioned argument. Moreover, despite the romantic stereotype of the solitary artist alone at his easel, the Impressionists frequently traveled together to sites of natural beauty where they could paint in each other's company. According to Farrell's description of their experiments painting in the Forest of Fontainebleau just outside Paris, "While working side by side, the young painters shared ideas about what art should be and began to develop their own vision. The group was like an amoeba that sends out a pod in one direction, pulls it back, then sends another one out in a new direction as it feels its way toward nourishment" (p. 34).

Collaborative circles like the French Impressionists are common fixtures in the history of popular culture and the arts. The tightest collaborative circles are *pairs* of cultural creators whose interpersonal dynamics propel their innovative discoveries. As author Joshua Wolf Shenk (2015) argues in *Powers of Two*, some creative pairs are known for their healthy competitiveness and differences in artistic vision, as was the Beatles' songwriting team of John Lennon and Paul McCartney, each trying to best one another in a productive rivalry buzzing with generative tension. (In 1965 Paul and John cowrote the No. 1 hit "We Can Work It Out," which fused Paul's lyrical optimism with John's perennial anxiety—"Life is very short / And there's no time for fussing and fighting, my friend.")

Apple chairman and cofounder Steve Jobs (left) unveils the portable Apple IIc computer in 1984 along with the company's CEO John Sculley (center) and cofounder Steve Wozniak (right). Jobs and Wozniak met in 1971 when they both worked at Hewlett-Packard, and the creative duo cofounded Apple Computer five years later.

According to Shenk, other creative duos work it out by adhering to a division of labor specifically designed to make the most optimal use of their respective talents and skill sets, as when electrical engineer and programming whiz Steve Wozniak collaborated with the more entrepreneurially minded Steve Jobs to bring the Apple II personal computer to market in 1977. On the set of the 1990s sitcom *Seinfeld*, the agreeable comedian Jerry Seinfeld smoothed out co-creator Larry David's prickly edges, just as the wildly imaginative Trey Parker needs the practical mindedness of his *South Park* and *The Book of Mormon* collaborator Matt Stone to bring his visions to the stage and screen. Sadly, our society's cult of the solitary genius often writes women who collaborate with men out of the picture altogether, which is why George Lucas is credited with creating the original *Star Wars* film but not his first wife, Academy Award—winning film editor Marcia Lucas, who worked tirelessly alongside him. (Mark Hamill, the lead actor who played Luke Skywalker in the first *Star Wars* trilogy, referred to her as "the warmth and the heart of those films"; see Shenk 2015, p. xviii.)

Ensemble work in television production provides another key illustration of how collaborative worlds lend themselves to the creation of innovative popular culture. Take the creative team behind the children's educational TV program *Sesame Street*, a motley bunch of puppeteers, writers, actors, stagehands, educators, composers, and animators, to say nothing of Jim Henson's hyperactive Muppets. According to Michael Davis's book *Street Gang* (2008), the show's cast and crew had always indulged in practical jokes, competition

The ensemble work of Jim Henson and his Muppet cast and crew was key to the success of Sesame Street *and also* The Muppet Show, *pictured here.*

among songwriters, and the myriad small-group interactions common among creative collaborators. According to Frank Oz, the puppeteer who lent his voice to beloved characters such as Bert, Grover, and Cookie Monster, "Fucking around [in the studio] was the key to *Sesame Street*. It allowed for that affectionate anarchy that Jim [Henson] reveled in" (p. 221).

The collective creativity generated by ensemble acting and tag-team writing has similarly made *Saturday Night Live* (*SNL*) one of the most successful sketch-comedy shows in TV history. Since its debut in 1975, the NBC late-night program has relied not only on the onscreen antics of its stars but the "affectionate anarchy" celebrated by its actors and writers off-camera as well. According to Tom Shales and James Andrew Miller's oral history *Live from New York* (2002), in its early years the show's studios at New York's Rockefeller Center resembled a 1970s coed college dormitory, with sketch writers and cast members pulling all-nighters, sharing drugs, sleeping with one another, and experimenting with all manner of jokes and outrageous performance. In this creative environment the Not Ready for Prime Time Players—Dan Aykroyd, John Belushi, Chevy Chase, Jane Curtin, Garrett Morris, Bill Murray, Laraine Newman, and Gilda Radner—reinvented television comedy, and future *SNL* stars such as Adam Sandler, Chris Rock, Will Ferrell, Jimmy Fallon, Tina Fey, Kristen Wiig, Amy Poehler, Seth Meyers, and Andy Samberg followed in their footsteps. (Tina Fey based her NBC comedy *30 Rock* on her experience as *SNL*'s first female head writer.)

Cultural Conventions

Creative collaborators from comedy writers to art collectives are able to work together with the help of *cultural conventions*, the taken-for-granted rules and agreed-on assumptions that make social activity possible (Becker 1982). In worlds of cultural creation, common conventions include the stable use of well-defined language and terminology; standardized materials, tools, and technology; systems of musical theory and notation (keys, scales, chords, time signatures); codified genre types and aesthetic styles; and rituals of participation, including the spatial and temporal boundaries that lend shape to performances.

Conventions make pop cultural production enormously more efficient than it would otherwise be. Picture a trio of rock musicians preparing to play "Smells Like Teen Spirit," the lead single from Nirvana's 1991 album *Nevermind*. Even if the players have never heard the song, standard conventions of musical structure, genre, and style can be mobilized to describe its fundamentals to the musicians, including its key (F minor), the four power chords that make up the song's dominant guitar riff (F5-B♭5-A♭5-D♭5), and instrumentation (guitar, bass guitar, vocals, drums). Like many rock songs, "Smells Like Teen Spirit" is organized in a conventional manner around a set of verses, a repeating first and second chorus, and a 16-bar guitar solo that echoes the vocal melody. (In fact, the simple formal structure of the song has been compared to other hit songs from the classic rock era, including "Louie Louie" by the Kingsmen and "More Than a Feeling" by Boston.) Armed with a familiarity of modern rock conventions, virtually any competent musician could perform a halfway-decent rendition of the Nirvana song with little practice—perhaps not as brilliant as the original, but passable nonetheless.

To further illustrate how conventions simplify and improve coordinated efforts among cultural creators, imagine how time-consuming it would be if every group of musicians had to invent an entirely new system of scales, chords, tones, and notation for themselves. Conventions are also reflected in the standardized tools and materials used to produce popular culture (e.g., digital video cameras, guitar effects pedals, oil and acrylic primers), and the physical infrastructure needed for its distribution and exhibition (e.g., fiber-optic cable networks, concert venues, multiplex cinemas, museum gallery spaces). Given the widespread adherence to cultural conventions, novelists need not program their own word-processing software, just as jazz musicians do not need to build their own brass instruments, nor do movie directors need to design their own screen projectors on which to show their films.

The stability of conventions eases the production of popular culture but ultimately limits its creative possibilities—that is, cultural *conventions* make culture *conventional*. Many pop songs sound so similar because they contain the same I-V-vi-IV chord progression, including Journey's "Don't Stop Believing," U2's "With or Without You," Lady Gaga's "Poker Face" and "The Edge of Glory," Miley Cyrus's "Party in the U.S.A.," Imagine Dragons' "Demons," and Adele's "Someone Like You" and "Hello." In fact, as in the case of Nirvana's "Smells Like Teen Spirit," pop music's reliance on cultural conventions often leads to accidental similarities among otherwise different song recordings. For example, note how Adele's 2015 song "Million Years Ago" from her album *25* sounds like Dusty Springfield's 1972 record "Yesterday When I Was Young," and Sam Smith's 2014 hit song "Stay with Me" resembles Tom Petty & the Heartbreakers' 1989 single "I Won't Back Down." Similarities like these often lead to lawsuits alleging copyright infringement, as when a federal jury decided that Robin Thicke, Pharrell Williams, and Clifford "T. I." Harris Jr. owed Marvin Gaye's estate royalties given the unmistakable similarities between their 2013 hit "Blurred Lines" and Gaye's 1977 classic disco record "Got to Give It Up."

How else do cultural conventions make popular culture more conventional? Jazz cabaret musicians cover a well-worn repertoire of standards when they perform, just as Chicago blues bands and wedding DJs do (Grazian 2003; Faulkner and Becker 2009). Pop music artists sometimes record double albums of brand-new material but rarely triple albums, which caused critics to call the 1999 release of the Magnetic Fields' three-CD set *69 Love Songs* "as much an eccentric New York art project as a pop album." Similarly, U.S. feature films are rarely longer than four hours, which is why Quentin Tarantino's 247-minute epic *Kill Bill* had to be split in half and released to theaters as two separate films in 2003 and 2004.

Meanwhile, some conventions are embedded in the tools and exhibition spaces employed by cultural creators. Alto saxophones have a more limited octave range relative to other instruments like the piano, just as calligraphers who rely on mass-produced inks may be hamstrung by the retail availability of certain colors, hues, or textures. Artists who create impossibly large sculptures or environmental "earthworks" like Robert Smithson's 1970 piece *Spiral Jetty* (a massive 1,500-foot-long sculpture of mud, salt crystals, and basalt rocks that juts off the coast of Utah's Great Salt Lake) may have difficulty finding gallery or museum spaces in which to exhibit their work. (Such works are usually erected in outdoor spaces, or else photographed or filmed for inclusion in art galleries and museums.) The physical characteristics of most local rock music venues (notably building size and age) prevent the use of pyrotechnics and stage effects

Robert Smithson's 1970 environmental sculpture Spiral Jetty *is a 1,500-foot-long "earthwork" located off Rozel Point in the Great Salt Lake of Utah.*

common to plus-sized arena and stadium concerts. The heavy metal band Great White learned this the hard way in 2003 when they headlined a show at the Station nightclub in West Warwick, Rhode Island. The spray of sparks set off at the beginning of their set accidentally ignited the flammable soundproofing material surrounding the stage, and the resulting fire claimed the lives of 100 people, including the band's guitarist.

Not all dismissals of convention leave behind this sort of tragic destruction. In fact, many conventions are relatively easy to break, although in doing so one risks confusing audiences and critics alike. For example, my word-processing software, Microsoft Office Word, gives me hundreds of fonts and styles to employ in my writing, but convention discourages me from **using** multiple **fonts** in the same **sentence** or paragraph. The use of unconventional tools or materials in popular culture can easily generate either delight or outrage. As noted in our discussion of George Harrison in the last chapter, the Beatles excited fans by featuring Indian tabla drums along with string instruments such as the sitar and tambura on their 1966 rock 'n' roll album *Revolver*, as heard on at least two tracks, "Love You To" and "Tomorrow Never Knows." The indie rock band the Decemberists opened their 2005 album *Picaresque* with a blast from a Jewish *shofar*, a ceremonial ram's horn traditionally blown during the holidays of Rosh Hashanah and Yom Kippur. Contemporary U.S. writers similarly experiment with cultural conventions, often to entertaining effect. The acknowledgments section of Dave Eggers's 2000 memoir *A Heartbreaking Work of Staggering Genius* is packed with seemingly irrelevant, nonliterary details—the amount he was advanced by his publisher (minus his agent's fee and taxes), his budgeted expenses for writing the book, a random drawing of a stapler—while much of the final third of Jennifer Egan's 2010 Pulitzer Prize—winning novel *A Visit from the Goon Squad* is written as a PowerPoint presentation.

On the other hand, British painter Chris Ofili generated political controversy by incorporating elephant feces into his work, most famously in 1999 when New York mayor Rudolph Giuliani threatened to pull the Brooklyn Museum of Art's municipal funds when it ran an art exhibit that included Ofili's dung-adorned *The Holy Virgin Mary*. The exhibit in question, fittingly called *Sensation*, also included Damien Hirst's *A Thousand Years*, a piece composed of flies, maggots, and a cow's head, and Marc Quinn's *Self*, a sculptural rendering of the artist's head made from nine pints of his own frozen blood. In keeping with the overall theme of the chapter, we must bear in mind the context-specific nature of these cultural unconventionalities and taboos—after all, the sitar is hardly an unconventional instrument in *Indian* popular music, and it is not uncommon for dried animal dung to be used on occasion in African arts and crafts from pottery to baskets and even paper.

A Reflection Theory of Culture

It has become commonplace to suggest that popular culture serves as a mirror that, as a society, we hold up to see our own reflection as illuminated in our songs and soap operas, our movies and myths. We imagine that the heroic characters of great American novels—Huck and Jim from Mark Twain's *The Adventures of*

Huckleberry Finn, Captain Ahab from Herman Melville's *Moby-Dick*, Dean Moriarty from Jack Kerouac's *On the Road*—reflect our frontier individualism and rugged fearlessness. We see our iconoclasm and revolutionary spirit in classic films such as *Rebel Without a Cause* (1955) and *One Flew Over the Cuckoo's Nest* (1975), and also in sci-fi epics such as *Star Wars* (1977). This same national rebelliousness and pride can be read into the poetry of Walt Whitman, the folksongs of Woody Guthrie and Pete Seeger, and the rock 'n' roll of Chuck Berry, Elvis Presley, and Bob Dylan. As Americans we know and accept these truths, just as we embrace baseball, Cracker Jack, hot dogs, roasted turkey, and apple pie as quintessential to our very being, our national soul.

Or do we? On a second look, the synchronicity between our popular culture and social order seems to slip. After all, pop culture is a complicated organism, more than simply a sponge that easily absorbs the multiple realities that make up a national way of life. (If only it were so easy—then *every* American novel would be as revelatory as those penned by Twain or Melville, just as every pop song would be as important as Bob Dylan's "Blowin' in the Wind" or "Ballad of a Thin Man.") As we have discussed, popular culture is the product of collective work coordinated among innumerable creators and support personnel, often under the auspices of a profit-seeking multinational company. If our novels and music are reflections of the cultural zeitgeist, they are also reflections of other sociological realities. Let us briefly discuss three such realities. They are (1) the *legal system* that regulates the production of popular culture; (2) the *organizational apparatus* that structures how media and culture are promoted and sold to audiences; and (3) the *technological constraints* that undergird the entire process. By analyzing the legal, organizational, and technological contexts in which novels, movies, and music are created, we can better see not only how popular culture reflects society and the social order but also how it reflects the *cultural production process itself*.

First, how exactly does popular culture reflect its surrounding legal context? To take just one example, changes in copyright law have an enormous impact on the content of popular culture. In fact, Wendy Griswold (1981), a sociology professor at Northwestern University, argues that the distinctiveness of the so-called American frontier character that emerged in nineteenth-century novels such as *The Adventures of Huckleberry Finn* and *Moby-Dick* can be attributed in large part to the specific quirks of U.S. copyright law. For most of the nineteenth century, U.S. publishers recognized the copyright of American authors yet refused to pay royalties to British and European writers. Since these publishers passed the savings along to consumers, novels by foreign authors were considerably less expensive than books penned by American writers. (For example, between 1876 and 1884 the average prices for imported and domestic books were $0.64 and $1.04, respectively.) To compete successfully in what had become an unfair market, American authors were therefore forced to create characters and plots that differed substantially from those found in British and European novels by writers like Charles Dickens and Gustave Flaubert—thus giving birth to distinctively "American" title characters from Melville's *The Confidence-Man*

What role did American copyright law play in the creation of cultural icons such as Huck Finn?

to Twain's *A Connecticut Yankee in King Arthur's Court.*

How do we know that these differences were a response to copyright law and not borne out of some essential American ideology or way of life? Because in 1891 Congress passed the Platt-Simmonds Act that finally extended copyright protections to foreign authors for the first time, and after this, the differences between British and American novels radically declined. While some characterizations and themes unique to American literature obviously persist, notably those concerning race, the convergence of national book cultures brought about by the transformation of U.S. copyright law is otherwise nearly undisputable. As Griswold observes, "The American authors had greater incentive to deviate from the norm, to write on nontraditional themes that European authors had not effectively monopolized. After 1891, there was no longer the same incentive for deviation, the novelistic imperatives took over, and the American authors swung into line with everyone else" (p. 760).

A more recent example of how changes in copyright law affect the content of popular culture can be found in two special rap albums: *Paul's Boutique*, recorded in 1989 by the rock-rap fusion group the Beastie Boys, and the 1990 Public Enemy album *Fear of a Black Planet*. Both of these records enjoy enormous critical acclaim: *Time* included *Paul's Boutique* on its list of the 100 greatest albums of all time, while *Spin* rated *Fear of a Black Planet* the second-best album of the 1990s. Both albums offer a sonic soundscape practically unmatched in the history of pop music, in part because of the sheer number of music and film samples packed within each of their tracks. *Fear of a Black Planet* alone samples at least 90 classic recordings, including those by James Brown, George Clinton, the Temptations, Eric Clapton, Grandmaster Flash, and Sly & the Family Stone. Meanwhile, *Paul's Boutique* features over *100* samples from the Beatles, Jimi Hendrix, Curtis Mayfield, Isaac Hayes, Pink Floyd, Led Zeppelin, the Ramones, the Sugarhill Gang, and, interestingly enough, Public Enemy.

Plenty of contemporary hip-hop tracks rely on sophisticated sampling techniques, but still, it is rare for an artist or producer to employ nearly as many samples as these two albums do; most usually include no more than one or two per song. Why? The answer lies in a highly influential judicial court case: *Grand Upright Music, Limited v. Warner Bros. Records Inc.*, in which the U.S. District Court for the Southern District of New York granted an injunction against Warner Bros., finding that the label had illegally released a recording by rapper Biz Markie that sampled the 1972 Gilbert O'Sullivan song "Alone Again (Naturally)" without first acquiring permission from the copyright owners. This ruling ultimately transformed hip-hop forever by discouraging music producers from oversampling copyrighted recordings, because while permissions were never guaranteed and were often prohibitively expensive, the threat of exposure to potential lawsuits from injured parties had now reached new heights. And guess when this court case was decided? That's right—in 1991, shortly after the release of *Paul's Boutique* and *Fear of a Black Planet*. Those two albums were among the last albums recorded by major labels (Capitol and Def Jam/Columbia, respectively) before *Grand Upright Music* changed the music industry irrevocably, perhaps forever. Today, such adventures in sampling require digging into the public domain for available recordings, or else releasing mash-ups and remixes online as illegal bootlegs, as renegade DJs such as Danger Mouse and Girl Talk have done.

These examples illustrate how popular culture reflects the specific legal system that regulates its production. Let us now move on to our next concern: How does popular culture reflect the organizational apparatus that structures the way music, film, books, and television programs are promoted and sold? For instance, of the thousands of music recordings released every year, only a small fraction of them ever receive any radio or television airplay, and the songs chosen (or rejected) for promotion through these public venues reflect the organizational arrangements that shape the selection and distribution process. Again, 1980s popular music provides a nice example—in this case early '80s British new wave music as represented by synthesizer-pop glam bands such as Duran Duran, Culture Club, the Human League, the Cure, and the Eurythmics. What explains the dominance of this music genre in the United States in the early 1980s? In fact, in many ways it seems downright *unreflective* of American society, or at least the musical styles performed by the most popular American artists at that time, particularly the R&B-influenced pop music of Michael Jackson and Prince and the hard rock of Journey and Van Halen.

However, the success of British new wave music in the early 1980s almost perfectly reflects the organizational apparatus of the music industry as exemplified by the emergence of MTV, which debuted as a 24-hour cable music channel in 1981. During the 1980s and 1990s, MTV relied heavily on promotional music videos produced by major record labels for a large proportion of its on-air content. (In the digital age, MTV has increasingly emphasized scripted teen comedies and reality television programs like *Real World, True Life*, and *Catfish* rather than music videos, given their availability on YouTube and other online sites.) But as sociologist Paul Lopes (1992, p. 68) points out, in the early 1980s "no significant video production of pop music existed in the United States." However, music videos *had* long been a source of television programming in—you guessed it—Great

The American success of 1980s British New Wave bands such as Duran Duran was due in large part to the programming decisions of MTV early in the decade.

Britain, as exemplified by the four cutting-edge films the Beatles made in the 1960s as cinematic companions to their classic albums *A Hard Day's Night, Help!, Magical Mystery Tour*, and *Yellow Submarine*. (Other British pop records eventually made into movies include the Who's *Tommy* and Pink Floyd's *The Wall*.) Given the high-quality production of music films and videos made in England (relative to its paucity in the United States), MTV was forced to rely almost entirely on imported videos promoting new British artists for its programming in the channel's first years of existence, thus inadvertently jump-starting the popularity of new wave music here in the United States. Sure enough, the success of the genre reached its peak shortly thereafter, in 1983, when new wave performers made up 43 percent of all new artists on *Billboard* magazine's annual albums chart, and 50 percent of new artists on the singles chart (p. 66).

Even before songs make it into MTV's rotation, they first must be selected for release by a profit-seeking record company. The music industry has long relied on market testing pop singles to potential consumers by playing them small bursts and snippets of music (Gladwell 2005, p. 166), and today marketers like HitPredictor (a subsidiary of iHeartMedia) ask listeners to rate entire songs by listening to their musical fragments online (Thompson 2014). This strategy privileges particular types of pop songs—short, fast tunes with studio effects and catchy hooks that are immediately gratifying but may not withstand repeat listening on overzealous Top 40 radio stations. It also effectively filters out certain kinds of recordings from the production process altogether, including songs that emphasize lyrical and/or sonic complexity that may demand more listener attentiveness than that required during market testing, and innovative forms of music that listeners may not immediately assimilate because they sit uncomfortably between traditional genres. In this manner, contemporary popular music directly reflects the organizational strategies employed during the production and selection process.

One may simply argue that today's pop music is more a reflection of *audience preference* than the production process, just as long as test marketing represents an accurate indicator of what people want. In fact, the record industry relentlessly seeks out digital signals of audience preference by mining data from online searches on Shazam (an app that identifies songs heard in public within seconds), Spotify, and even Wikipedia (Thompson 2014). But despite these attempts at unearthing musical preferences through computational science, the fact remains that listeners cannot "prefer" new music that they have never heard. It bears remembering that some of pop music's most successful artists began their careers with small fan bases and only over time gained the kind of traction and consumer approval that test marketing presupposes should be instantaneous and effortless. In 1973, Columbia Records took a chance by releasing two albums by a relatively unknown male singer-songwriter who had developed a following along the New Jersey shore, and although the recordings received critical acclaim, they sold poorly. In today's era of test marketing, data mining, and immediate profit-seeking, he surely would have been dropped by the record label.

Fortunately, Columbia released his third album in 1975, and although it garnered no hit singles, a handful of its songs found a home on album-oriented rock (AOR) radio stations, including "Thunder Road," "Tenth-Avenue Freeze Out," "Jungleland," and the album's title track, "Born to Run." Since then, that singer-songwriter, Bruce Springsteen, has sold more than 65 million albums in the United States and 120 million worldwide, including his 1984 album *Born in the U.S.A.*, which at 30 million copies sold worldwide makes it one of the best-selling albums of all time. (He has also won 20 Grammy Awards, and in 1999 he was inducted into the Rock and Roll Hall of Fame.) My point here is not only to celebrate "The Boss," as Springsteen is known to fans, but to illustrate how his music and career reflect an older (and now outdated) organizational apparatus that structured product selection in the music industry during the 1970s—an industry that in recent years has embraced more formal test-marketing and data-mining strategies that for better or worse have transformed what popular music looks and sounds like in today's global cultural marketplace.

Finally, how does popular culture reflect the technological constraints that shape its production and distribution to the public? On one level, the answer is as obvious as the shift in music from acoustic jazz to electric R&B to synthesized pop to digital techno beats, or the transformation in film from silent black-and-white cinema to "talkies" to Technicolor to CGI animation. Of course, the reality is more complicated, particularly since technologies of the past have a strange way of influencing the present. For example, why are most pop songs about three or four minutes long? The technological context of music production in the earliest years of the recording industry provides an answer. From the 1910s until the end of the 1940s, popular music was typically recorded on "seventy-eights": double-sided, 10-inch shellac discs that spun at 78 rpm (or revolutions per minute). These discs could hold only about three minutes of sound per side, so naturally the hit songs of the 1920s, 1930s, and 1940s were produced as three-minute recordings. (The less standard 12-inch disc could hold a whopping three-*and-a-half* minutes per side.) This probably does not seem like a big deal, except that until the age of recorded music, composers and performers had never really been constrained in this particular way—consider the expansive length of most classical symphonies or operas. Early American blues and folk music were even less inhibited because they were based on oral traditions in which songs were passed along from musician to musician without a written score and often included improvisational passages that the player would invent anew with every performance. In such a context, songs had *no* determined length: They simply ended when the performer stopped playing. Therefore, the technology of the early recording era not only determined what a song sounded like—it determined what a song, in fact, *was*.

How did the technological limitations of early records shape the form of popular music?

Still, none of this explains why most pop songs *today* should be only three or four minutes long. After all, long-playing (or LP) records were invented in 1948, while digital recording technologies and data storage capacities allow us to record songs of virtually *any* length, from three minutes to three hours, or days or months. But few contemporary listeners would sit through a three-hour song (I can barely get my students to sit through a one-hour lecture), because over time we have become conditioned as a society to define down the duration of our songs. In this manner, the three-minute pop song is what sociologists call a *cultural survival* from the past: Created out of technological necessity but now destined to remain a constraining cultural convention all its own, today's three-minute pop song is a reflection of the technological context in which popular music was recorded between 1910 and 1948.

The technologies of the digital age—namely the conversion of music to data files that can be purchased or streamed online, shared among users, inserted into homemade playlists, and turned into smartphone ringtones—have transformed the way we habitually experience music in many other ways. One in particular stands out: We are more likely to think about songs as cultural and aesthetic entities unto themselves than as component parts of entire albums. After the invention of the LP record in 1948, artists increasingly began releasing music in album format, which soon gave rise to the *concept album* as a cohesive musical work intended to be heard in its entirety in one sitting, its songs woven together by common stylistic virtues and lyrical themes. The first concept albums were jazz recordings such as Duke Ellington's *Black, Brown and Beige* (1958) and John Coltrane's *A Love Supreme* (1965). During the 1960s and 1970s critics

Prince's best-selling concept album Purple Rain *was released as a soundtrack to the movie of the same name in 1984.*

began to take popular music more seriously with the release of a series of experimental rock concept albums, notably the Beach Boys' *Pet Sounds* (1966), the Beatles' *Sgt. Pepper's Lonely Hearts Club Band* (1967), and the Kinks' *The Kinks Are the Village Green Preservation Society* (1968). Later concept albums include Marvin Gaye's *What's Going On* (1971), David Bowie's *The Rise and Fall of Ziggy Stardust and the Spiders from Mars* (1972), Pink Floyd's *The Wall* (1979), Radiohead's *OK Computer* (1997), the Flaming Lips' *Yoshimi Battles the Pink Robots* (2002), Green Day's *American Idiot* (2004), Jay Z's *American Gangster* (2007), Arcade Fire's *The Suburbs* (2010), and Beyoncé's *Lemonade* (2016). (This last smash was released as a "visual" album with accompanying video, just as classic concept albums like the Beatles' *Yellow Submarine* and Prince's *Purple Rain* were originally released as soundtracks to films featuring those artists.)

Despite *Lemonade*'s runaway success, the concept album as a work of pop art may be destined to remain a relic of the past, if only because digital technology makes it so much easier to download or stream individual songs rather than entire albums. In fact, in 2015 total album sales (CDs and full-album downloads) dropped to 241.4 million, while 964.8 million individual songs were purchased that same year (Caulfield 2016). This does not also count the 317.2 *billion* songs consumers streamed that year from Spotify, Apple Music, and other subscription or ad-based services, a doubling from the previous year (Christman 2016).

What makes this digitally driven market shift extra-fascinating is that for all practical purposes, it revives the emphasis on recorded three-minute singles that dominated the popular music industry in the 1940s, albeit as a response to a set of technological conditions not likely dreamed of by the pop stars of yesteryear.

Arts and Crafts

In his book *Art Worlds*, sociologist Howard S. Becker (1982) observes that we often distinguish between two kinds of cultural creativity closely identified with one another: arts and crafts. According to Becker, when making *art* one relies on aesthetic skill and judgment to produce a genuine articulation of one's individuality, creativity, and unique vision. In this sense the creator produces art for purely expressive or otherwise nonutilitarian reasons—"art for art's sake," as they say. Examples might include abstract painting, avant-garde poetry, or performance art. In contrast, *crafts* refer to similarly creative endeavors performed for the purposes of making a useful object or providing a specific service, usually for a paying client or consumer. Like art, craft production relies on aesthetic skill and judgment as well, as illustrated by the talents of commercial artists, TV camera operators, shipbuilders, photojournalists, and pastry chefs.

Yet as dissimilar as these categories may seem, in many cases arts and crafts refer to the *exact same types* of activities made different only because they are infused with alternative meanings as shaped by their cultural context; when circumstances shift, their social designations as art or craft may change as well. For instance, the production of motorcycles is typically thought of as a craft: While they can possess a certain aesthetic beauty in their design, motorcycles are generally appreciated as vehicles purchased by consumers to be driven at high speeds on highways and roads rather than shown in an art museum—that is, until 1998, when the Solomon R. Guggenheim Museum in New York hosted an exhibit titled "The Art of the Motorcycle," which showcased 114 motorcycles of all vintages and models. This is an example of *craft becoming art*, as utilitarian commodities are consecrated as art objects by legitimizing institutions such as museums (Becker 1982, pp. 273—88). Perhaps oddly, home and office furnishings provide another example: Desks and armchairs designed by the architect Frank Lloyd Wright appear on permanent display at the Art Institute of Chicago, and office furniture is regularly exhibited at the Smithsonian's Cooper-Hewitt National Design Museum in New York. While wedding planners commonly hire disc jockeys to play preselected music for party guests, since the late-1970s disco, dub, house, and hip-hop DJs have become pop artists in their own right by spinning, sampling, scratching, and remixing records (Brewster and Broughton 2000). By employing twin turntables as expressive musical instruments, DJs transform craft into art.

How common is this transformation from craft to art? In many ways the consecration of early Renaissance art itself represents such a categorical shift. In an examination of fifteenth-century Italian painting, Michael Baxandall (1972) observes that frescoes and portraits during that time were funded not by benevolent patrons but by wealthy clients who commissioned "great works"

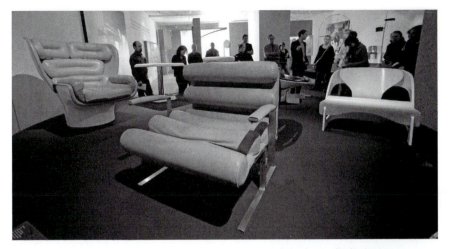

Armchairs by the mid-twentieth-century furniture designer Joe Colombo, on display in an art museum.

by negotiating complex contractual arrangements with artists for hire. These contracts obligated the artist to conform to the aesthetic wishes of the buyer in excruciating detail, from the use of certain paints and colors (especially gold, silver, and ultramarine, given their high cost) to the specificity of the artwork's subject matter. In 1485, the Florentine painter Domenico Ghirlandaio contractually agreed to incorporate "figures, buildings, castles, cities, mountains, hills, plains, rocks, costumes, animals, birds, and beasts of every kind" into a set of frescoes for the choir of the Basilica of Santa Maria Novella in Florence (pp. 17–18). When his 1488 masterpiece *Adoration of the Magi* was commissioned, Ghirlandaio was contracted to "color and paint the said panel all with his own hand in a manner shown in a drawing on paper . . . in every particular according to what *I, Fra Bernardo [the client] think best* . . . with powdered gold on such ornaments as demand it . . . and the blue must be ultramarine of the value about four florins the ounce" (p. 6; emphasis added). Today we honor Ghirlandaio and his most accomplished apprentice, Michelangelo, as inspired and expressive artistic geniuses rather than commercial craftspeople, yet in many ways that is exactly what they were. (This observation does not take anything away from their talents but simply asks us to reevaluate the context of social relations in which they produced their work.)

Just as social circumstances can transform craft into art, examples of *art becoming craft* abound as well (Becker 1982, pp. 288–96). Struggling theatrical actors sometimes take on roles in industrial training films and corporate promotional videos. Meanwhile, U.S. movie stars frequently earn big paychecks acting in TV commercials shown in foreign countries abroad: Examples include Academy Award winners Leonardo DiCaprio peddling Jim Beam bourbon in Japan, George Clooney selling Nespresso in France, and Gwyneth Paltrow shilling for Martini vermouth. Recently, Hollywood actors have begun regularly appearing in TV commercials in the United States for Budweiser (Amy Schumer and Seth

George Clooney is the face of Nespresso. Many American movie stars lend their celebrity to promote brands both here and abroad.

Rogen), Lincoln (Matthew McConaughey), J'adore perfume by Dior (Charlize Theron), Capital One (Alec Baldwin, Jimmy Fallon, Jennifer Garner, and Samuel L. Jackson), and, again, Jim Beam (Mila Kunis). Other movie stars appear as fashion models in magazine ads, notably for prestige luxury brands such as Louis Vuitton, whose celebrity endorsers include Angelina Jolie, Scarlet Johansson, Jennifer Lopez, Uma Thurman, and Michelle Williams. Meanwhile, it has traditionally been common for the biggest pop music artists to appear in commercials for Coke or Pepsi, including Michael Jackson, Elton John, Madonna, Britney Spears, Beyoncé, Katy Perry, Nicki Minaj, Janelle Monae, and Taylor Swift. Among less famous musicians and performers, orchestral violinists, cellists, clarinetists, and other instrumentalists often make ends meet by working as commercial studio musicians in the Hollywood film and television industry, as do classical music composers and conductors (Faulkner 1971). Celebrity rock musicians age into this professional craft as well. When he reached his mid-40s, Nine Inch Nails frontman Trent Reznor began scoring films for director David Fincher, including *The Social Network* (2010), *The Girl with the Dragon Tattoo* (2011), and *Gone Girl* (2014). (A version of his song "Closer" also appears during the opening credits of Fincher's 1995 thriller *Seven*.)

For artistic creators, performing the work expected of craftspeople—that is, producing culture in a commercialized context for a paying clientele or audience—often requires that they compromise their expressive or aesthetic vision in the interests of satisfying the mainstream tastes of consumers. As Gary Alan Fine (1992), a professor of sociology at Northwestern University, observes in his research on restaurant cooking, chefs must balance their own culinary judgment against the expectations and desires of average customers who, as a group, tend to prefer their meat and fish entrees overcooked and add too much salt and pepper to otherwise optimally seasoned dishes. In chain restaurants like Applebee's, Bennigan's, Chili's, and T.G.I.Friday's, chefs are also bound to corporate promises and customer expectations that the same dishes—Loaded Potato Skins, "Oh, Baby" Back Ribs, Death by Chocolate—will taste exactly the same in any restaurant location, from Carlisle, Pennsylvania, to Cartersville, Georgia, to Carlsbad, New Mexico. (Chili's has outlets in each location.) And since restaurant diners will wait only so long for their orders to be prepared, behind kitchen walls chefs regularly cut corners to an unsettling degree; this is why, according to Fine, "when food falls on a dirty counter or floor after being cooked, cooks will wipe or rinse it, and then serve it, with the customer none the wiser" (p. 1281).

Buying In and Selling Out

The myth of the romantic artist is an endur-ing one: It is easy to imagine the lonely painter or poet isolated in his garret studio, tortured by his inner demons as he creates his imaginative masterpieces. Unconcerned with money, his art alone—the unique expression of his human vision and inspired genius—keeps him alive. This myth easily lends itself to the world of popular music. Exemplars of the beatified singer-songwriter include John Lennon in his post-Beatles career; Jim Mor-rison, the lead singer of the 1960s rock band the Doors; Kurt Cobain, vocalist and lead guitarist of the 1990s Seattle grunge band Nirvana; the 1990s indie rock troubadour Elliot Smith; and the British sultry song-stress Amy Winehouse, whose 2006 album *Back to Black* featured songs chronicling her bouts with drug and alcohol addiction. Not coincidentally, all five tragically died young in the prime of their careers, solidifying their mythical status as pop cultural martyrs.

Grammy Award–winning British singer Amy Winehouse died tragically of alcohol poisoning in July 2011 at the age of 27.

But sociology punches a number of holes in this timeless myth of the solitary artist. As this chapter illustrates, cultural producers tend to work collectively in collaborative circles and other social groups (just as Cobain performed closely with Nirvana's bassist Krist Novoselic and drummer Dave Grohl), and their cre-ations are modeled in accordance with prevailing cultural conventions and social expectations. While popular culture may express something of the artist's per-sonality or identity, his or her output also reflects its social context, particularly the production process in which it is embedded. These contextual realities include the technological constraints that shape the manufacture and performance of pop culture, the organizational apparatus that structures its promotion and distribution, and the legal system that governs the overall process. At the same time, institutions of cultural consecration and legitimacy such as the Guggenheim Museum, the Art Institute of Chicago, and the Rock and Roll Hall of Fame help to mold and shift public perceptions of cultural value and propriety.

As for the obvious suggestion that authentic artists are far more concerned with expressing themselves creatively than with making money, it bears remembering how many try to excel at both. Certainly, almost all pop culture creators strive for aesthetic expressiveness and artistic excellence on even their most commercially oriented projects. Recent Hollywood blockbusters have managed to combine commercial demands with artistic vision: As the *New York Times* critic Manohla Dargis (2008) wrote of the Batman film *The Dark Knight*, "Pitched at the divide between art and industry, poetry and entertainment, it goes darker and deeper than any Hollywood movie of its comic-book kind." According to Stephen Oakes, a director of animation and special effects who produces television advertisements and promotional spots, commercial artists use client-based projects as outlets for their own creative vision: "In the production companies, in the creative teams at the ad agencies, I would say that we don't spend much time worrying about the home viewer. It is mostly ourselves as peers. We are trying to entertain ourselves and our friends—we are trying to get away with as much fun as possible while doing the job that the brand manager has set forth for us" (Ohmann 1996, p. 79). In fact, Oakes and his colleagues rely on TV advertising and music videos as testing grounds for developing experimental concepts and techniques. Regarding his work creating promotional ads for MTV during the 1980s, he recalls:

> It was a wonderful opportunity, because they said, "Here is the budget; do whatever you want; just make sure it ends up with the MTV configuration, the logo." Well, that was my dream job. And we did come up with some pretty wild stuff that came from the artist's interest. We did one that was based on a woman's personal watercolors, and she was the director of it. We did some sculptural model things. We did an MTV logo made out of time lapse of frozen chemicals that did funny things during its melting. We ran it in reverse so all this glop sort of swirled together and made the MTV logo. Each one of those was like a little visual experiment. Some were more successful than others, but the stakes weren't that high. It was a kind of novelty workshop. (pp. 78–79)

At the same time, pop cultural creators in most fields of production, particularly in fashion, television, filmmaking, and popular music, typically seek out professional and commercial success at least as much as any artistic ideal. In rap music, artistic success is *specifically* defined in monetary terms, as baldly proclaimed by the title of the rapper 50 Cent's 2003 multiplatinum album *Get Rich or Die Tryin'*. In a context of commercialized culture, money connotes artistic status; or, in the words of the late blues singer Barkin' Bill Smith, "It's not about havin' fun. It's about *makin' money*—now *that's* what it's all about! . . . Hell, then you can go out and *buy* your own fun!" (Grazian 2003, p. 151).

Of course, occasionally pop artists can overdo it. As part of a $100 million promotional campaign, in 2014 the band U2 partnered with Apple for an undisclosed sum to release its album *Songs of Innocence* to 500 million iTunes customers in 119 countries for free—regardless of whether individual consumers actually wanted the record. (The music files just showed up on their smartphones and other devices.) Many music fans objected to having the album unwittingly foisted on them.

But generally speaking, licensing songs for use in television commercials, soundtracks, and video games—branding strategies that for years musicians, critics, and fans lambasted as "selling out" (Klein 2009)—are today considered business as usual, even among bands with serious DIY punk ethics or indie credibility, simply because there are so few alternative ways of earning a livable wage as a recording artist. In his memoir *Black Postcards*, Dean Wareham (2008), the lead vocalist for the indie rock bands Galaxie 500 and Luna, explains that most touring bands on independent labels must forgo musicians' salaries and typically only make money on the road from T-shirt sales and other merchandising schemes (p. 181). As for performers on major labels, album royalties are often only paid out to blockbuster acts like Madonna and U2, whose records earn enough to recoup their original production, marketing, and touring costs. According to Wareham, "All the money that gets spent on making and promoting your record means that sometimes you are only digging yourself a hole, a deep pit of record company debt. You may get a 14 percent royalty rate, but with all those expenses being charged to your account you are never going to see royalties anyway" (p. 111). (Worse, record labels have recently begun taking a cut of their bands' merchandising revenues as well, as will be discussed in the next chapter.)

In contrast, licensing fees for TV commercials and other ancillary markets are guaranteed and generally paid up front. As the *New York Times* pop music critic Jon Pareles (2008) observes, "Musicians have to eat and want to be heard, and if that means accompanying someone else's sales pitch or video game, well, it's a living." Another *Times* writer, John Leland (2001), puts this in recent historical perspective: "Fourteen years after Nike outraged Beatles fans, and the surviving Beatles, by using 'Revolution' in a sneaker ad—Michael Jackson controlled the publishing rights to the song—the revolution is over, and the advertisers have largely won." If this is "selling out," writes Leland, then many bands today are more than willing to "buy in."

While comic book adaptations like *Avengers: Age of Ultron*, which raked in more than $1.4 billion globally, seem like surefire box-office wins, the reality is that all hits are flukes.

6

nobody knows

HOW THE MEDIA AND CULTURE INDUSTRIES WORK

I**T COULDN'T MISS. HOLLYWOOD TYPICALLY EQUATES FILM** adaptations of comic books with box-office gold, especially since Marvel's *The Avengers* earned more than $600 million domestically and $1.5 billion worldwide in 2012. It was therefore no wonder that in 2015, Twentieth-Century Fox released *Fantastic Four*, featuring Marvel superheroes Mr. Fantastic, the Human Torch, the Invisible Woman, and the Thing. (The film was actually a franchise reboot—the 2005 version of *Fantastic Four* grossed more than $150 million in the United States and more than $330 million worldwide.) Made at a cost of $120 million, *Fantastic Four* showcased a promising cast of young actors, including Jamie Bell, a former BAFTA winner for Best Actor in a Leading Role (the BAFTAs are the British equivalent of the Oscars), and the Emmy-nominated actress Kate Mara. And yet in spite of its great promise, the film was roundly panned by critics, a $56.1 million U.S. box-office bomb.

That same year, Sam Taylor-Johnson directed a sadomasochistic film based on a collection of erotic fan-fiction web postings involving the characters of Stephenie Meyer's *Twilight* vampire series. Filmed on a relatively small budget of $40 million, the picture featured two little-known television actors in its lead roles. Upon the release of *Fifty Shades of Grey*, organizations from the American Family Association to the National Center on Sexual Exploitation urged theaters and audiences to boycott the film. Critics hammered the movie, including *New York Times* film critic A. O. Scott (2015), who wrote, "*Fifty Shades of Grey* might not be a good movie—O.K., it's a terrible movie," and *USA Today* reviewer Claudia Puig (2015), who called it "plodding, inane and wretchedly acted." Upon its release Puig wrote, "Sitting through the turgid and tedious S&M melodrama that is *Fifty Shades of Grey* may feel like its own form of torture. . . . The dialogue, based on E. L. James's best-selling book, is laughable, the pacing is sluggish, and the performances are one-note." *Fifty Shades of Grey* went on to gross $166 million in domestic box-office receipts and $571 million worldwide, making it the third-top-grossing film of all time directed by a woman and the fourth-highest-grossing R-rated movie ever (Mendelson 2015).

One of the most firmly held truths in the media industry is that "all hits are flukes," or as the Academy Award—winning screenwriter William Goldman has suggested of the uncertainties surrounding success in Hollywood, "Nobody knows anything" (Faulkner and Anderson 1987; Bielby and Bielby 1994). And yet media and pop culture—producing firms exert a great deal of effort seeking out talent, trying however futilely to predict box-office winners, ratings champions, best-selling authors, and multiplatinum artists. This raises an interesting question: Given the strong uncertainty of success in today's mass media market, how do the culture industries go about choosing the films, books, television programs, and music projects on which to take their chances?

One might think that in such cases, quality would be paramount. But what *is* quality? How does one recognize it, and according to whose standards? Instead, I would argue that decision making in the media industries is primarily driven by the *minimization of risk*. In the absence of a crystal ball that can predict commercial success, decisions are usually made rationally in a context of risk aversion and caution. Of course, this contradicts the wild image of corporate media instigators in the popular imagination—MTV, Comedy Central, VH1, Def Jam Recordings, Jerry Bruckheimer Films. And yet behind their façade of racy content portrayed in spring-break specials, reality TV dating shows, hip-hop videos, and shoot-'em-up blockbusters, these and other media outlets operate no differently than insurance companies that employ great bureaucratic mechanisms to effectively manage risk.

Conventional wisdom might suggest that a two-and-a-half hour movie set in 1823 featuring little dialogue wouldn't have much commercial appeal, especially if its good-looking star spent most of the movie roughed up beyond all recognition, grunting and scavenging for bush meat. But in fact, Alejandro González Iñárritu's 2015 film The Revenant, starring Leonardo DiCaprio, went on to gross $184 million domestically and $533 million worldwide.

The Organization of the Media Industries

To understand how this process works, one must remember that the stuff of popular culture—movies, music, television shows, video games, graphic novels, magazines—are products sold by multinational corporations in the interest of making billions of dollars in annual profit under market capitalism. In emphasizing this, I do not intend to belittle or disparage pop culture, particularly given that this capitalist system has generated many of the most innovative artistic works of the last century. Nevertheless, aesthetic and cultural brilliance should not prevent the sociologically minded from observing how our favorite cultural products are just that—products for sale that are selected for production, manufactured, marketed, and distributed within a highly regimented organizational system.

Sociologist Paul Hirsch (1972) illustrates how this system operates as if it were a giant processing machine. The production process begins with a surplus pool of creative talent made up of starving artists, guitar heroes, table-serving actors, cutting-edge filmmakers, and would-be great American novelists. To eventually succeed as cultural producers, these creative workers must meet the immediate needs of profit-seeking firms, whether music companies such as Warner Bros. Records, film studios such as Sony Pictures, or book publishing behemoths such as Penguin Random House. In organizational jargon, we might say that this labor pool of willing artists, musicians, and actors pushes up against the edge of what Hirsch would call a protective *input boundary*. This input boundary operates as a filter used by record labels, movie production houses, and other firms to hand select a small group of creative talent from the enormous pool of media hopefuls for eventual mass cultural diffusion and possible stardom.

Facilitating in this winnowing process are *boundary spanners*, responsible for making connections between individual artists and corporate media firms. Some of these boundary spanners are managers, agents, or other emissaries representing creative personnel. They include talent manager Scooter Braun, perhaps best known for discovering an unknown 12-year-old boy from Canada singing on YouTube. (The boy's name was Justin Bieber.) Other boundary spanners serve as talent seekers for media companies, such as A&R (artists and repertoire) scouts in the music industry, casting directors in film and television, and acquisitions editors in book publishing. Through countless auditions and evaluations, networking at meetings, and other assorted trust-building exercises, a select number of creative artists who manage to break through the aforementioned input boundary are eventually hand-picked for temporary contract work (more

Anna Wintour, editor-in-chief of *Vogue*, is one of the most powerful cultural gatekeepers in the United States. She was also the inspiration for Meryl Streep's character in the film The Devil Wears Prada.

on this shortly) with a media company, whether it be to write and submit a novel for publication, costar in a motion picture, or record a hip-hop album.

After manufacturing a variety of cultural products, mass media firms must successfully market these wares to a set of media and communication outlets that will promote them on glossy magazine covers, newspaper features pages, entertainment TV programs, and popular websites. To do this, a second group of boundary spanners—in-house support personnel that include publicists, press coordinators, radio promoters, and sales representatives—selectively champion their firm's most promising films, albums, or other offerings with every available means at their disposal across a second filter, a fittingly named *output boundary* that must be successfully traversed if these products are to gain the attention of the entertainment press, and eventually the public.

The boundary-spanning personnel situated at the receiving end of this deluge of corporate solicitation serve as *gatekeepers* responsible for selecting and disseminating an even smaller set of cultural products to the public. Whether magazine editors, television news producers, entertainment journalists, movie reviewers, book critics, or social-media celebrities, gatekeepers are theoretically entrusted with the responsibility of making thoughtful recommendations to pop music fans, fiction readers, film buffs, fashion followers, and other consumers. And so, in a funny way, the primary audience for movies, books, and music is not everyday people but those professional evaluators charged with offering reliable suggestions to the public. Given their importance to the overall output of the media and culture industries, Hirsch refers to these gatekeepers as *surrogate consumers*, since they are expected to make choices on behalf of their readers and viewers, ordinary paying customers like you and me. Of course, gatekeepers are not merely marketing pop culture but also selling their own version of it—as magazine covers, podcasts, or content for their YouTube channels.

The Need for Blockbusters

As one can see, at the input and output boundaries within this organizational system, industry professionals are required to make multiple decisions in a context of uncertainty, in which success is virtually impossible to predict with any reliability. Traditionally the media industries have managed this risk by relying on a strategy of *overproduction*, in which they flood the marketplace with a diverse array of content. In 2013, U.S. book publishing houses released 304,912 new titles and editions. According to the Motion Picture Association of America (MPAA), 708 films were released in the United States and Canada in 2015. Most of those books and films never made a dime, but no matter. For years, TV studios, film distributors, publishers, and record labels have made big bets that out of their plentiful annual offerings, a few big-budget blockbusters, along with a smattering of surprise "sleeper" hits, will generate enough profit to cover the losses incurred by everything else.

For example, in 2015 the second-top-grossing film was *Jurassic World*. Released by Universal Pictures at a cost of $150 million, the film brought in a whopping $652 million at the U.S. box office and $1.67 billion worldwide, making it the fourth-highest-grossing motion picture of all time. Fortunately for its parent company, Comcast, the film's tremendous success allowed Universal to subsequently take a loss on *Blackhat*, a $70 million action thriller starring Chris Hemsworth released in January of that same year. With a U.S. box-office take of only $8 million and $19.7 million worldwide, the movie cost more than triple what it grossed, and after only three weeks it dropped out of theaters. But no matter—just one *Jurassic World* can pay for itself along with more than 10 commercial bombs as expensive and underachieving as *Blackhat*.

Of course, such a business model can only work if media firms are assured that blockbusters as triumphant as *Jurassic World* can rise from their offerings—no easy feat, given that "blockbusters are nearly impossible to predict" (Faulkner and Anderson 1987, p. 891). In the motion picture industry, the considerable rewards to be gained by investing in potential blockbusters drive the demand for highly visible directors, producers, and cinematographers, but only those who have enjoyed recent box-office success (hence the oft-quoted Hollywood truism, "You're only as good as your last credit"). To increase their chances of creating a smash hit, this select pool of A-list filmmakers—today they include J. J. Abrams (*Star Wars: The Force Awakens, Star Trek, Mission: Impossible III*), Christopher Nolan (*Inception, Interstellar, The Dark Knight* trilogy), Peter Jackson (*King Kong, The Lord of the Rings* trilogy, *The Hobbit* trilogy), Joss Whedon (*The Avengers, Avengers: Age of Ultron*) and David Fincher (*Fight Club, The Curious Case of Benjamin Button, The Social Network, The Girl with the Dragon Tattoo, Gone Girl*)—controls multimillion-dollar budgets that have grown exponentially in the last 40 years.

The drastic overspending on such film projects only increases the need among studios to produce windfall profits to simply break even, which generates an even *greater* demand for blockbusters. Taken to its logical conclusion, this cycle of bet-raising resembles an endless round of no-limit gambling, "an enormously high-rolling crap game" (Faulkner and Anderson 1987, p. 885). Moreover, the current digital landscape has made genuine breakout successes more important than ever for an industry with tighter profit margins. To take just one example, in the film industry the rise of streaming video has spelled the death knell for the once-dominant DVD home-video market, which used to bring in far more revenue for studios than theatrical box-office ticket sales.

In this crazed financial context, the need for blockbusters encourages movie studios to invest heavily in films with a built-in audience and promotional apparatus, particularly sequels, prequels, remakes, and spinoffs of previously successful entertainment properties from comic books to sci-fi novels. Given their expensive production and marketing budgets, studios then depend on the devoted fans of franchises such as *Star Wars* and *The Avengers* to purchase multiple tickets for repeat viewings to turn a profit (Barnes 2016). The success of this strategy is evident if we look at the Top 20 all-time box-office hits in the United States (see Table 6.1). Of these motion pictures, 16 represent box-office franchises, and the vast majority (13) are sequels or prequels of previously successful films. (Meanwhile, only *three* of the original films released in these series—*Star Wars, The Avengers*, and *The Hunger Games*—made this exclusive list.) Also, more than half of the films are spinoffs or adaptations from best-selling novels (*The Hunger Games, Jurassic Park*), comic books and graphic novels (*The Avengers, Batman, Captain America, Iron Man*), and even a Disney World theme-park ride (*Pirates of the Caribbean*). Even *Titanic* could be considered a loose remake of the award-winning 1958 film *A Night to Remember*.

The celebrated triumphs enjoyed by these types of films suggest a predictable, low-risk formula for engineering a blockbuster smash: instant brand recognition and popularity, youth appeal, expensive computer-generated graphics, dumbed-down dialogue, and explosive pyrotechnics. In his *Times* review of the 2016 DC Comics—inspired action movie *Suicide Squad* starring Will Smith and Margot Robbie, A. O. Scott (2016) emphasizes the conventionality indicative of the superhero genre: "In spite of all the mayhem and attitude, the overall mood is cautious. For a film about a gang of outlaw brawlers, *Suicide Squad* is awfully careful to stay inside the lines." Scott notes that the film's shortcomings represent the "systemic" failure of Hollywood to take creative risks with comic-book pictures by keeping their directors "on a short leash," forcing them to adhere to "the most rigid" of formulaic genre conventions. His concluding take on *Suicide Squad* is a depressing one: "This movie, for all its rebellious posturing, is nothing but business as usual."

The irony is that despite the predictability of *Suicide Squad* and other promising big-studio tent-pole extravaganzas (after all, the Will Smith film did make more than $320 million in U.S. box-office receipts), all hits are still flukes in the end, as illustrated by many other movies that colored "inside the lines" yet still proved dreadfully disappointing at the U.S. box office. In spite of the eventual success of the *Pirates of the Caribbean* franchise, the similarly themed 1995 stinker *Cutthroat Island*, budgeted at $98 million, collected a paltry $10 million at the box office, driving its production company Carolco Pictures into bankruptcy. Then there is the sad case of the 2002 flop *The Adventures of Pluto Nash*, a $100 million film starring Eddie Murphy that managed to gross a measly $4.4 million. In 2004, Academy Award—winning director Oliver Stone made *Alexander*, a film based on the life of the mighty conqueror Alexander the Great, for $155 million. The film featured two previous Oscar winners—Anthony Hopkins and Angelina Jolie—along with a long list of stars that included Colin Farrell, Val Kilmer, Christopher Plummer, and Rosario Dawson. In melodramatic fashion, the film was brutally defeated at the box office, grossing only $34.3 million.

Need more evidence? In 2006, Wolfgang Peterson, the director of the wildly successful hit *The Perfect Storm* (2000), took the creative reins of *Poseidon*, a $160 million remake of a 1970s cult classic about yet another sinking ship. Although the film's disaster plot shared a passing resemblance to that of *Titanic* (at one time the highest-grossing movie ever), it was the film itself that eventually sank, making only $60.7 million. In 2010, James L. Brooks directed *How Do You Know*, a romantic comedy starring Oscar winners Reese Witherspoon and Jack Nicholson, along with stars Owen Wilson and Paul Rudd. Filmed on a $120 million production budget, it earned only $30 million at the U.S. box office. In 2015, Cameron Crowe directed *Aloha*, starring Bradley Cooper, Emma Stone,

TABLE 6.1

Top 20 All-Time USA Box Office (as of September 2016)

1. *Star Wars: The Force Awakens* (2015)
2. *Avatar* (2009)
3. *Titanic* (1997)
4. *Jurassic World* (2015)
5. Marvel's *The Avengers* (2012)
6. *The Dark Knight* (2008)
7. *Finding Dory* (2016)
8. *Star Wars: Episode I: The Phantom Menace* (1999)
9. *Star Wars* (1977)
10. *Avengers: Age of Ultron* (2015)
11. *The Dark Knight Rises* (2012)
12. *Shrek 2* (2004)
13. *E.T. The Extra-Terrestrial* (1982)
14. *The Hunger Games: Catching Fire* (2013)
15. *Pirates of the Caribbean: Dead Man's Chest* (2006)
16. *The Lion King* (1994)
17. *Toy Story 3* (2010)
18. *Iron Man 3* (2013)
19. *Captain America: Civil War* (2016)
20. *The Hunger Games* (2012)

Source: Box Office Mojo (2016a).

Rachel McAdams, Bill Murray, and Alec Baldwin. Even though the budget only came in at $37 million, the movie *still* lost money, grossing only $21 million in domestic receipts. Many other so-called can't-miss films starring celebrity actors Johnny Depp (*Mortdecai*), Will Ferrell (*Land of the Lost*), Sandra Bullock (*Our Brand Is Crisis*), Daniel Craig (*Cowboys and Aliens*), and Angelina Jolie and Brad Pitt (*By the Sea*) have met similar box-office fates.

The music business provides an even clearer example of how important blockbusters have become in the digital age. Record companies used to make money by selling entire albums' worth of music to consumers who would have otherwise only purchased two or three songs from any particular release. As a result, in 1999, the music industry touted global revenues of $28.6 billion. But sales began to plummet once music fans could purchase and download single songs on iTunes for $0.99 rather than pay $16.98 for cheaply manufactured compact discs packed with lots of filler. This led to a 46 percent drop in revenue for the music business from 2002 to 2010 (Seabrook 2015, p. 134), and by 2015 global revenues in the music industry remained at $15 billion, nearly half what they were at their height in the late 1990s.

Today, fewer people than ever purchase music or own record collections at all. The music industry's fastest-growing source of revenue comes from fees from streaming services such as Apple Music and Spotify. After all, why purchase songs from iTunes when you can rent a 30-million-song library for less than $10 a month? In the United States, streaming music made up 34.3 percent of all industry revenues in 2015, besting earnings from digital downloads (34 percent) and physical sales (28 percent). The problem for the music industry is that the profit margins in earned royalties from streaming music are razor thin. Spotify only pays out an average of $0.006 to $0.0084 per stream to publishers, artists, and other rights holders.

So what keeps the current pop music industry afloat? You guessed it—blockbusters. Powerhouses such as Adele and Taylor Swift have never been more important to the survival of the music business than they are today. Across all formats, superstars—those representing the top 1 percent of artists based on revenue—make up a gigantic 77 percent share of all profits earned in the music industry (Seabrook 2015, pp. 15—16). Similarly, today's pop charts are dominated by a relatively small number of blockbuster performers. In 1985, a total of 27 songs made it to No. 1 on the *Billboard* pop chart, including Madonna's "Like a Virgin," Dire Straits' "Money for Nothing," Tears for Fears' "Everybody Wants to Rule the World," Whitney Houston's "Saving All My Love for You," and Duran Duran's "A View to a Kill." Thirty years later, in 2015, only *nine* songs hit No. 1, by a total of just seven artists: Adele ("Hello"), Taylor Swift ("Blank Space" and "Bad Blood"), OMI ("Cheerleader"), Justin Bieber ("What Do You Mean?"), The Weeknd ("Can't Feel My Face" and "The Hills"), Wiz Khalifa with Charlie Puth ("See You Again"), and with the biggest song of the year, Mark Ronson and Bruno Mars ("Uptown Funk"). The vast inequality of the record business represents what Cornell economist Robert H. Frank (Frank and Cook 1995) calls a *winner-take-all* market.

Not only do fewer artists claim more attention space in the pop culture universe, but their songs also have more staying power than did the hits of yesterday.

For example, it is instructive to look at the 11 songs that hold the record for having spent the most weeks on the *Billboard* Hot 100 pop chart (see Table 6.2). All have been released in the last 20 years, and most in the last decade. This includes the record-breaking "Radioactive" by Imagine Dragons, which managed to stay on the pop charts for 87 weeks, just a few months shy of two years.

Since the music business generates most of its revenue from blockbuster successes, the industry has transformed itself into an engine for manufacturing catchy pop music hits. Forget risk—nothing is left to chance. As *New Yorker* writer John Seabrook (2015) chronicles in his aptly titled book *The Song Machine*, when super-

TABLE 6.2

Most Total Weeks on the *Billboard* Hot 100 Pop Chart

1.	Imagine Dragons, "Radioactive" (2014)—87 weeks
2.	Awolnation, "Sail" (2014)—79 weeks
3.	Jason Mraz, "I'm Yours" (2009)—76 weeks
4.	LeAnn Rimes, "How Do I Live" (1998)—69 weeks
5.	LMFAO, "Party Rock Anthem" (2012)—68 weeks
6.	OneRepublic, "Counting Stars" (2014)—68 weeks
7.	Jewel, "Foolish Games"/"You Were Meant for Me" (1998)—65 weeks
8.	Adele, "Rolling in the Deep" (2012)—65 weeks
9.	Carrie Underwood, "Before He Cheats" (2007)—64 weeks
10.	The Lumineers, "Ho Hey" (2013)—62 weeks
11.	Lifehouse, "You and Me" (2006)—62 weeks

Source: *Billboard* magazine (2014).

stars such as Rihanna make a record, professional songwriters and producers set up camp for weeks at a time crafting songs for consideration. According to Seabrook's look "inside the hit factory," pop songs today are less likely to be recorded by actual musicians than by studio whizzes who build tracks from prerecorded beats, computer samples of acoustic and electric instruments, and digitally perfected vocals, so nothing ever sounds out of tune. These internationally recognized writer-producers—they include Max Martin, Lukasz "Dr. Luke" Gottwald, and the Norwegian production team Stargate—rely on a formula of hit-making in which every musical element defers to the rhythm track, including the melody and even the lyrics, all calibrated in the service of generating irresistible hooks and often an explosive chorus with an emotional payoff. While many of the decade's pop stars sparkle with personality and charm, their music emphasizes the craft-like precision and formulaic conventions developed by these song-makers behind the scenes—a sound that has dominated the pop music industry for at least a generation. Stargate's monster hits that went to No. 1 on the *Billboard* Hot 100 singles chart include Beyoncé's "Irreplaceable," Katy Perry's "Firework," and Rihanna's "Take a Bow," "Rude Boy," "Only Girl (In the World)," "What's My Name?" "S&M," and "Diamonds." From 1999 to 2016 Max Martin wrote no less than 22 No. 1 hit songs, including Britney Spears's ". . . Baby One More Time"; Pink's "So What" and "Raise Your Glass"; Katy Perry's "I Kissed a Girl," "Part of Me," "Last Friday Night (T.G.I.F.)," and "Roar"; The Weeknd's "Can't Feel My Face"; Justin Timberlake's "Can't Stop the Feeling!"; and Taylor Swift's "We Are Never Ever Getting Back Together," "Shake It Off," "Blank Space," and "Bad Blood." (That's more No. 1 singles than the Beatles or Elvis Presley ever had—and unlike them, Martin is still making music.) Meanwhile, in addition to Britney Spears, Rihanna, and Katy Perry, Dr. Luke has produced records for Kelly Clarkson, Shakira, Pitbull, Ne-Yo, Nicki Minaj, Kesha, Ciara, One Direction, Flo Rida, Miley Cyrus, Usher, Wiz Khalifa, and Maroon 5.

In an age of streaming services such as Apple Music and Spotify, superstars like Taylor Swift (left) are more important to the pop music industry than ever before. Behind the success of stars like Swift are writer-producers like Max Martin (right), who wrote "We Are Never Getting Back Together," "Shake It Off," "Blank Space," and "Bad Blood" for Swift.

Going with What You Know

These examples from the film and music industries highlight how risk-averse media firms work within fairly traditional genre categories (comic-book superhero films, contemporary pop music) and other types of cultural conventions. As discussed in previous chapters, the use of established genres represents an attempt to classify similar kinds of music recordings, films, and other media or cultural products according to recognizable stylistic criteria, audience expectations, and market efficiencies. For example, daytime soap operas (*Days of Our Lives, The Young and the Restless*) are notable for their melodramatic scripts; overly theatrical acting; consistent themes of love, lust, betrayal, and revenge; and their largely female audiences. Exemplars of neo-noir films (*Memento, Collateral, Drive*) take place in modern cities haunted by shadows and feature casts of morally complicated characters that include lonely heroes, confidence men, and femme fatales, while teen comedies (*Mean Girls, Superbad*, and *The Edge of Seventeen*) take place almost exclusively in middle-class suburbs and emphasize the social politics of high school and the anxieties of adolescent dating and developing a sexual identity.

Within the media and culture industries, these genres serve as organizational devices useful for making the production process more efficient, particularly given that teams of support personnel often work on genre-specific projects. Creative departments in the recording industry are organized by music genre, and boundary spanners in a number of media-related fields (A&R personnel in the music industry, acquisitions editors in book publishing) work in dedicated genre areas as well. (In the music business, genre distinctions are even represented geographically—particularly in the case of country music, which the major labels typically produce out of studios and offices headquartered in Nashville, rather than New York or Los Angeles.) At the distributional end of the media industry, promotional outlets such as radio stations are studiously classified by genre (especially satellite radio channels, which can be further classified by subgenre, decade, etc.), and the sales floors of bookstores and record shops are similarly organized into conventional categories: true crime and women's studies, classical music and R&B, science fiction and horror. Meanwhile, online retailers like Amazon allow for genre categorization at an even more specified level. (As an example of this specificity, while Barnes & Noble shelves books under the category "sociology," Amazon further differentiates among "suburban sociology", "research and measurement," "social situations," and the "sociology of death.")

As a result, it is exceedingly uncommon for the media industries to promote cultural products that do not cleave to common types of genre categories or stylistic conventions, particularly in a context of unpredictability. Music artists who defy industry-defined genres are far less likely than others to be signed to a recording label, attract radio airplay, be sold in retail venues that measure and evaluate sales for industry publications, matched with similar performers for live touring opportunities, succeed abroad in the international market, or have their songs covered by other artists. According to author Malcolm Gladwell (2005), such unconventional artists also tend to perform poorly in market tests, since mainstream audiences may initially regard their music with suspicion or confusion. For this reason, as an emergent music genre, rap music took years to gain acceptance in the recording business during the 1980s despite its proven popularity and commercial success (Lopes 1992; Negus 1998).

American television has demonstrated similar biases throughout its history. Traditionally, TV programming schedules have been insistently dotted with highly formulaic types of offerings, including police mysteries, family-based situation comedies, period dramas, and game shows. In recent years, a number of breakout hits have succeeded in challenging these genre distinctions, creating new hybrid categories in their wake. For example, *comedy verité* alters the traditional sitcom formula by making use of conventions associated with reality TV, including a documentary filming style and characters that directly address the camera—these shows include *Modern Family* and earlier hits such as *Parks and Recreation* and *The Office*. Some shows illustrative of this style even send up former sitcom stars by exposing fictional versions of themselves to the aesthetic and narrative trappings of reality TV, such as *Curb Your Enthusiasm* (featuring Larry David from *Seinfeld*), *Episodes* (Matt LeBlanc from *Friends*), and

The Comeback (Lisa Kudrow from *Friends*). Another is the *dramedy* format, a hybrid of drama and comedy genres. Beginning in 1972 with *M*A*S*H*, one of the most critically acclaimed and popular shows in television history, more recent examples include HBO's *Girls*, Amazon's *Transparent*, and Netflix's *Orange Is the New Black*. Of course, thanks to the success of all these programs, their hybrid styles have become enshrined as cultural conventions in their own right, spawning untold numbers of copycat programs of greater or lesser success.

Just as television studios rely on standardized (or emergent) genre categories as a means of minimizing risk, they also turn to personnel with proven track records, including actors. Zooey Deschanel performed in critically acclaimed films such as *Almost Famous* and *500 Days of Summer* before starring in her own Fox sitcom, *New Girl*. Aziz Ansari appeared in NBC's *Parks and Recreation* before starring in his own Netflix show, *Master of None*. Jeffrey Tambor performed in the HBO comedy *The Larry Sanders Show* and later on Fox/Netflix's *Arrested Development* before taking on the title role in *Transparent*. Before Julia Louis-Dreyfus was cast as the vice president of the United States in HBO's *Veep*, she'd won an Emmy for her title performance on CBS's *The New Adventures of Old Christine*, and before that she played Elaine Benes for nine seasons on *Seinfeld*. Before *that*, she was a reliably hilarious cast member on *Saturday Night Live* from 1982 to 1985.

This isn't only the case with actors. In fact, network executives are even more likely to hire prominent writer-producers or showrunners with successful projects under their belts than potentially bankable actors or celebrities (Bielby and Bielby 1994). Shonda Rhimes was only able to develop ABC's *Scandal* and *How to Get Away with Murder* because of the massive success of her earlier smash hit, the

Writer-producer Shonda Rimes (second from right) sits alongside the stars of her hit shows: (from left to right) Viola Davis (How to Get Away with Murder), Kerry Washington (Scandal), and Ellen Pompeo (Grey's Anatomy).

long-running medical dramedy *Grey's Anatomy*. Since Netflix began developing its own original shows, beginning with *House of Cards* and *Orange Is the New Black* in 2013, it has turned to previously successful television writer-producers such as Tina Fey (*30 Rock*) and Judd Apatow (*The Ben Stiller Show, Freaks and Geeks, Funny or Die Presents, Girls*) for much of its programming. (Fey's *Unbreakable Kimmy Schmidt* premiered on Netflix in 2015; Apatow's *Love* debuted in 2016.) Other successful TV writer-producers in recent years have included Michael Schur (*The Office, Parks and Recreation, Brooklyn Nine-Nine*), Greg Berlanti (*The Mysteries of Laura, Blindspot, Arrow, The Flash, Legends of Tomorrow, Supergirl*), and Mark Burnett (*Survivor, The Apprentice, Shark Tank, The Voice*).

The Secondary Market

In recent years the proliferation of 24-hour cable networks in addition to Amazon, Hulu, and other video-on-demand services has permanently altered our temporal experience of television and cinema. Thirsty for available quality programming, cable channels and streaming websites offer a never-ending buffet of reruns of popular shows. In fact, the *secondary market* for popular culture, which represents all opportunities to generate profit from a cultural product beyond its domestic sale in its original format, competes with its more glamorous primary market counterpart as an alternative revenue stream in music, television, and film.

Secondary markets are associated with a number of strategies for minimizing risk because they create a host of profit-making opportunities without incurring additional development or production costs. For example, as noted in Chapter 5, licensing the rights to a music recording for use in another media format can provide a new source of untapped revenue as well as increase public exposure for the artist. As media and communication scholar Bethany Klein (2009) observes, in an era of decreasing album sales, song licensing for commercial use in television advertising or movie soundtracks has become a lucrative way for musicians and their record companies to generate compensatory income and added promotional buzz. According to Klein, the results have altered the calculus of how pop music today is marketed and sold. Starting in 1999, the electronic dance music artist Moby successfully licensed all 18 tracks of his album *Play* for use in motion pictures, television shows, or commercials. The late singer-songwriter Nick Drake's 1972 title track recording from the album *Pink Moon* was licensed for a Volkswagen commercial in 2000, an appearance that revived interest in Drake's largely forgotten catalog. According to journalist Naomi Klein (2002), the late-1990s reissue of Louis Prima's big band hit "Jump, Jive An' Wail" for use in a Gap commercial practically jump-started the neo-Swing revival of that decade. The secondary market often transforms dormant product into big sales by disengaging it from its original context, sometimes to strange effect—witness the placement of Iggy Pop's 1977 recording of "Lust for Life," a driving, energetic song about the punk singer's heroin addiction, in a commercial for Royal Caribbean Cruise Lines (Klein 2009, pp. 101–4). (The ad conveniently edits out all references to drugs, liquor, torture films, and stripteases.)

Other efforts at tapping into the secondary market can be similarly advantageous as strategies of leveraging ready-made cultural products for risk-free gain. A domestic movie can easily be repackaged for the global marketplace, where it may make more than double its original box-office take. In 2015, *Terminator: Genisys* only took in $90 million domestically but later earned an additional $351 million in the non-U.S. market. The following year, *Warcraft* grossed a meager $47 million in the United States, only to then grab up a whopping $386 million abroad. These examples illustrate how the global market can save a film that bombed its first time around, and plenty of others abound. Directed by Peter Berg in 2012, the over-the-top science-fiction action flick *Battleship* (nominally based on the board game) cost $220 million to produce, only to gross $65 million in the United States. Megan Lehmann (2012) of the *Hollywood Reporter* panned the picture and its "armada of cinematic clichés" and "truly awful dialogue." She writes, "At once silly and overly ponderous, it is a long-winded exercise in cartoonish war games pitting a splinter section of the U.S. Navy against invading aliens—a sort of just-add-water *Transformers*." No matter—this turkey of a film earned more than $237 million abroad, which accounted for 78 percent of its total box-office take.

It takes a particular kind of movie to find success in the international cinema marketplace—namely superhero flicks and animated films. By drawing on the recognition of global brands from *Harry Potter* to *Spider-Man* while emphasizing endless action sequences and slick effects over witty dialogue and character development, these movies effortlessly translate to non-English-speaking audiences. (In comic-book films laden with special effects, explosions,

Warcraft, a movie adaptation of the popular video game of the same name, earned 89 percent of its total box office receipts outside North America, including more than half from China.

and fight scenes pitched to global audiences, subtle acting performances rarely get noticed, which may partially explain why Keanu Reeves and Vin Diesel still have movie careers.) The all-time box-office blockbusters worldwide (see Table 6.3) include two films each from the *Avengers, Transformers*, and *Pirates of the Caribbean* franchises, and one film apiece from the reliable *Star Wars, Harry Potter, Jurassic Park, Lord of the Rings, Fast and the Furious, Batman, Iron Man, Despicable Me, Captain America, Toy Story*, and James Bond series. Meanwhile, the remaining three motion pictures in the Top 20 all rely on either computer-generated imagery (CGI), artful animation, or fireballs galore: *Titanic, Frozen*, and *Avatar*.

Further diving into the secondary market, these kinds of blockbuster films easily lend themselves to video-game tie-ins and other branding and merchandising opportunities, as best exemplified by the *Star Wars* juggernaut. Hasbro maintains an exclusive license to manufacture and sell all manner of *Star Wars* toys, collect-

TABLE 6.3

Top 20 All-Time Worldwide Box Office (as of September 2016)

1. *Avatar* (2009)
2. *Titanic* (1997)
3. *Star Wars: The Force Awakens* (2015)
4. *Jurassic World* (2015)
5. Marvel's *The Avengers* (2012)
6. *Furious 7* (2015)
7. *Avengers: Age of Ultron* (2015)
8. *Harry Potter and the Deathly Hallows Part 2* (2007)
9. *Frozen* (2013)
10. *Iron Man 3* (2013)
11. *Minions* (2015)
12. *Captain America: Civil War* (2016)
13. *Transformers: Dark of the Moon* (2011)
14. *The Lord of the Rings: The Return of the King* (2003)
15. *Skyfall* (2012)
16. *Transformers: Age of Extinction* (2014)
17. *The Dark Knight Rises* (2012)
18. *Pirates of the Caribbean: Dead Man's Chest* (2006)
19. *Toy Story 3* (2010)
20. *Pirates of the Caribbean: On Stranger Tides* (2011)

Source: Box Office Mojo (2016b).

ible dolls, action figures, Lego sets, games, puzzles, and candies until 2020. They include a "Darth Tater" Mr. Potato Head, *Star Wars* 3-D Monopoly game, light-saber lollipops that actually light up, and a Destroyer Droid Yo-Yo. Meanwhile, shorter-term promotional deals associate the films' heroes, villains, and Wookies with CoverGirl, Subway, Taco Bell, KFC, Pizza Hut, Pepsi, Frito-Lay, Kellogg's, Colgate, Duracell, and Fruit of the Loom. In addition to generating secondary sources of revenue, licensing and merchandising schemes like these help movie studios promote their action pictures directly to their target markets—generally young and impressionable consumers already addicted to cola, fast-food burgers, and video games.

Studios also generate secondary market revenue by licensing their films to cable channels such as HBO and subscription-based streaming providers such as Netflix and Hulu, often for handsome fees. Regarding the latter, typically services like Netflix contract with studios like Disney to stream entire packages of films, rather than individual movies. This means that even films that failed to capture an audience during their theatrical release can help generate profits for the studio. In certain instances, such films can actually find popular acclaim their second time around. When *The Shawshank Redemption* debuted in 1994, it was a commercial

Movie tie-in merchandise, like this "Darth Tater" Mr. Potato Head, allows studios to promote their movies directly to young consumers.

failure, grossing a paltry $18 million, and no wonder: It was a 142-minute prison film with an incomprehensible title and no obvious audience. Even after receiving seven Academy Award nominations, including Best Picture, it went on to earn only an additional $10 million at the box office. And then, after years of late-night watching on home video—originally on cable TV and DVD rentals, and more recently on streaming video—it finally broke free from its darkened cell. As of July 2016, *The Shawshank Redemption* was the No. 1-rated film on the Internet Movie Database's worldwide poll of the 250 best movies of all time.

In television's secondary market, the most profitable risk-minimizing strategy is literally in reruns, as prime-time shows that have already demonstrated their durability as hits find repeat success in syndication. However, syndication is lucrative in another way as well. While the licensing fees networks pay to studios for first-run prime-time programs do not typically cover even the costs of production, the earnings to be gained from syndicated programming are exceedingly more remunerative, and this is where studios recoup their investments. For example, in 2014 CBS sold the syndication rights to its show *Elementary* to cable giant WGN and Hulu Plus for $3 million per episode.

This secondary market is so profitable that television producers create programs specifically designed to perform well in syndication, notably procedural police dramas such as *NCIS* (and its spinoffs), *Criminal Minds, Hawaii 5-0,* and, of course, *Elementary*. Procedural police dramas emphasize plot-driven narratives in which teams of criminalists made up of police detectives, federal agents, prosecutors, medical examiners, forensic scientists, and lab technicians—all characters whose interior lives rarely seem to change—work on cases assured to be solved within the temporal confines of each episode. Moreover, such shows feature last-minute plot twists that encourage (or at least do not discourage) multiple viewings among fans who may remember the basic outlines of a rerun show without quite recalling how it ends. By avoiding the serialization common to other kinds of dramas like soap operas, the producers of procedural dramas make it easier for audiences to view episodes out of sequence, a clear advantage for syndicated programming. It is therefore no wonder that these aforementioned shows—all CBS series, incidentally—are among the most ubiquitous of any syndicated dramas currently available on cable television and subscription-based streaming platforms.

Procedural police dramas like Elementary *are specifically designed to perform well in syndication, where television studios make the bulk of their earnings.*

Gaming the Gatekeepers

The conventional view of popular culture suggests that in a market system, mass media firms target everyday people and their desires, and it is the fickleness of those desires that makes success so unpredictable. However, this is not entirely the case, given that the primary audiences for movies, books, and recordings are not everyday consumers but the gatekeepers responsible for distributing and marketing culture directly to the public. As explained earlier, professional evaluators of mass culture can be thought of as *surrogate consumers*; therefore, for media firms to get their products out to the public requires that they promote their wares to *Entertainment Weekly* and *People* editors, *Washington Post* book reviewers, *Chicago Tribune* film critics, and radio programmers for iHeartMedia and local independent stations. These editors, critics, and journalists choose a small percentage of the thousands of records, movies, and books released each year to incorporate into their publications' editorial content, whether as short reviews, lengthy profiles, or even as a magazine cover. These surrogate consumers also include buyers for big-box retail outlets such as Barnes & Noble, Wal-Mart, and Target.

How do surrogate consumers make decisions regarding which cultural products to promote? The history of popular culture is filled with sordid tales of bribery and other criminal activities designed to manipulate the cultural dissemination process. During the early days of rock 'n' roll, it was discovered that radio disc jockeys had been accepting side payments from record companies to play specific singles on the air. This abusive practice, known as *payola* (a mash-up of "pay" and "Victrola," an early record player model manufactured by the Victor

Talking Machine Company), eventually attracted attention from the U.S. Congress and became illegal in 1960. From the 1980s to the 2000s, record companies attempted to get around this inconvenience by hiring *independent record promoters* to serve as middlemen who could indirectly pass money along to radio stations and thereby evade payola laws. But in 2005 and 2006 the New York State attorney general (and later governor) Eliot Spitzer prosecuted and eventually received settlements from the four major labels (Warner, Sony BMG, Universal, and EMI) for exploiting this loophole, with the Federal Communications Commission (FCC) ruling this practice illegal as well.

Of course, similar kinds of strategies are still legal (if ethically problematic) and widely practiced. Book publishers pay bookstore chains to prominently place their titles on their front tables, aisle endcaps, and in other high-visibility areas (Miller 2007). Film critics enjoy lavish, all-expenses-paid press junkets in return for previewing and hyping upcoming movies. And as business writer Daniel Gross (2005) points out, "The Web is one gigantic payola machine, from Amazon to the exploding realm of paid search."

But the contemporary age of giant multinational media conglomerates offers an even simpler model of gatekeeper cooptation. Making side payments to disc jockeys requires conspiratorial cooperation, but parent companies have a much easier time simply marketing their products across their own promotional platforms. In this manner, the *synergy* existing among the acquired subsidiaries or merged parts of a large media corporation represents a more contemporary strategy of minimizing risk within the culture industries. For example, Sony Pictures Television owns the popular game shows *Jeopardy!* and *Wheel of Fortune*, both of which it promotes by showing reruns on its Game Show Network (GSN). Disney owns both ESPN and Marvel Entertainment, which is why a number of athletes have graced the cover of *ESPN* magazine in the likenesses of Marvel's comic-book heroes. A November 2010 NBA Preview issue featured LeBron James wielding Captain America's striped and starred shield, Kevin Durant with Thor's hammer, and Kobe Bryant pumping an Iron Man fist. Disney also owns *Star Wars*, which is why in 2015 ESPN's *SportsCenter* presented a special on the "Evolution of the Lightsaber Duel." Narrated by Mark Hamill, who played Luke Skywalker in the three original *Star Wars* films, the "documentary" also featured sneak peeks from the movie *Star Wars: The Force Awakens*, which opened in theaters later that December. Pitchmen for *SportsCenter* have included Statler and Waldorf from the Muppets, which Disney also owns. (ESPN once featured the Swedish Chef as the station's cafeteria cook. The Chef has also appeared on ESPN's *Sunday NFL Countdown*, as have Kermit the Frog, Miss Piggy, Sam the Eagle, and Animal.)

Flexible Production and the Economics of Reality TV

Once we get used to thinking about decision making in the culture industries in terms of minimizing risk, certain recent cultural trends suddenly begin to make more sense. Take reality television. Many critics explain the proliferation of reality TV by pointing out the blurring of news and entertainment and the democratization of celebrity in American popular culture, yet a candid look at the economics of reality TV provides an even better explanation. First, reality TV programs are relatively inexpensive to produce, especially when compared to star-studded comedies and dramas. In its 2014 season, the three lead cast members of the CBS hit show *The Big Bang Theory*—Jim Parsons, Kaley Cuoco, and Johnny Galecki—were each paid $1 million *per episode*. Even anonymous character actors are typically paid competitive union wages as members of the Screen Actors Guild.

Meanwhile, reality TV participants are often paid little more than small stipends to cover their expenses, and many dip into their savings to finance their hiatus from their day jobs. Since reality television shows do not rely on traditional scripts, producers also avoid the high costs of hiring writers and paying out their royalties. It bears observing that it was during the 1988 Writers Guild of America strike that networks introduced the first generation of reality-based television programs, notably the bare-knuckled law enforcement shows *Cops* and *America's Most Wanted*. The union-resistant nature of this type of programming was reaffirmed during the 2007 Writers Guild strike two decades later when reality shows were left virtually unaffected even as TV production work in more mainstream sectors came to an abrupt halt.

Another way that reality TV programming contributes to an overall strategy of minimizing risk concerns the flexible norms of production permitted by the genre. Conventional television comedies and dramas are produced over the course of a season in which major networks and studios often plan for a 22-episode run. (Series premiering on premium cable networks or streaming services like Netflix tend to air shorter episode runs per season.) But the flexibility of reality television allows for much smaller, low-commitment runs of five or six episodes per season, like the 2015 HBO true-crime documentary miniseries *The Jinx: The Life and Deaths of Robert Durst*. The shortened lengths of these seasons allow producers to take chances on cutting-edge programming with minimal risk, and unlike with narrative comedies and dramas, producers can tinker with the most basic premises of their reality shows during hiatuses. This is best illustrated by programs like *Survivor* and *Real World*, both of which switch locales as well as casts each season. (A small number of fictional dramatic series have similarly experimented with different casts and contexts from season to season, including HBO's *True Detective* and FX's *American Horror Story*.)

Finally, the proliferation of reality programming represents an industry shift toward genres that most easily lend themselves to product-placement advertising campaigns. The insertion of product placement by sponsors into the content of film and television has a long and storied history, ranging from the subtle (such as the appearance of Stella Artois beer in the films *No Strings Attached, Birdman*, and *The Intern*, and the Netflix drama *House of Cards*) to the awkwardly obvious, as when a character on CBS's *Hawaii 5-0* launched (or lunched?) into a monologue praising the "serious culinary fusion" of Subway's turkey BLT sandwich in a 2012 episode. In recent years the rise of technological advances that allow for commercial-free television viewing have increased

During Season 13 of Project Runway *contestants made use of the Aldo Style Wall when dressing their models for competition.* Project Runway *has featured brands such as Banana Republic, Macy's, Bluefly, Piperlime, Lord & Taylor, Belk, and JustFab.*

anxieties among networks, which have looked to product placement as a means of recouping lost ad revenue.

Regardless of their merit or entertainment value, reality TV shows are perfect platforms for incorporating the brands of corporate sponsors. Like traditional game shows such as *The Price Is Right*, competitive reality programs can easily feature branded products as prizes. On *Survivor*, starving contestants often win name-brand sodas, chips, and candy bars during reward challenges and savor them on camera. Branded sponsors from Babies "R" Us to Barbie to Campbell's Soup have each been awkwardly featured as inspirations for design challenges on Lifetime's *Project Runway*. Meanwhile, narrative reality shows can get away with introducing brands of cola and designer fashion as simply part of the organic fabric of everyday life. In extreme cases such as the E! network's reality soap opera *Keeping Up with the Kardashians*, in which the central characters lounge around in Givenchy and Gucci, sip Diet Coke and SmartWater, dine at Nobu, shop at Bloomingdale's, and pose for *GQ*, it is unclear who exactly is promoting whom.

Shifting the Burden of Risk

The low-to-nonexistent wages paid to reality TV stars suggest a final set of strategies employed by the media industries to minimize risk under volatile market conditions. Sociologists Gina Neff, Elizabeth Wissinger, and Sharon Zukin (2005) observe that in a variety of creative occupations, from computer software design to fashion modeling, workers increasingly take on risks and expenses formerly shouldered by their employers. Neff and her coauthors appropriately depict these jobs as *entrepreneurial labor* since these workers invest their own capital and sweat equity in their careers for the improbable opportunity to gain potentially lucrative rewards in return. In the culture industries, creative workers often contract out their labor on a short-term basis to work on specific earmarked projects: a photo shoot in Acapulco, a webpage for an advertising agency, a seasonal run of a television series, the index for a nonfiction book, the final editing of a feature film. These short-term contracts prevent companies from having to absorb the expenses associated with hiring creative workers on a full-time basis (including their training costs, health insurance, retirement benefits, and vacation time) as well as the financial liabilities involved in maintaining a highly paid workforce during unpredictable economic downturns.

Instead, these risks and costs are borne by the creative workers themselves. Serving as independent contractors, a variety of entrepreneurial workers—graphic designers, photojournalists, digital animators, commercial studio musicians, video game designers—often pay continually out of pocket for training courses (or in the case of fashion models, gym memberships, yoga or Pilates classes, and personal trainer sessions), equipment, self-promotional materials, and one or more dedicated websites. Given that résumé-boosting prestige projects (e.g., modeling work for high-fashion magazines) frequently pay less than more mundane yet consistent media and cultural work (e.g., chain store catalog modeling), building an impressive portfolio often requires workers to accept high-profile but low-paying assignments over more lucrative opportunities. Additionally, these freelance workers endure the risks associated with job instability in an already mercurial marketplace and the pressure to constantly market themselves to potential clients and employers at professional networking events.

By shifting the burden of risk to the worker, the corporate strategy of hiring entrepreneurial labor allows media and culture-producing firms to minimize fixed overhead costs such as employee training and benefits. Another strategy for transferring risk involves the *royalty system* commonly used to organize payment in a variety of creative fields, particularly music recording and book publishing. According to this system, musicians, songwriters, and novelists are contracted to work for a small percentage of the earnings generated by their product. By distributing this royalty payment after the product has eventually been released to the public (provided it is released at all), media companies insure themselves against the unpredictability of the marketplace since they are only obligated to pay their creative artists *after* they have proven their financial viability.

These kinds of royalty-based deals also require the cultural worker to shoulder market risk in an additional way. Rather than invest in their creative artists' initial production and promotional expenses, media companies bill such costs to the artists themselves, as a charge against their future royalties. Musicians of all genres unfortunate enough to sign a run-of-the-mill record deal may receive an advance on their royalties to be disbursed for recording studio time, music video production, and a national road tour, only to find themselves eventually in debt to their own music label, even if their album is a moderate hit. Moreover, now that profits from music sales have declined so precipitously, record companies try to make up some of the difference by encouraging their artists to sign *360 deals*, arrangements in which labels give artists additional financial backing upfront for a share of the revenue that artists generate through live performances, publishing, and ancillary sales of T-shirts and other branded merchandise.

One way that some artists have dealt with the overreach of their record labels is to opt out of the system entirely by digitally recording and distributing their music themselves. In 2013, the shoegazer rock band My Bloody Valentine released its third album, *MBV*, for sale on its website as a digital download. (Consumers also had the option of ordering the record on CD or vinyl.) Similarly, Aziz Ansari and Louis C.K. have both bypassed the traditional cable TV industry by profitably recording and releasing comedy specials on their own websites, where fans can download or stream the shows for $5 each. In 2016, Louis C.K. also began releasing episodes of his self-produced online series *Horace and Pete*, which he described to the *New York Times* as "a handmade, one guy paid for it version of a thing that is usually made by a giant corporation" (Egner 2016).

Of course, My Bloody Valentine, Ansari, and Louis C.K. succeeded outside the system only after they had already become known quantities with devoted fan bases as well as the financial resources to invest in their online ventures. In contrast, a large percentage of anonymous workers in the creative industries make no money at all. Many web publications like the *Huffington Post* do not monetarily compensate their freelance writers, bloggers, and other contributors, claiming that the exposure offered by their platforms should be compensation enough. Similarly, since the early 1990s the so-called glamour industries represented by popular name-brand record companies, fashion houses, hip-hop magazines, film studios, advertising firms, and television networks have increasingly relied on the free labor provided by unpaid internships. These are typically jobs in which college students perform menial tasks—photocopying, answering phones, cold calling, filing, proofreading, fact checking, ordering lunch, fetching coffee—without being paid anything other than the opportunity to gain the "professional experience" thought necessary for eventual longer-term employment in the creative sector. As Jim Frederick (2003) observes, these lousy jobs sell themselves on false promises and inflated credentials while seducing impressionable youth eager

Comedians such as Aziz Ansari (shown here) and Louis C.K. have opted out of the industry system by self-releasing special performances on their own websites.

to subject themselves to certain drudgery and untold humiliations for the cachet signaled by the coolness quotient of celebrity companies like MTV, *Vogue*, and *Rolling Stone*—especially if the perks include free concert tickets, record release party invitations, invitations to movie premieres, and the slim opportunity for a chance encounter with a supermodel, action hero, or rock star. In violation of the 1938 Fair Labor Standards Act, most of these internships fail to provide young employees with useful professional skills while even the *symbolic* value of internship "experience" declines as these demeaning, unpaid jobs grow ever more popular among collegiate and postgraduate workers. Meanwhile, the surplus of giddy pop culture fanatics clamoring to work for free drives down wages and salaries for all *other* creative workers throughout the mass media industries at all levels of the job hierarchy. In doing so, the intern economy represents yet another attempt by culture-producing firms to minimize risk and decrease expenses under conditions of unpredictability and volatility, albeit on the young backs of their biggest fans.

How do films such as *Titanic* portray different types of culture and use them to represent

7

living in the material world

CULTURAL CONSUMPTION
AND SOCIAL CLASS IN AMERICA

THE 1997 BLOCKBUSTER FILM *TITANIC* IS AS MUCH A STORY ABOUT social stratification on the high seas as it is about the 1912 disaster itself. One of the top-grossing motion pictures of all time, James Cameron's *Titanic* presents, in its first half, a world divided economically and culturally on the basis of social class, where the wealthy live on the upper decks and luxuriate in first-class accommodations—private cabins, formal dining, fine cigars—while third-class passengers enjoy raucous parties full of music and dancing, albeit while cooped up in steerage. Just as in other films and television shows about social class and cultural mores (*The Help, Downton Abbey*), in *Titanic* the lines dividing the culture and tastes of the affluent classes from the poor could hardly be drawn in a more stark manner.

Rightly or wrongly, we commonly distinguish among different kinds of culture by relying on labels such as "highbrow" and "lowbrow" and associate them with their respective class affiliations. (The terms are an unfortunate survival from the nineteenth-century pseudoscience of phrenology, in which intelligence was measured by the size of one's forehead, or literally the height of his or her brow.) In the most stereotypical sense, *highbrow* culture (or simply *high* culture) refers to the fine arts consumed by the affluent classes—classical music and opera, ballet and modern dance, abstract painting and sculpture, poetry and literary fiction. We might also include less traditional forms of high culture enjoyed by contemporary cosmopolitan audiences: National Public Radio programs such as *This American Life* and *All Things Considered*, expensive farm-to-table fare such as locally sourced kale and roasted bone marrow, and world music recordings from Sufi chanting to Tuvan throat singing. In many ways high culture is merely synonymous with the traditionally humanist conception of culture itself, as the most intellectual and civilizing of leisurely pursuits. (When we say someone is *cultured*, we usually mean that he or she is familiar with *high* culture, just as we might go to an art museum or the symphony to "get some culture" [Grisword 2004, p. 4].)

Meanwhile, *lowbrow* or *low* culture typically refers to the kinds of mass culture stereotypically associated with working-class (or so-called *lower*-class) audiences, including rap, blues, heavy metal, and country music; professional wrestling, stock car racing, rodeos, and monster truck rallies; and gory horror films, gross-out comedies, and pornography. This pejorative label—*low* culture—suggests a set of activities and amusements lacking in virtue and associated with sexuality and the *lower* half of the body, certainly relative to its highbrow counterparts. Outrageous moral panics surrounding the imagined sexual and moral degradations of lower-class American culture seem to be a routine occurrence in our national discourse. In a 1985 *Newsweek* article about heavy metal titled "Stop Pornographic Rock," the writer complains:

> My 15-year-old daughter unwittingly alerted me to the increasingly explicit nature of rock music. "You've got to hear this, Mom!" she insisted one

afternoon . . . , "but don't listen to the words," she added, an instant tip-off to pay attention. The beat was hard and pulsating, the music burlesque in feeling. . . . Unabashedly sexual lyrics like these, augmented by orgasmic moans and howls, compose the musical diet millions of children are now being fed at concerts, on albums, on radio and MTV. (quoted in Binder 1993, p. 761)

These kinds of anxieties about lower-class culture in the United States have historically emphasized the liveliness and ribaldry of African American popular culture, often in hysterical overtones. In 1921, *Ladies' Home Journal* published a piece that asked, in all seriousness, "Does Jazz Put the Sin in Syncopation?"

Jazz disorganizes all regular laws and order; it stimulates to extreme deeds, to a breaking away from all rules and conventions; it is harmful and dangerous, and its influence is wholly bad. . . . The effect of jazz on the normal brain produces an atrophied condition on the brain cells of conception, until very frequently those under the demoralizing influence of the persistent use of syncopation, combined with inharmonic partial tones, are actually incapable of distinguishing between good and evil, right and wrong. (quoted in Appelrouth 2005, p. 1503)

Today it is admittedly difficult to imagine that the brilliant (not to mention thoroughly inoffensive) music performed by 1920s jazz greats such as Duke Ellington and Louis Armstrong could have ever generated such fearful hysteria. Another article that same year exclaimed, "Unspeakable Jazz Must Go!"

Those moaning saxophones and the rest of the instruments with their broken, jerky rhythm make a purely sensual appeal. They call out the low and rowdy instinct. All of us dancing teachers know this to be a fact. We have seen the effect of jazz music on our young pupils. It makes them act in a restless and rowdy manner. . . . They can be calmed down and restored to normal conduct only by playing good, legitimate music. (p. 1505)

Considered lowbrow at the time, jazz in the 1920s was even attacked for ruining the culture of elites, especially classical music. In 1929 the *New York Times* ran a piece titled "Composer Sees Jazz as Feverish Noise," in which Sir Hamilton Harty, the conductor of Great Britain's Halle Orchestra, warns readers, "When future historians look upon the present epoch they will call it a machine age of music. They will see that in an age that considers itself musically enlightened we permit gangs of jazz barbarians to debase and mutilate our history of classical music and listen with patience to impudent demands to justify its filthy desecration" (quoted in Appelrouth 2003, p. 125).

Do these kinds of cultural class divisions still hold in contemporary American life? In terms of a high/low distinction, our national culture sometimes seems schizophrenic. At the second inauguration of President Barack Obama in 2013, award-winning poet Richard Blanco read from the same grandstand where pop

Beyoncé sings the National Anthem at President Barack Obama's inauguration in 2013. Pop artists Kelly Clarkson and James Taylor also performed.

stars Kelly Clarkson and Beyoncé performed. Past honorees of the John F. Kennedy Center for the Performing Arts in Washington, D.C., include orchestral conductor Zubin Mehta and rock legends Pete Townshend and Roger Daltrey of the Who; ballet dancer Mikhail Baryshnikov and country music singer Willie Nelson; opera singer Luciano Pavarotti and R&B performer James Brown. Blues music, an expressive cultural form that grew out of the life experiences of impoverished descendants of African American slaves, is regularly performed at Carnegie Hall, Lincoln Center, and the White House (as is the jazz music once defamed by the *Ladies' Home Journal* and in the *New York Times*), while classical music is now performed at chic downtown nightclubs in New York City (McCormick 2009). Affluent white teenagers adore hip-hop music, while underprivileged African American youth appropriate Tommy Hilfiger's yacht-club clothes and other preppy brands (Polo Ralph Lauren, Nautica) as inner-city fashion (Klein 2002, pp. 75—76). Meanwhile, much of our mass culture—notably professional men's football, baseball, and basketball—is celebrated by audiences from all social classes and walks of life.

At the same time, we live in an extraordinarily unequal society in which the very poor live on as little as $2 a day (Edin and Shaefer 2015) while rich politicians can't remember how many houses they own (that would be Vietnam war hero and former Republican presidential nominee John McCain, speaking on the campaign trail in 2008). The United States has the highest poverty rate among all other wealthy capitalist countries, while *half* of all U.S. income goes to the top 10 percent of Americans (Wright and Rogers 2015, pp. 267—282). The top 1 percent alone accounts for about one-fifth of all income earned in the United States (p. 277). In terms of wealth, the differences are even starker: The average net worth of the top 1 percent is approximately 137 times that of the bottom 90 percent (p. 280).

Accompanying these enormous disparities, cultural differences among social classes abound. Affluent urban professionals are far more likely than working-class consumers to listen to classical music and opera, decorate their homes with abstract art, and read books for pleasure (Peterson 1992; Halle 1993; Griswold 2008). Their children are more likely to participate in competitive extracurricular activities such as chess, dance, and soccer (Lareau 2003; Friedman 2014). While the previous two chapters emphasized the social and institutional worlds in which popular culture is created, we now turn toward an exploration of taste and *consumption*—the reception, interpretation, and experience of culture. In what ways are cultural tastes patterned according to class status? In this chapter, we will attempt to tease out the complex relationship between cultural consumption and social class in the United States by examining the fluid nature of taste and class cultures and how they change over time. We will try to understand how the persistence of certain cultural differences among audiences helps to maintain socioeconomic inequality among social classes. At the same time, we will try to explain why the class boundaries surrounding the consumption of American popular culture sometimes seem blurry and confusing, and have been for the last 150 years or so.

The Invention of Class Cultures in America

Like all cultural conventions, distinctions between highbrow and lowbrow culture and taste are socially fabricated and prone to dramatic change over time. How do we know this? A brief cultural snapshot of nineteenth-century American society may be instructive. Today, we think of the plays of William Shakespeare as decidedly highbrow, largely considered the height of artistic and literary accomplishment. Students study *King Lear* and *Hamlet* in university courses and write PhD dissertations on the allegorical design of *Othello*. Audiences sit in silent awe during live performances of Shakespeare's tragedies, particularly those staged by the most prestigious thespian troupes in the world: Britain's Royal Shakespeare Company, the Shakespeare Theater Company in Washington, D.C., and the Public Theater in New York.

Yet during the nineteenth century, Shakespeare's plays were considered *popular culture*—not only in England but also in the United States. Working-class Americans as well as elites shared a deep familiarity and fondness for his plays. In his 1840 publication of *Democracy in America*, Alexis de Tocqueville reports, "There is hardly a pioneer's hut which does not contain a few odd volumes of Shakespeare. I remember reading the feudal drama of *Henry V* for the first time in a log cabin" (1988, p. 471). According to historian Lawrence W. Levine (1991), Shakespeare's plays were regularly performed on steamboats and makeshift stages in mining camps and breweries as well as in more metropolitan theaters in Philadelphia and San Francisco. As Levine observes, "Shakespeare was performed not merely alongside popular entertainment as an elite supplement to it; Shakespeare was performed as an integral part of it. Shakespeare *was* popular entertainment in nineteenth-century America" (p. 163).

When did Shakespeare become highbrow? An 1849 portrait of Charlotte and Susan Cushman as Romeo and Juliet in Act 3, Scene 5. Charlotte (left) was considered the most powerful actress on the nineteenth-century stage and was the first American actress to attain critical theatrical acclaim.

In many ways, Shakespeare's widespread popularity among Americans in the mid-nineteenth century should not be particularly surprising. His plays matched the mass tastes of the period: They are laden with dry humor and wit, as are the novels of Mark Twain, and his scenes are melodramatic and full of ghosts, just like the poems and short stories of Edgar Allan Poe. His most famous soliloquies, such as *Hamlet's* "To be or not to be . . ." speech, offer the kind of oratory familiar to a nation whose public life required studied attentiveness to lengthy preachers' sermons and political speeches and debates. Unlike contemporary readers, nineteenth-century Americans would have had little trouble deciphering Shakespeare's Elizabethan English, since the most popular book of the era was the King James Bible, first published by the Church of England in 1611—the same year that Shakespeare introduced his comedies *The Winter's Tale* and *The Tempest*. Moreover, American audiences would have sympathized with Shakespeare's worldview that placed the individual human being at the center of the universe, a creature of free will with ultimate responsibility for his or her own destiny. Indeed, this is how Americans viewed themselves.

But perhaps the biggest reason that Shakespeare's plays were considered popular culture has to do with the social organization of American entertainment in the nineteenth century. Unlike the highbrow/lowbrow distinctions of today, 150 years ago Americans enjoyed a national popular culture consumed and experienced collectively by the masses, by people from *all* social classes. Live entertainment performances were attended by a microcosm of society, arranged according to socioeconomic status—aristocratic gentlemen and ladies luxuriated in box seats, the merchant and professional middle classes sat in the orchestra, and working-class audiences crowded the gallery, or balcony. (As an illustration of the racial segregation of the period, African American attendees of all classes were relegated to the balcony as well.) During performances of Shakespeare, those in the cheap seats would express their derision of an inept actor by pelting him with eggs, apples, potatoes, carrots, lemons, cabbages, pumpkins, and, in at least one reported instance, a dead goose (Levine 1991, p. 168).

Likewise, American entertainment blended diverse genres and styles in ways that would be thought blasphemous by today's standards. Theaters presented

Shakespearean plays alongside acts by magicians, dancers, acrobats, and comics (p. 164). According to NYU sociologist Paul DiMaggio's (1982) research on nineteenth-century Boston, concerts featured the mingling of classical music compositions, Italian opera, devotional and religious songs, and popular tunes (p. 34). As for other entertainment spaces,

> Museums were modeled on Barnum's: fine art was interspersed among such curiosities as bearded women and mutant animals, and popular entertainments were offered for the price of admission to a clientele that included working people as well as the upper middle class. Founded as a commercial venture in 1841, Moses Kemball's Boston Museum exhibited works by such painters as Sully and Peale alongside Chinese curiosities, stuffed animals, mermaids and dwarves. For the entrance fee visitors could also attend the Boston Museum Theatre, which presented works by Dickens and Shakespeare as well as performances by gymnasts and contortionists, and brought to Boston the leading players of the American and British stage. The promiscuous combination of genres that later would be considered incompatible was not uncommon. As late as the 1880s, American circuses employed Shakespearean clowns who recited the bard's lines in full clown make-up. (p. 34)

Today, the idea of *King Lear* being performed at the circus stretches and boggles the mind, as does the image of rowdy working-class audiences hurling rotten vegetables down from the balconies of the Metropolitan Opera House. What happened? Well, the Industrial Revolution happened, creating a new upper-class American elite of successful entrepreneurs, bankers, and businesspeople. (The richest men in American history—John D. Rockefeller, Cornelius Vanderbilt, John Jacob Astor, Stephen Girard, Andrew Carnegie—first amassed their great fortunes in the nineteenth century.) This *nouveau riche* (literally "new rich") class enjoyed untold wealth but few of the refinements that grow from an aristocratic upbringing—in fact, many came from rather humble backgrounds. These increasingly status-conscious industrialists therefore drew on the trappings of European nobility—family crests, indulgences in French cuisine, classical art and music—in crafting newfound cultural tastes and symbols of distinction for themselves (Beisel 1993). To this end, in the late nineteenth century this new bourgeoisie began erecting class boundaries concretized in elite arts and cultural organizations, including the Boston Symphony Orchestra and the Museum of Fine Arts, the Art Institute of Chicago, New York's Metropolitan Museum of Art, and the Philadelphia Academy of Music (Zolberg 1981; DiMaggio 1982).

With these elite institutions, the upper classes of the Gilded Age successfully *invented* the highbrow/lowbrow class-based cultural distinctions that Americans now take for granted. This invention of class cultures required conscious efforts at boundary maintenance and social exclusion, most obviously through the development of special entertainment venues, so-called legitimate theaters and museums in which to consecrate and present classical music, opera, drama, and art as "serious" culture for upper-class audiences. By making ticket prices and subscriptions prohibitively expensive and strictly enforcing dress codes and rules of social etiquette (no throwing cabbages allowed, I presume), the elite effectively excluded members of the working classes from participating in these new worlds of cultural esteem. By the turn of the twentieth century, the American upper classes had eventually succeeded in bifurcating the nation's once diverse mélange of popular culture—Shakespearean tragedy, circus clowns, acrobats, contortionists, mermaids, dwarves—into separate stylistic offerings of "serious" and "popular" culture, each redefined on the basis of class and prestige. Given the wholly manufactured nature of this prestige, it is perhaps fitting that the word *prestige* itself was originally used to describe the illusions, tricks, and fakery of magicians and jugglers.

Class Status and Conspicuous Consumption

For the American upper classes, attendance at symphony halls and Shakespearean theater performances represented part of a larger set of rituals and customs designed to exhibit status and distinction in public. In his classic work *The Theory of the Leisure Class*, Thorstein Veblen (1899/1994) coined the term *conspicuous consumption* to describe these status displays since they represented attempts to show off one's wealth through the flagrant consumption of expensive and luxurious goods and services, particularly those considered wasteful or otherwise lacking in obvious utility, like diamond bangles or high-heeled shoes. Even today, upper-class tastes tend to emphasize *form over function* as well as *quality over quantity*, which is why expensive restaurants often serve tiny portions of elaborately presented foods, such as salmon sashimi or Spanish tapas. Of course, the very wealthy not only enjoy an excess of money but also free time, as displayed in pursuits that Veblen called *conspicuous leisure*. They include playing sports that emphasize specialized technical skill and elaborate training, such as sailing, golf, polo, fencing, or equestrian riding, and studying dead languages like ancient Greek.

The conspicuous consumption of luxury SUVs, summer homes, ski vacations, and spa treatments has a noteworthy counterpart—the purposeful *avoidance* of popular culture associated (rightly or wrongly) with working-class tastes. Health crazes among the affluent typically revolve around the denigration of foods preferred by working-class people, chiefly inexpensive yet efficient sources of protein, fat, and carbohydrates: fried chicken, cheeseburgers, tacos, pizza, and so forth. According to sociologist Bethany Bryson (1996), when asked about their music preferences and dislikes, American respondents are most likely to express disapproval for those genres associated with less educated audiences: heavy metal, country, gospel, and rap. Pejorative class-based characterizations like "ghetto," "trailer park," and "white trash" are commonly affixed to low-status behaviors and styles as a strategy of dismissal.

If affluent Americans studiously avoid symbolic or cultural associations with the working class, the opposite is almost certainly not true, since the members of all social classes often try to emulate the conspicuous consumption of the superrich, at least in superficial ways. While low-income African American youth embrace Tommy Hilfiger and Polo country-club fashion, young inner-city mothers adorn their babies in expensive brand-name clothes like Reebok and Nike (Anderson 1990, p. 125). Another example might be the widespread popularity of designer knockoff handbags, wallets, earrings, and sunglasses, replicas of high-priced brands from Prada to Chanel to Louis Vuitton. (Perhaps as a means of competing with the imitation jewelry industry, Tiffany & Co. sells a small heart-shaped charm for $80, which caters to a significant market of consumers who desire the celebrity luster of the Tiffany brand but cannot afford its $7,100 diamond bracelet.) More audacious emulators of the rich and famous hire personal paparazzi

Members of the lower classes emulate the conspicuous consumption of the superrich by purchasing counterfeit luxury goods.

firms like Celeb 4 a Day to follow them around with cameras while clubbing. Meanwhile, the success of the $51 billion U.S. wedding industry depends on the strength of the fantasy that everyday people deserve the trappings of wealth—limousines, glamorous clothing, catered cocktail parties, ice sculptures, champagne toasts—if only for one special evening (Mead 2007; Grose 2013).

Cultural Capital and Class Reproduction

One might reasonably ask what is at stake here. If cultural consumption is all about image making, why do the images matter so much? After all, the billionaire who drives a beat-up pickup truck and wears discount-store clothes (as Wal-Mart's founder Sam Walton did) still has his overflowing bank accounts. Yet in fact, quite a lot might be at stake, if we bear in mind that cultural tastes and consumer habits have social consequences that extend far beyond one's wardrobe or music playlists. Rather, cultural tastes have value and can be transferred to others, converted into financial wealth, and ultimately help to reproduce the class structure of our society. As George Harrison and Madonna have both sung in different songs, we are living in a material world.

Let us start with the basics. In his venerable book *Distinction*, French sociologist Pierre Bourdieu (1984) discusses his concept of *cultural capital*—one's store of knowledge and proficiency with artistic and cultural styles that are valued by society, and confer prestige and honor on those associated with them. Cultural capital refers to one's ability to appreciate and discuss intelligently not only the fine arts but elite forms of popular culture as well, such as art-house cinema and foreign films, critically acclaimed novels, public television and NPR programs, and sophisticated magazines like *Harper's* and the *New Yorker*. It also includes one's familiarity with global culture, including one's fluency in foreign languages and the cultivation of taste for exotic cuisines from around the world (Johnston and Baumann 2007). Cultural capital also refers to one's familiarity and competence with the rules of dress and etiquette appropriate for upper-class social situations, such as knowing how to tie a necktie in a Windsor knot, when to applaud during chamber music concerts, and how to order sushi in an expensive Japanese restaurant.

Why call this kind of knowledge cultural capital? Bourdieu uses the term *cultural capital* because it shares many of the same properties as economic capital or wealth. Like wealth, cultural capital is unevenly divided among the social classes, largely because it tends to be *inherited*, passed among generations within families. One's taste and appreciation for the fine arts is never derived naturally but taught through constant exposure and positive reinforcement, often at a young age. The homes of upper-class families are brimming with collections of novels and nonfiction books, paintings and drawings, atlases and maps, and all kinds of music. Wealthy families introduce their children to the arts by taking them to museums, plays, and concerts, and by sending them to private piano, violin, and ballet lessons. They take them to gourmet restaurants, bring them on European vacations to world capitals such as Paris and Rome, and send them to college preparatory private schools, or else well-funded public schools in affluent suburbs. In doing so, parents try to cultivate in their children the same sense of respect and esteem (if not actual affection) for the fine arts and cosmopolitan culture that they themselves have come to appreciate, or at least value.

Of course, the transfer of cultural capital from upper-class parents to their children can be a pricey proposition—think of the expense of all those years of ballet and music lessons, foreign travel, and private school. In this sense, economic capital itself can be *converted* into cultural capital as an investment. In fact, the returns on such an investment can be substantial given that once accumulated, cultural capital can be converted back into economic capital, in part by increasing one's chances of landing a respectable salaried job. According to Northwestern sociologist Lauren Rivera (2015), high-paying investment banks, law firms, and management consulting agencies screen their applicants not only on the basis of their work experience, intellect, and academic achievement but also on their "cultural fit" with the organization and its employees. During interviews, recruiters evaluate candidates on how well polished they appear, with attention paid to their display of ease, poise, and effortlessness in social interactions, their articulateness and ability to take the lead in conversation, and their professional business attire and hygienic appearance. Applicants are often expected to have competed in a high-status athletic sport such as football, lacrosse, or field hockey in high school or college, and enjoy elite recreational pursuits such as world travel, scuba diving, or triathlon training as adults.

By instilling in their children an appreciation for the fine arts, wealthy parents pass along their cultural capital to the next generation.

Once hired, new employees may be expected to socialize with their bosses or associates while skiing or playing golf (both expensive hobbies requiring years of training), or else they may be asked to entertain clients at dinner parties at fancy restaurants—they will need to know how to order wine from a sommelier, correctly distinguish between their salad and entrée forks (the salad fork is always on the outside), and know how to properly break and butter their dinner roll (in small pieces). In much of the business world, the rules of the game privilege those with impressive levels of cultural capital, and access to high-income occupations (or otherwise prestigious jobs in higher education, publishing, or the performing arts) may require it. During the application process and on the job itself, recruits who make the most of their cultural capital are able to convert it back into economic wealth, as represented by the financial rewards of the high-paying job itself.

If cultural capital is therefore transferable (from parents to kin) and convertible (to economic rewards), then it is hardly a stretch to hypothesize that over time the organization of cultural tastes and consumer habits might work to reproduce the class structure of our society. Upper-class adults use their cultural capital to secure lucrative jobs and invest their incomes in cultivating the same tastes and cultural skills in their children, who eventually generate enough cultural capital of their own that they can effectively continue the cycle. In doing so, the upper classes reproduce themselves over and over again, in perpetuity if they wish, leaving behind those who lack basic competence in elite cultural consumption themselves and the resources to train their children to do all that much better.

When assessing how cultural capital operates in the United States, we must remember that our industries and social institutions not only discriminate on the basis of socioeconomic class but race, ethnicity, and gender as well. As UCLA anthropologist Philippe Bourgois (2002) discovered during his research among a group of young Puerto Rican men in New York City, the tough style of interpersonal communication they developed while on the streets of East Harlem was completely incompatible with the white-collar culture of the corporate world, a sad fact that consistently resulted in job termination for these otherwise hardworking employees. Research also suggests that within the business world, familiarity with professional and college sports (as demonstrated by one's ability to fill out an NCAA basketball tournament bracket, or follow the weekly travails of a local NFL team) probably matters much more than knowledge of the fine arts (Erickson 1996). This could theoretically give males an advantage over equally qualified women when competing for jobs and promotions. (Since the 1970s, the female audience for U.S. sports has grown tremendously, particularly among active women who participated in high school or intercollegiate athletics, and so to a large extent this is changing.)

We should also bear in mind that different professions may reward different kinds of knowledge. For example, in today's global postindustrial economy, *technical* expertise likely matters just as much as cultural capital, especially in professions such as financial services, investment banking, insurance, engineering, and software development. These fields employ many smart workers admired more for their

Office dress codes are often more relaxed in the tech sector compared to other white-collar work settings, as demonstrated by Mark Zuckerberg, who often dons a T-shirt and sneakers to give presentations.

mathematical prowess and computer coding abilities than their aesthetic or fashion sensibilities. For this reason, many Internet entrepreneurs and knowledge workers follow the lead of Apple's former head Steve Jobs and Facebook founder and CEO Mark Zuckerberg by dressing casually for work, wearing jeans, T-shirts, and sneakers or sandals in the workplace. (Zuckerberg famously wore a black hoodie to meetings with investors and bankers during the run-up to Facebook's IPO.) In fact, in the postindustrial knowledge economy, workers often work from home, which spares them the challenge of negotiating office dress codes and face-to-face social norms altogether. Alternatively, many jobs in the media industries—advertising, publishing, website design, music and film editing—obviously *do* demand a wide set of aesthetic skills, while employment in high-end retail, dining, entertainment, and other service industries in which workers interact with affluent customers may require cultural competencies and communicative skills that resonate with those with upper-class lifestyles (Grazian 2008b, p. 47).

From Cultural Snob to Omnivore

In search of understanding the aesthetic and cultural tastes of Americans, UCLA sociologist David Halle (1993) interviewed a variety of people from different neighborhoods in the New York City metropolitan area about their consumption of modern abstract art (such as the work of Wassily Kandinsky, Paul Klee, Piet Mondrian, and Jackson Pollock) typically regarded as highbrow culture enjoyed by contemporary elites. Sure enough, he discovered that 55 percent of the residents he sampled from Manhattan's ritzy Upper East Side display abstract art on the walls of their homes, while *none* of his respondents from a lower-middle-class urban neighborhood in Brooklyn did. But while Manhattan professionals are more likely to collect abstract art than other cultural consumers, they are also more likely to collect a wider variety of other kinds of art as well. Among Halle's urban elites, 58 percent display non-Western art in their homes, including African, Oceanic, and Native American figurines, masks, weapons, baskets, jewelry, pottery, textiles, musical instruments, and other artifacts, higher than any other group sampled in his research (p. 149).

Sociological research on cultural consumption suggests similar findings. According to sociologist Richard A. Peterson (1992), highly educated professionals are more likely than others to attend opera, jazz and classical music concerts, Broadway musicals and dramatic plays, art museums, ballet and modern dance performances, as we might expect of the stereotypical upper-class snob. (Think of Benedict Cumberbatch's portrayal of Holmes in the BBC hit *Sherlock*.) However, they are also more likely to participate in almost *all other* recreational activities than their lower-class counterparts as well, including attending sports events, exercising, gardening, boating, camping, hiking, and photography. This suggests that in the context of American life, elite status is signified not only by an affinity for highbrow culture but an appreciation for practically *all* major kinds of leisure activities, creative pursuits, and cultural consumption, highbrow *and* lowbrow.

Peterson (1992) calls these affluent consumers *cultural omnivores* because of their far-ranging cosmopolitan and inclusive tastes, as illustrated by President Barack Obama's wildly eclectic Spotify summer playlist released by the White House in 2016, which featured tracks by jazz greats Miles Davis and Charles Mingus, pop artists from Prince to Sara Bareilles to the Beach Boys, alternative Latin fusion artist Manu Chao, soul singers Aretha Franklin and Nina Simone, and hip-hop rappers Jay Z, Nas, and Common. (Vice President Joe Biden's playlist similarly featured artists of different musical genres and styles, including Lady Gaga, Coldplay, Frank Sinatra, Tina Turner, the Beatles, and the cast of *Les Misérables*.)

Like Obama, cultural omnivores rely on their cultural capital not only to consume highbrow fare but also to successfully inhabit several different kinds of social universes, each with a different set of taste expectations, rules of etiquette, and codes of subcultural behavior, language, and style. Yale sociologist Elijah Anderson (1999, p. 36) refers to this ability to negotiate among multiple and varied cultural worlds simultaneously as *code-switching*—a social dexterity famously illustrated by rapper Jay Z, who moves easily between underground hip-hop clubs and the executive suites of Def Jam Recordings, having served as its president and CEO. (Perhaps Rose, the *Titanic* heroine played by Kate Winslet, who smoothly transitions from elegant dining to Irish dancing below deck, provides a suitable fictitious example.)

What can explain the inclusive tastes of the cultural omnivore? One possible explanation could be the rising accessibility of non-Western culture among educated

Jay Z is a platinum-selling rapper, entrepreneur, and CEO. How is he an example of Elijah Anderson's concept of code-switching?

cosmopolitan consumers in the United States. Restaurants in U.S. cities serve Ethiopian *injera* and *gomen wat*, El Salvadoran *pupusas* and *pastelitos*, and Korean *bulgogi* and *bibimbop* to satisfied customers of all racial and ethnic backgrounds. Amazon promotes a global array of novelists from Nigeria's Chimamanda Ngozi Adichie to Japan's Haruki Murakami. Spotify invites its digital users to sample playlists from a range of folk and world music traditions from Jamaican ska and rocksteady to Brazilian bossa nova. On Netflix, subscribers can stream movies made in India, China, Nigeria, and the Middle East. Of course, the inclusive consumer habits among affluent Americans can also be explained by the increasing ethnic and international diversity of the nation's upper class itself (Khan 2011) and the persistence of formative tastes among upwardly mobile immigrants who themselves carry traditional ethnic and religious customs and cultural practices—Sicilian cooking, Hindu wedding rituals, Mexican folk art, Senegalese dance—into the high-society world of the American elite (Peterson 1992, p. 255).

We might also consider how the inclusive tastes of the U.S. upper class may be a product of our national ideals concerning democracy and equality. American ideology emphasizes the promise of egalitarianism, as reflected in our typically casual dress and informal norms of etiquette, at least when compared to our European counterparts. In her book *Money, Morals, and Manners*, Harvard sociologist Michèle Lamont (1992) shows how disparaging Americans are of "social climbers" and "phonies" who "put on airs" (p. 26). Along these lines, the capacity for code-switching and omnivorous cultural consumption signifies class status without necessarily appearing snobbish, which is why young affluent nightlife consumers not only drink expensive Prohibition-era cocktails but cheap cans of Pabst Blue Ribbon beer as well. In *Bobos in Paradise*, David Brooks (2001) argues that the new upper classes combine elite bourgeoisie tastes with bohemian sensibilities, rejecting traditional luxury goods for Costa Rican fair-trade handicrafts, Ethiopian coffee beans, Malaysian curries, Salvadoran fleece sweaters, organic elk and ostrich burgers, tickets to hip music festivals such as Coachella and South by Southwest, and vacations to Global South outposts such as Vietnam and Cambodia.

Given how Americans so readily identify with the promise of equality as a symbolic ideal, perhaps it should come as no surprise that some elites try to downplay their class status altogether, particularly candidates running for office. In U.S. politics, wealthy candidates often emphasize their humble roots or working-class tastes, especially when TV news cameras are around. For example, during her 2016 U.S. presidential campaign, former secretary of state Hillary Clinton used her speeches as opportunities to emphasize her modest middle-class background, rather than her degrees from Wellesley and Yale. As reported in the *Washington Post* during a 2015 campaign stop through Iowa, "You may think of her as the wife of a president or as a globe-trotting diplomat, but Hillary Rodham Clinton wants voters here to see her as the granddaughter of an immigrant factory worker and the daughter of a small businessman who printed fabric for draperies and then went out and sold them. 'A waste-not, want-not kind of a guy,' she said, 'and he provided a good living for us'" (Rucker and Gearan 2015). During that same campaign, Clinton's vice-presidential running mate, Senator Tim Kaine of Virginia, touted his blue-collar bona fides as the son of an iron welder. Meanwhile,

Clinton's Republican opponent, self-described billionaire Donald J. Trump, tried to connect with blue-collar voters by posting on his Facebook, Instagram, and Twitter feeds images of himself feasting on McDonald's burgers and fries and a bucket of KFC fried chicken—all on his private jet (Parker 2016).

One is reminded that although former president George W. Bush was a graduate of Phillips Academy, Yale, and Harvard, and the eldest son of a former U.S. president, his political career greatly benefited from his handlers' ability to depict the scion as a rough-riding cowboy and all-around "regular guy." During Bush's two terms in office, he customarily took his vacations at his ranch in Crawford, Texas—a more ruggedly populist setting than his family's oceanfront retreat in Kennebunkport, Maine:

> President Bush has spent the last three Augusts at his ranch in the scorched flatlands of Crawford, Tex., where he has cleared brush, gone for runs in 105-degree heat and summoned sweaty cabinet members to eat fried jalapeño peppers at the only restaurant in town. No one ever confused the place with that white-wine-swilling island in the Atlantic Ocean, to reprise the president's put-down of Martha's Vineyard, and so Mr. Bush has loved it all the more. (Bumiller 2004, p. A12)

At the same time, one should not forget the cultural excesses of the ultra-wealthy whose tastes may be cosmopolitan but far from humble. Boston University sociologist Ashley Mears (2015) chronicles how business elites surround themselves with fashion models and spend tens of thousands of dollars a night on bottle service in the VIP lounges of nightclubs in New York, the Hamptons, Miami, and Cannes, all to impress clients and competitors. In the high-end art world represented by Christie's and Sotheby's auction houses in New York, rich collectors bid on modern and contemporary paintings by Andy Warhol and Jasper Johns, and headline-grabbing pieces by Jeff Koons and Damien Hirst, for millions of dollars (Thornton 2008). (Hirst's most infamous works include *The Physical Impossibility of Death in the Mind of Someone Living* [1991], a tank containing an actual tiger shark preserved in formaldehyde, and *For the Love of God* [2007], a platinum cast of a human skull covered in 8,601 flawless diamonds made at a cost of $23.6 million. At the time of its unveiling, its original asking price was $100 million.) In 2014, Christie's and Sotheby's brought in $1.78 billion in a single week, with two Warhol works fetching $81.9 million and $69.6 million. It is perhaps ironic that although they sold in the rarefied elite world of the New York art market, the Warhols depicted two celebrity icons synonymous with postwar American *mass* culture: Elvis Presley and Marlon Brando (Fontevecchia 2014).

The Blurring of Class Boundaries in American Popular Culture

I began this chapter by suggesting that our national culture today sometimes seems schizophrenic, but the evidence indicates that class boundaries in the United States have always been a bit blurry—in the live entertainment of the nineteenth century, replete with Shakespearean actors, clowns, and acrobats;

in the conspicuous if purely symbolic emulation of the wealthy by the working classes through the purchase of designer baby clothes; in the cynical posturing of wealthy politicians and the filthy rich; and finally, in the mixing of pop culture and high-end art. As historian Michael Kammen (1999) reminds us, the blending of highbrow, lowbrow, and mass culture has been a recognizable quality of American popular culture, entertainment, and art since at least the 1920s. In the late part of that decade, Duke Ellington's harmonious compositions and performances blended together European classical music, ragtime jazz, and the Mississippi blues, as best illustrated by his 1927 recording of "Black and Tan Fantasy," a song that combines the blues melodies of the Deep South and the muted trumpets and stride piano of Harlem's jazz sound with, of all things, Frédéric Chopin's Funeral March from his Piano Sonata No. 2 in B-flat minor (Grazian 2003, pp. 28–29). In Walt Disney's 1940 film *Fantasia*, animated elephants, hippopotamuses, ostriches, and Mickey Mouse are accompanied by selections from the classical music canon: Bach's Toccata and Fugue in D Minor, Tchaikovsky's *Nutcracker Suite*, Beethoven's sixth symphony (the *Pastoral Symphony*), and Stravinsky's *The Rite of Spring*. Starting in the 1950s, Hugh Hefner's *Playboy* magazine began publishing serious short fiction along with its pictorial centerfolds: Its authors have included such luminaries as Vladimir Nabokov, Saul Bellow, Norman Mailer, John Cheever, Gabriel García Márquez, John Updike, Joyce Carol Oates, and Philip Roth. Citing creative influences as canonical as Bach, Vivaldi, Paganini, and Pachelbel, progressive rock and heavy metal artists such as Rush, Deep Purple, Van Halen, Randy Rhoads, and Yngwie Malmsteen incorporated complex classical music techniques (harmonic progressions, sliding chromatic figures, minor modalities, fast arpeggios) into their performances during the 1970s and 1980s (Walser 1994).

This blurring of aesthetic boundaries continues in American popular culture today, especially as the fine arts absorb more democratic influences in the interests of remaining relevant to contemporary audiences. Choreographer Twyla Tharp's creations include ballet, interpretive modern dance, and theatrical performances set not only to Brahms and Haydn but also the jazz music of Jelly Roll Morton and the pop songs of Frank Sinatra, Bob Dylan, and Billy Joel, just as in 1993 the Joffrey Ballet premiered a rock ballet performed to the recorded music of Prince. Minimalist composer Philip Glass has written symphonies based on the albums of David Bowie. Recent Broadway musicals have included a 2010 adaptation of Green Day's punk rock album *American Idiot*; a 2011 production of *Spider-Man: Turn Off the Dark*, with music and lyrics by U2's Bono and the Edge; and a 2015 adaptation of the Richard Linklater film *School of Rock*. Lin-Manuel Miranda's libretto for his Broadway musical *Hamilton* features traditional musical theater compositions alongside hip-hop-inspired raps by actors playing Thomas Jefferson and the Marquis de Lafayette, in addition to Miranda himself in the title role as the former U.S. Treasury secretary.

Meanwhile, mainstream film and television liberally borrow from the fine arts as well as avant-garde influences. The 1995 movie *Clueless*, starring Alicia Silverstone, is a modernization of the Jane Austen novel *Emma*, just as the Julia Stiles teen films *10 Things I Hate About You* and *O* are based on Shakespeare's *The Taming of the Shrew* and *Othello*, respectively. (Similarly, the 2006 Amanda

In his Broadway blockbuster Hamilton, *based on the life of Founding Father Alexander Hamilton, Lin-Manuel Miranda drew on influences as diverse as the Notorious B.I.G. and* The Pirates of Penzance.

Bynes rom-com *She's the Man* is an adaptation of *Twelfth Night*.) The final season of the TV comedy *Seinfeld* included an episode loosely based on the experimental Harold Pinter play *Betrayal*: Like the original, the episode's scenes were presented in reverse chronological order, with punch lines delivered before their setups (Johnson 2006, p. 88).

More to the point, one should consider the central attractions of American popular culture consumed by vast audiences whose members hail from all social classes. The most successful talk show in television history, *The Oprah Winfrey Show* had 30 million weekly viewers from all walks of life tune in during its heyday. Late-night TV is similarly inclusive as well as popular: In August 2016, NBC's *Tonight Show Starring Jimmy Fallon* enjoyed season-to-date ratings of 3.63 million viewers, while CBS's *Late Show with Stephen Colbert* drew in another 2.81 million viewers. Professional men's sports, particularly football, basketball, and baseball, attract fans from all social classes, with games enthusiastically followed on TV sets in working-class bars and flat-panel home theaters, in upper-deck bleachers as well as in corporate skyboxes. Of all U.S. sporting events, perhaps the Super Bowl is the most celebrated, watched in 2016 by an estimated 112 million American viewers of all social classes, its inclusiveness illustrated by the diversity of pop music stars that have performed during its live halftime shows since 2007: Beyoncé, Lady Gaga, Coldplay, Bruno Mars, Katy Perry, Lenny Kravitz, Red Hot Chili Peppers, Black Eyed Peas, Madonna, Usher, the Who, Prince, and Bruce Springsteen and the E Street Band. Like Shakespeare's comedies and tragedies during the nineteenth century, the sporting event best represents the nationwide reach of our mass entertainment and popular culture.

Pop culture pilgrims flock to Ong Jmel, in southern Tunisia, where several scenes from the first *Star Wars* film were originally shot.

don't stop believing

AUDIENCES AND THE QUEST
FOR MEANING IN POPULAR CULTURE

ACCORDING TO *STAR WARS* LORE, A LONG TIME AGO JEDI KNIGHT Luke Skywalker hailed from a desert planet called Tatooine, its two suns burning bright in the galaxy's Outer Rim. Today, Tatooine attracts a small but devoted following of fans that make pilgrimage to its sandy landscape, or at least the North African outpost in Tunisia where George Lucas filmed numerous scenes that appear in the original 1977 movie. Writing in *Harper's*, Jon Mooallem (2009) chronicles the archaeological exploits of David West Reynolds, who used his *Star Wars* trading cards from his youth to locate the Saharan salt flats and craters that serve as the backdrop for the film's early scenes of Skywalker's homestead. According to Reynolds (as quoted in Mooallem 2009, p. 68), "I felt like I actually succeeded in stepping up from the seat in the movie theater when I'm an eight-year-old kid and stepping up into the screen. The action has wound down, and Luke and C-3PO have run off on the landspeeder, and the dust has settled. . . . But I'm still there—on Tatooine." Meanwhile, in Finland, tour guides lead visitors over the snowy glaciers that make up the scenic landscape of the ice planet Hoth in *The Empire Strikes Back*. Other adventurers excavate Buttercup Valley in the southwestern United States, the site of the Imperial Sand Dunes in *Return of the Jedi*, for left-behind scraps from the 1983 movie set.

What attracts tourists to these remote and otherwise nondescript locales in the wilderness, often to dig up decades-old garbage left behind by film crews of yesteryear? Like religious pilgrims, such crusaders are on a quest for meaning, only their sacred texts and myths are not biblical but the stuff of popular culture. As Mooallem (p. 63) argues, "Somewhere under the sand lay the actual relics of a fake, futuristic past—which were also the set pieces from the actual past that had helped bring that fiction into being. It was hard to keep it all straight. But I sensed that, as with any archeological endeavor, whatever physical objects we recovered would somehow tie us, in our time, more closely to the truths and mythologies of the era they survived."

Like *Star Wars* superfans, avid followers of the *Harry Potter* novels and movies trek to the real-life Alnwick Castle in Northumberland County in England, which appears in the first two *Harry Potter* films as the Hogwarts School of Witchcraft and Wizardry. When touring London, *Harry Potter* enthusiasts also visit Platforms 4 and 5 at Kings Cross railway station, where some of the Hogwarts Express scenes were shot. (Tourists also take selfies in front of a sign there reading "Platform 9¾.") Other real-world sites that appear onscreen in the series include the Reptile House at the London Zoo (where a Burmese python speaks to the boy-wizard before its escape in *Harry Potter and the Sorcerer's Stone*) and the city's Leadenhall Market, which plays the "role" of Diagon Alley in numerous films.

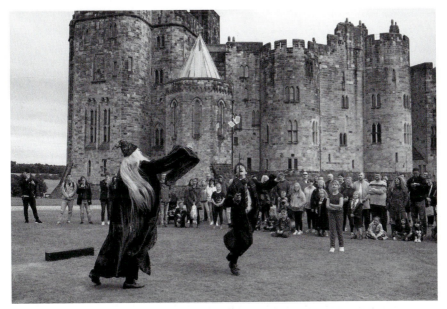

Diehard Harry Potter fans re-create a game of Quidditch on the grounds of Alnwick Castle in Northumberland County, England. The castle served as the real-life stand-in for the Hogwarts School of Witchcraft and Wizardry in the first two Harry Potter films.

The last chapter followed the consumer habits of audiences in an attempt to understand the impact of social class on one's cultural tastes and patterns of consumption. In doing so, we discovered the complexities of American popular culture and the frequently shifting boundaries that define identity and status in our society. In this chapter, we look beyond consumer preferences and proclivities to assess how people invest popular culture with significance and meaning. Scholars from a variety of disciplines in the social sciences and the humanities agree that cultural meaning is a product of human engagement and interpretation. While a traditional model of culture might imagine that texts, dramatic plays, songs, film, and visual art are like walnuts, to be cracked open so that their hidden interiors can be revealed and consumed, most social scientists today recognize that cultural meanings are actively created by audiences themselves, albeit in socially patterned ways.

Audiences and Interpretive Communities

If audiences actively construct and attribute meaning and significance to popular culture, it follows that some of their experiences consuming culture will be uniquely singular and intimately personal. Some of those experiences are of a psychological or neurological character. For instance, in his book *Musicophilia*, the late neurologist and author Oliver Sacks (2007) reports on an epileptic patient whose seizures are provoked by a wildly diverse array of music from operatic Verdi arias to romantic Frank Sinatra tunes to rock music (he must wear earplugs when out of the house), while another patient with a temporal lobe abnormality regularly experiences convulsions after listening to recordings of her favorite Neapolitan songs (pp. 26–27). Even mentally healthy music lovers may swoon over a personally captivating song (as when Elaine's boyfriend has a near-hypnotic reaction to the Eagles' hit "Desperado" during a 1996 episode of *Seinfeld*). Some married couples strongly identify with a featured slow dance number played at their wedding—according to Spotify, popular examples include "All of Me" by John Legend, "Thinking Out Loud" by Ed Sheeran, "Come Away with Me" by Norah Jones, "First Day of My Life" by Bright Eyes, and the classic hits "At Last" by Etta James and "Can't Help Falling in Love" by Elvis Presley—while others still wax nostalgic for the song featured as their high school prom's theme, whether "A Moment Like This" by Kelly Clarkson, "Don't Want to Miss a Thing" by Aerosmith, or "Don't Stop Believing" by Journey.

When attributing meaning and significance to songs, movies, and other kinds of media and popular culture, audiences not only draw on their personal memories or individual psyches but their social circumstances as well. Consumers whose common social identities and cultural backgrounds (whether organized on the basis of nationality, race, ethnicity, gender, sexuality, religion, or age) inform their shared understandings of culture in patterned ways are called *interpretive communities* (Radway 1991; also see Fish 1980). As we discussed in Chapter 1, despite their historically negative depiction in film, Native American men tend to be ardent fans of Hollywood Westerns, an enthusiasm that derives in part from the value many place on the principles of hard work and self-reliant country living. Upon viewing the 1956 John Ford film *The Searchers*, starring John Wayne, American Indians surveyed by sociologist JoEllen Shively (1992) emphasized the free and independent cowboy lifestyle commonly celebrated in such films: "Westerns relate to the way I wish I could live"; "The cowboy is free"; "He's not tied down to an eight-to-five job, day after day"; "He's his own man"; "Indians today are the cowboys" (pp. 729–30). Similarly, LGBT audiences have historically dealt with the invisibility or otherwise negative depiction of homosexuality in film by resisting such readings of mainstream culture, finding gay-positive messages in classic films like *The Wizard of Oz* (1939), *Rebel Without a Cause* (1955), and *Ben-Hur* (1959) (Ross 2015, p. 125).

Interpretive communities often share a specific intellectual, religious, or political worldview within a larger institutional context (Fish 1980). For example, Christian organizations greatly differed in their interpretation of director Martin Scorsese's critically acclaimed yet controversial 1988 motion picture *The Last Temptation of Christ*, in which Jesus Christ (played by Willem Dafoe) is presented as a truly human figure tortured by inner demons and grave doubts; in keeping with the 1951 revisionist novel by Nikos Kazantzakis on which the film is based, during his crucifixion Jesus dreams of marrying and making love to Mary Magdalene, impregnating her and going on to lead the life of a normal man. A spokesperson for the National Council of Churches called the movie "an honest attempt to tell the story of Jesus from a different perspective," and the Reverend Michael Himes, a Notre Dame theologian, referred to the film as

What spurred interpretive communities to protest the release of Martin Scorsese's film The Last Temptation of Christ?

"fairly distinguished art" (Hunter 1991, pp. 233—34). Meanwhile, conservative Catholic and Evangelical groups were outraged by the film and its depiction of Christ. The right-wing fundamentalist group Focus on the Family attacked the Scorsese film for portraying Jesus "as a confused, lustful wimp who denies his divinity and struggles with his sinful nature," and an organization called Morality in Media proclaimed it "an intentional attack on Christianity" (p. 234). In 2004, religious and civil rights organizations similarly fought over the meaning and ideological implications of Mel Gibson's box-office blockbuster *The Passion of the Christ*. Focus on the Family's James Dobson called the film "the most heart-wrenching, powerful portrayal of Christ's suffering that I have ever seen," while other Evangelical leaders criticized *Passion* for its Roman Catholic themes. The Anti-Defamation League criticized the film's depiction of "bloodthirsty" Jewish mobs as historically inaccurate and anti-Semitic.

Interpretive communities materialize during public debates surrounding the value or potential harm of certain types of popular culture. In 1985, the U.S. Senate held hearings on the so-called dangers of heavy-metal rock music lyrics. Led by Tipper Gore (the wife of future vice president Al Gore), the Parents' Music Resource Center (PMRC) demanded that warning labels be placed on metal albums by artists such as Ozzy Osbourne, whose song "Suicide Solution" from the 1980 album *Blizzard of Ozz* had been dubiously blamed for the death of John McCollum, a depressed teenage boy who killed himself with a bullet to the head while listening to the record. At the Senate hearings, one child psychiatrist representing the PMRC attacked the music of Black Sabbath (Osbourne's previous band) and AC/DC for encouraging violent behavior:

> One of the most pathological forms of evil is in the form of the cult killer or deranged person who believes it is OK to hurt others or to kill. The Son of Sam who killed eight people in New York was allegedly into Black Sabbath's music. . . . Most recently, the individual identified in the newspapers as the Night Stalker has been said to be into hard drugs and the music of the heavy metal band AC/DC. . . . Every teenager who listens to heavy metal certainly does not become a killer. [But] young people who are seeking power over others through identification with the power of evil find a close identification. The lyrics become a philosophy of life. It becomes a religion. (quoted in Binder 1993, p. 758)

Meanwhile, an interpretive community made up of a strange mix of music industry executives, newspaper journalists, and musicians—from Twisted Sister lead singer Dee Snider to experimental rock guitarist Frank Zappa to acoustic folk and country star John Denver—defended the content of contemporary popular music, citing the small minority of songs containing explicit lyrics, the cartoonish and therefore harmless character of heavy metal, and the negligible role that rock lyrics play in the increasing proliferation of images of sex and violence in the media overall (Binder 1993, p. 759).

In later years, another public debate emerged among interpretive communities concerning the so-called dangers of popular music, specifically rap and hip-hop. In 1990, the Miami rap group 2 Live Crew's third album *As Nasty as They Wanna Be* was ruled obscene by a U.S. District Court judge in Fort Lauderdale, Florida, and the proprietor of a record store in Broward County was arrested for continuing to sell the album. (The album contains songs with titles such as "Me So Horny," "Put Her in the Buck," "Dick Almighty," "The Fuck Shop," and "Get the Fuck Out of My House." In addition to including more than 200 utterances of the word *fuck*, the album features more than 150 mentions of *bitch* and more than 80 descriptions of oral sex; see Hunter 1991, p. 232.) On the CBS news program *48 Hours*, an attorney accused 2 Live Crew's lead singer Luther Campbell of being "a psychological child molester" (p. 232), while conservative commentator George Will warned in *Newsweek* that the rap group not only threatened young listeners but all of society:

> Fact: some members of a particular age and social cohort—the one making 2 Live Crew rich—stomped and raped [a] jogger to the razor edge of death, for the fun of it. Certainty: the coarsening of a community, the desensitizing of a society will have behavioral consequences. (quoted in Binder 1993, p. 762)

As in the previous controversy surrounding heavy metal, an interpretive community of perhaps uncommon bedfellows came to defend rap music (if not 2 Live Crew itself) from its critics, including African American university professor and ordained Baptist minister Michael Eric Dyson, who writes in an essay on "Gangsta Rap and American Culture" (1996):

> At their best, rappers shape the torturous twists of urban fate into lyrical elegies. They represent lives swallowed by too little love or opportunity. They represent themselves and their peers with aggrandizing anthems that boast of their ingenuity and luck in surviving. . . . Before we discard the genre, we should understand that gangsta rap often reaches higher than its ugliest, lowest common denominator. Misogyny, violence, material-ism, and sexual transgression are not its exclusive domain. At its best, this music draws attention to complex dimensions of ghetto life ignored by many Americans. Of all the genres of hip-hop—from socially conscious rap to black nationalist expressions, from pop to hardcore—gangsta rap has most aggressively narrated the pains and possibilities, the fantasies and fears, of poor black urban youth. (pp. 177, 184—85)

Likewise, during the 2 Live Crew controversy, pop music journalist Jon Pareles (1990) pointed out in the *New York Times* that "not all rap machismo should be taken entirely at face value. Like other black literary and oral traditions, rap lyrics also involve double-entendre, allegory and parody. Some rap machismo can be a metaphor for pride or political empowerment; it can be a shared joke, as it often is in 2 Live Crew's wildly hyperbolic rhymes." According to UCLA anthropologist Philippe Bourgois (whom Pareles interviewed for his *Times* piece):

> I see rap as reflective, and what people should be scared about is the extent to which the songs reflect reality. That there is such unbelievable violence in these communities is a national tragedy, while the fact that people express themselves in terms of violence is a part of American culture, a way of thinking that goes back to the Wild West. I wouldn't worry about rap music leading to violence. On the contrary, rap music leads to a productive expression of alienation and oppression, and it's good that it gets channeled into creative outlets rather than drug addiction or physical violence. I see people, high-school dropouts, who carry around notebooks in their back pockets so they can compare their latest rhymes. (quoted in Pareles 1990)

The interpretive communities depicted in the preceding examples are engaged in what James Davison Hunter (1991) refers to as *culture wars*, cultural conflicts fought among ideological adversaries in the public arena. But while interpre-tive communities may disagree about the fundamental meanings of cultural texts, objects, or events, we need not think of such differences as necessarily combative or even oppositional.

For instance, during the 1980s the British rock band the Smiths and its morose lead singer Morrissey attracted a U.S. fan base of shy, pale-skinned white teenagers who identified with the band's melancholic view of life as expressed in morbidly titled songs such as "Heaven Knows I'm Miserable Now,"

"Unhappy Birthday," "Girlfriend in a Coma," "The Boy with the Thorn in His Side," "Still Ill," "Suffer Little Children," "I Want the One I Can't Have," "That Joke Isn't Funny Anymore," "Death of a Disco Dancer," "Barbarism Begins at Home," and "Meat Is Murder." Today, Morrissey and the Smiths continue to be popular in the United States—but among young Latino men, particularly those from Mexico and Southern California. As East Los Angeles native Javier Cabral (2014) reported in the *Washington Post*, "Mexican Americans can't get enough of him. The onetime lead singer of the Smiths is as central to the culture [of East L.A.] as bean-and-cheese burritos." Interpretive communities rely on common social experiences to frame their collective readings of popular culture, which is why some Latino fans explain their embrace of Morrissey and the Smiths in terms of their shared ethnic heritage and immigrant experience. Gloria Antuez, a 23-year-old junior high school teacher, explains, "Morrissey's family emigrated to England from Ireland, and they were kind of socially segregated from the rest of the country. . . . That is very similar to the Latino experience here in Los Angeles. We see things within his songs that we can particularly relate to. He sings about loneliness. He sings about solitude. Those are things any minority group can relate to." According to Martha Barreras, another Latina fan, "We're passionate people. He's passionate like us. . . . The music our parents played when we were growing up was always about love and emotion, and it's the same thing with Morrissey." As Cruz Rubio, a 20-year-old male fan, insists, "He speaks to us, man. As Latinos. He addresses us personally. . . . His music fits our lifestyle" (Klosterman 2006, pp. 49–52). Then again, other Latino fans associate Morrissey's pompadour and rockabilly sensibility with 1950s icon Ritchie Valens, the Mexican American rock 'n' roll pioneer whose hits included "Donna," "Come On, Let's Go," and, most famously, "La Bamba."

Meaning-Making and the Changing Significance of Popular Culture

While interpretive communities may attribute differing meanings and significance to popular culture, often it is the meanings themselves that shift among audiences over time. We have already seen examples of this in earlier chapters, as when contract-based craft production, like Italian Renaissance painting, gains prestige as an art form, or when mass cultural attractions, like Shakespearean drama, are recast as highbrow culture. We have also seen examples of cultural genres once contested among interpretive communities for their so-called threatening and dangerous character rehabilitated in the public imagination, such as the "demoralizing" and "unspeakable" African American jazz music of the 1920s (Appelrouth 2005).

Occasionally this reputational augmentation in the national consciousness reaches transformative heights, as in the case of the late American folk singer Pete Seeger. The progressive songwriter and beloved performer of songs like "Where Have All the Flowers Gone?" and "If I Had a Hammer," Seeger was demonized as a communist sympathizer during the McCarthyism of the 1950s.

He was called to testify before the House Un-American Activities Committee in 1955 and blacklisted for years from performing on prime-time network television. But as a result of the 1960s folk music revival and his subsequent fame as a cultural icon (as well as the eventual discrediting and dissipation of anti-communist hysteria among mainstream Americans), Seeger was selected as an Honoree of the John F. Kennedy Center for the Performing Arts in 1994, its publicity materials identifying him as "arguably the most influential folk artist in the United States" (Bromberg and Fine 2002, p. 1147). Just weeks later, President Bill Clinton awarded Seeger the coveted National Medal of Arts, the highest possible award given to an artist by the U.S. government.

Seeger's gradual transformation from national pariah to official recognition as an American treasure is a testament to the socially constructed character of the interpretive meanings and significance attributed to popular culture. But how common are these kinds of changes in meaning, particularly with regard not simply to individual artists but to entire forms of mass media themselves? In fact, these kinds of shifts occur more frequently than one might think. The reception of film in the United States provides an interesting case. Today we attach great artistic significance to movies, at least those easily recognized by socially conventional standards as worthy of critical praise—recent examples might include Academy Award winners and nominees such as *American Hustle, 12 Years a Slave, Birdman or (The Unexpected Virtue of Ignorance), The Revenant, Spotlight, The Grand Budapest Hotel, Selma*, and *Boyhood*. Yet historically this interpretation of cinema as art is a relatively recent development in American culture and dates back only as far as the 1960s. Earlier in its history, moviegoing was an inexpensive and therefore devalued form of urban entertainment. In New York City, nickelodeons—turn-of-the-century storefront theaters where film screenings could be enjoyed for a nickel—were typically concentrated in blue-collar tenement districts and attracted crowds of predominantly working-class patrons, particularly women and immigrants (Peiss 1986). According to sociologist Shyon Baumann (2007), from its beginnings through the 1930s wealthy and educated cultural snobs looked down on movies for their "lack of sophistication or aesthetic value," "tackiness," "tastelessness," and "corrupting and immoral" influence, while shunning the theaters themselves for attracting audiences of low social status, including ethnic minorities and the poor (pp. 24–25). Movies were considered entertainment for the lowest common denominator of audiences, inferior to more "legitimate" live theatrical performances.

In his book *Hollywood Highbrow*, Baumann (2007) argues that the work of prestige-granting institutions in concert with industry shifts and broader social changes can help explain the rising significance of film among American audiences. Believe it or not, the introduction and rapid popularity of television in American homes during the 1940s and 1950s was a crucial factor. As noted in Chapter 1, in 1953 two-thirds of family households in the United States owned at least one television, and by the mid-1960s that figure had grown to 94 percent (Cohen 2003, p. 302). Television's enormous mainstream appeal allowed film to emerge as a more distinctive and status-signaling cultural alternative, and by the 1960s,

The Criterion Theater in New York City's Times Square in 1931. Why did many cultural elites in the early twentieth century look down on movies?

motion pictures seemed especially smarter and more sophisticated than network television, particularly in light of the formulaic commercial TV programming popularized during the 1940s and 1950s, as represented by shows such as *Bozo the Clown, Howdy Doody, Candid Camera*, and *What's My Line?* Meanwhile, the growth of the middle class and the expansion of colleges and universities in the United States after World War II created newly educated audiences who were both hungry for rich cultural experiences and prepared to critically engage with cinema as something more than simply trivial entertainment.

At the same time, a set of legitimizing institutions had succeeded in canonizing American films as worthy of intellectual and artistic cultural merit. In 1927, Louis B. Mayer of MGM and other studio heads created the Academy of Motion Picture Arts and Sciences as a means of bolstering the industry's image, and in 1929 the organization began nominating and bestowing its Academy Awards—today more popularly known as the Oscars—for achievement in film. By showcasing a small number of films every year, the Academy Awards helped contribute to the creation of a canon of American motion picture "masterpieces," just as prizes such as the National Book Award and the Nobel Prize in Literature serve to establish a literary canon over time. The American Film Institute (AFI) was similarly created during the

1960s to recognize achievement in cinema, and in 1998 the AFI established a list of the 100 greatest American movies of all time. The AFI last updated its list in 2007, when the AFI 100 top five films were, in descending order, *Citizen Kane* (1941), *The Godfather* (1972), *Casablanca* (1942), *Raging Bull* (1980), and *Singin' in the Rain* (1952). More recent films on the updated list include *Toy Story* (1995), *Titanic* (1997), *Saving Private Ryan* (1998), *The Sixth Sense* (1999), and *The Lord of the Rings: The Fellowship of the Ring* (2001).

The American film canon was also developed during the 1960s by growing numbers of academic departments offering advanced degree programs in film and cinema studies at major colleges and universities such as New York University, Columbia, UCLA, and the University of Southern California. Movies and their directors gained social prestige and scholarly significance as they were gradually incorporated into the university curriculum in courses on film history and theory. The early 1960s also saw the American importation of French auteur theory, which credits the director (rightly or wrongly) with providing the artistic vision for their movies, as if he or she were the sole author of their films. The theory of the auteur gained particular prominence as visionary directors such as Alfred Hitchcock and Stanley Kubrick gained more creative autonomy both behind the camera and in the editing room. Contemporary examples of the Hollywood director-as-auteur include Martin Scorsese, Woody Allen, Steven Spielberg, Sofia Coppola, Christopher Nolan, Spike Lee, Wes Anderson, Lisa Cholodenko, Alejandro González Iñárritu, and Quentin Tarantino. In addition, by the 1950s and 1960s cosmopolitan U.S. cities—Chicago, San Francisco, New York, Boston, Seattle— began hosting international film festivals showcasing new films as worthy of critical and intellectual consideration.

These changes helped reshape the heightened meaning and artistic significance that American audiences today attach to popular film. Baumann (2007) cleverly illustrates this interpretive shift by examining the differences between movie reviews published before and after the 1960s. Whereas earlier film reviews were short write-ups with little more than plot summaries and consumer recommendations, starting in the mid-1960s movie critics began employing an increasingly sophisticated language in lengthier discussions of films. Contemporary reviewers characterize film using an analytic voice featuring a critical terminology usually reserved for dissecting great works of literature and art—"composition," "irony," "metaphor," "symbol," "tone." Critics today refer to the creative vision and authorial control of the director by using laudatory adjectives such as "art," "brilliant," "genius," "inspired," and "master," and modifiers such as "Hitchcockian" or "Tarantinoesque" when comparing the cinematographic styles of different directors (pp. 119—20).

Of course, one could (incorrectly, I think) argue that contemporary critics are more likely to describe films as artistic and intellectually significant simply because movies *are* actually more artistic and culturally significant today—except that Baumann also discovered these differences among earlier and later reviews of the *same movies*, including *Casablanca, Gone with the Wind*, and *The Wizard of Oz* (pp. 128—33). As an illustrative example, Baumann presents early and

While Disney's Snow White and the Seven Dwarfs *drew criticism when it first premiered in 1937, it was later named the greatest animated movie of all time by the American Film Institute.*

more recent reviews of the Disney animated classic *Snow White and the Seven Dwarfs*. As the *New Yorker* told readers in 1938, shortly after the film's premiere:

> He has perhaps overdone the wicked stepmother, and just for a moment or two has tinted the film with too lurid a touch. In one other element, too, I think Mr. Disney's judgment has erred. The language of the dwarfs is funny, but it must be called a little tough. It smacks too much of the language of the streets, and in a film like this it should be most literate, punctilious, and polite. No nice dwarf, Mr. Disney, ever says "ain't." (quoted in Baumann 2007, pp. 131—32)

Note the differences between this recap from the late 1930s and a more recent *Village Voice* review from 1973:

> Disney is for children as much as Chaplin and Keaton are, by which I mean that children understand the broadest aspects of these artists—the lowest slapstick comedy and, in the case of Disney, the terror—but little else. "Bambi," for example, with its subtle mood studies, its deliberate lack of story-line and identification figures, left the largely children's audience I saw it with restless. . . . On a narrative level this sense of the past and emphasis on family relationships make the films, like fairy tales, fertile ground for Freudian

analysis. As in the Grimm original, "SNOW WHITE AND THE SEVEN DWARFS" centers around a sexual jealousy between an overweeningly vain queen and her innocent step-daughter. (quoted in Baumann 2007, p. 132)

In this latter review from the 1970s, the *Village Voice* compares Disney's work to that of Charlie Chaplin and Buster Keaton (both directors as well as comedic actors) and draws on terminology such as "Freudian" and "narrative." Since then, *Snow White and the Seven Dwarfs* has been added to the U.S. National Film Registry (founded in the 1980s to honor and preserve "culturally, historically or aesthetically significant films"), named by the American Film Institute as the 34th greatest American film of all time and the *greatest* animated movie ever. (So much for Mr. Disney's "erred" judgment.)

In today's popular cultural environment, few American audiences would deny that filmmakers possess the potential to create transcendent works of artistic import and significance, and in hindsight the success of cinema's socially engineered shift from entertainment to art almost seems inevitable, a foregone conclusion. Moreover, in the contemporary era of high-quality programming and digital distribution, television has enjoyed a renaissance of similar proportions as plenty of entertaining shows have achieved the status of art in the popular consciousness. (A short list of such programs would include HBO's *Game of Thrones, The Sopranos,* and *The Wire*; AMC's *Mad Men* and *Breaking Bad*; Showtime's *Homeland* and *Masters of Sex*; Netflix's *House of Cards* and *Orange Is the New Black*; and Amazon's *Transparent*.)

However, a less prestigious brand of popular culture, such as rock music, may better emphasize the conflicts and contestation surrounding these kinds of transformations in cultural meaning-making. During its emergence in the 1950s, cultural authorities vilified rock 'n' roll, calling it juvenile, simplistic, and coarsely sexual, but in the last several decades rock critics and the remaining major record labels have worked tirelessly to increase its prestige as a respectable American art form, in part by relying on the same strategies as the Hollywood film industry and its institutional enablers. The National Academy of Recording Arts and Sciences annually honors rock artists with its Grammy Awards. Founded in 1983, the Rock and Roll Hall of Fame and Museum canonizes rock artists in much the same way that the American Film Institute attributes significance to Hollywood movies. (Inductees have ranged from Chuck Berry and Elvis Presley to more contemporary acts such as U2 and Madonna.)

Rock magazines such as *Rolling Stone* also engage in canon formation by generating lists of classic albums and singles; for example, in May 2012 *Rolling Stone* released its definitive list of "The 500 Greatest Albums of All Time." Its top 10 included albums by the Beatles (whose *Sgt. Pepper's Lonely Hearts Club Band* was honored with the coveted No. 1 spot on the list), the Beach Boys, Bob Dylan, Marvin Gaye, the Rolling Stones, and the Clash. College professors at Columbia and Northwestern University teach courses with titles such as "Issues in Rock Music and Rock Culture" and "Special Topics: The Music of Radiohead," while Liverpool Hope University now offers a master of arts degree in "The Beatles, Popular Music and

Society" (Kozinn 2009). Harvard classics professor Richard F. Thomas teaches a first-year seminar on the music of Bob Dylan, who surprised the world when he was awarded the 2016 Nobel Prize in Literature (Schuessler and Kraft 2016). Academics and journalists organize scholarly conferences around the intellectual study of rock music as well. At the 2016 annual Pop Conference of the Experience Music Project in Seattle, participants presented papers that included the following titles:

- "'Reality Ruined My Life': Lesbian One Direction Fandom and Disruptive Desires"
- "I Am Not a Hipster and Other White Lies: Seeing the Voice of Indie Rock"
- "A Blank Space Where You Write Your Name: Taylor Swift's Early Late Voice"
- "'My Presence Is a Present': Kanye West, Nicki Minaj, and the Laughter of the Rapper"
- "Of Whistles, Coos, and Doo-Wops: The Racial Kitsch of Mariah Carey's Vocal Theatrics"
- "Accidental Post-Racism in a Southern Voice: What Country Music Did and Didn't Say as the Obama Era Began"
- "Feeling the Human and the Politics of Vocal Pitch Correction: Notes from the Field"

Finally, today's music critics lionize canonical rock albums by relying on the same critical terminology and intellectualizing discourse employed by contemporary film reviewers, as illustrated in the above examples. In his book *It Ain't No Sin to Be Glad You're Alive: The Promise of Bruce Springsteen*, Eric Alterman (1999), a columnist for the *Nation* as well as a professor of journalism and English, writes:

> *Born to Run* exploded in my home and my mind and changed my life, just as Elvis and the Beatles had done for Bruce a decade earlier. I never could have articulated it at the time, but *Born to Run* offered me an alternative context for my life, a narrative in which hopes and dreams that felt ridiculous were accorded dignity and, no less important, solidarity. . . . The poetry and power of *Born to Run* lie in its unwillingness to compromise, in the refusal of its protagonists to accept passively the hand dealt to them by circumstance. . . . The album's stories are internal monologues and dramatic renderings of Springsteen's own personal struggles with his parents, with authority, with women, and with the expectations of the world, universalized and ennobled through the language of the radio. . . . It is an album about the unsung heroism of everyday life, the quiet glory of unflinching personal integrity in a world where virtue is deemed to be its own reward. (pp. 73–76)

Note the language Alterman employs to characterize *Born to Run*, Springsteen's celebrated 1975 album: He emphasizes its "narrative," "poetry and power," and "internal monologues and dramatic renderings," all "universalized and ennobled," just as if he were dissecting Fyodor Dostoyevsky's *Crime and Punishment* or William Faulkner's *The Sound and the Fury*. This artistic and literary characterization of rock among music journalists and critics, along with the formation of a classic rock canon, university courses and scholarly conferences, an endowed museum, and award-granting institutions, all shape the heightened meaning and artistic significance that American audiences today attach to rock 'n' roll music.

However, unlike cinema, rock has had more than its fair share of dissenters and party-poopers, and not just among the psychiatrists and politicians' wives associated with the Parents Music Resource Center of the 1980s culture wars. In *The Closing of the American Mind*, the renowned University of Chicago philosophy and classics professor Allan Bloom (1987) writes:

> Though students do not have books, they most emphatically do have music. . . . This is the significance of rock music. I do not suggest that it has any high intellectual sources. But it has risen to its current heights in the education of the young on the ashes of classical music. . . . Ministering to and according with the arousing and cathartic music, the lyrics celebrate puppy love as well as polymorphous attractions, and fortify them against traditional ridicule and shame. . . . Picture a thirteen-year-old boy sitting in the living room of his family home doing his math assignment while wearing his Walkman headphones or watching MTV. He enjoys the liberties hard won over centuries by the alliance of philosophic genius and political heroism, consecrated by the blood of martyrs; he is provided with comfort and leisure by the most productive economy ever known to mankind; science has penetrated the secrets of nature in order to provide him with the marvelous, lifelike electronic sound and image reproduction he is enjoying. And in what does progress culminate? A pubescent child whose body throbs with orgasmic rhythms; whose feelings are made articulate in hymns to the joys of onanism or the killing of parents; whose ambition is to win fame and wealth in imitating the drag-queen who makes the music. In short, life is made into a nonstop, commercially prepackaged masturbational fantasy. . . . People of future civilizations will wonder at this and find it as incomprehensible as we do the caste system, witch-burning, harems, cannibalism and gladiatorial combats. (pp. 68–75)

Bloom's vitriol betrays a wide generational gap as well as his inability to code-switch between classical and pop music worlds. But while he launches his attack on the significance of rock from outside its cultural universe, plenty of rock musicians *themselves* fight against the emergent production of prestige surrounding popular music, arguing that attempts to fabricate its critical and canonical "legitimacy" deprive rock of its rebelliousness and subcultural cool. British rock vocalist and guitarist Elvis Costello has been quoted as asserting that "writing about music is like dancing about architecture—it's a really stupid thing to want to do." And in February 2006, the surviving members of the 1970s punk band the Sex Pistols reacted to their upcoming induction into the Rock and Roll Hall

Jann Wenner, founder of Rolling Stone *magazine and chairman of the Rock and Roll Hall of Fame Foundation, reads the note from the Sex Pistols declining to attend the ceremony inducting them into the Rock and Roll Hall of Fame.*

of Fame by posting the following announcement (replete with grammatical and spelling errors) on their website explaining their refusal to attend the induction ceremony at New York's Waldorf-Astoria Hotel:

Next to the SEX PISTOLS rock and roll and that hall of fame is a piss stain. Your museum. Urine in wine. Were not coming. Were not your monkey and So what? Fame at $25,000 if we paid for a table, or $15000 to squeak up in the gallery, goes to a non-profit organisation selling us a load of old famous. Congradulations. If you voted for us, hope you noted your reasons. Your anonymous as judges, but your still music industry people. Were not coming. Your not paying attention. Outside the shit-stem is a real SEX PISTOL.

By refusing to donate thousands of dollars for a table at the black-tie event, the Sex Pistols railed at what many consumers recognize as the worst excesses of the rock music industry: the prohibitive cost of stadium and arena concerts, the endless celebration of passé or otherwise forgotten musicians, the commodification of beloved rock songs, and, most of all, the lack of rabble-rousing authenticity among millionaire rock stars.

Popular Culture and the Search for Authenticity

Perhaps no other desire motivates consumers of contemporary popular culture more than the search for authenticity. In recent years, reality television has proliferated not only because it is very inexpensive to produce (as we discussed in Chapter 6) but also for its brazen attempts to capture "ordinary" people in unscripted moments of everyday life, warts and all (Grindstaff 2002). African American hip-hop music artists sell millions of albums based on their ability to "keep it real" by remaining "true" to "the street," even when they hail from middle-class suburbs (McLeod 1999). Television news anchors and on-air media personalities go so far as to downgrade their résumés for fear of seeming inauthentic and insufficiently populist. On Fox News, cable TV host Bill O'Reilly has asserted that "I understand working-class Americans. I'm as lower-middle-class as they come," even though he hails from the decidedly well-off neighborhood of

Westbury, Long Island, and earned advanced degrees from Harvard and Boston University without financial aid (Murphy 2002).

Since the onslaught of the Industrial Revolution in the nineteenth century, the search for authenticity has been a middle-class reaction to the soulless-ness of monopoly capitalism and the ravaging of the countryside, whether as expressed by Karl Marx's critique of alienated labor or Walt Whitman's and Henry David Thoreau's pastoral odes to the natural landscape. Today, as contempo-rary media and popular culture grow ever more processed and manufactured, many consumers place increasing value on that which appears less prone to manipulation and thus more authentic. For instance, in our postmodern age of high-tech frivolity—as exemplified by the proliferation of Botox and filtered Instagram photos, Hollywood artifice and Auto-Tuned pop music, virtual real-ity and vampire chic—some consumers nostalgically seek out the authenticity suggested by symbols of agrarian simplicity (organic beets, raw honey) and old-fashioned folkways (handlebar mustaches, homemade taxidermy).

Authenticity can refer to a variety of desirable traits: credibility, originality, sincerity, naturalness, genuineness, innateness, purity, or realness. Like a badge of honor, authenticity connotes legitimacy and social value, but like honor itself it is also a social construct with moral overtones rather than an objective and value-free appraisal. Given its socially constructed and thus elusive nature, authenticity *itself* can never be authentic but must always be performed, staged, fabricated, crafted, or otherwise imagined (MacCannell 1976; Peterson 1997; Fine 2003; Grazian 2003). The performance of authenticity always requires a close conformity to the expectations set by the cultural context in which it is situated. For instance, in American politics authenticity is marked by straight talk, plain speech, and working-class cultural sensibilities, whereas foodies evaluate the authenticity of ethnic cuisine according to its closeness to national, local, or regional sources of tradition (Lu and Fine 1995; Johnston and Baumann 2007).

Consumers attribute authenticity to cultural objects and symbols as a means of creating distinction, status, prestige, or value; it is therefore ironic that authen-ticity is so often associated with hardship and disadvantage. Collectors assign legitimacy to the childlike artwork of uneducated, self-taught artists on the basis of its unmediated purity, its expression of the wild but innocent creativity of an unrefined mind (Fine 2003). Music fans and ethnomusicologists romanticize the Mississippi Delta blues melodies of poor sharecroppers as rural expressions of African American primitivism and Anglo-Saxon folk ballads for their association with working-class country living (Roy 2002). For similar reasons, international tourists and consumers delight in their purchases of indigenous crafts hand-made in developing countries such as Thailand and Costa Rica (Wherry 2008).

While these examples illustrate how the search for authenticity can serve as an exercise in snobbery or condescension, other cases reveal how consumers and cultural authorities can establish distinction through a more democratizing discourse of authenticity attribution. Gourmet food writers, cooks, and diners alike validate ingredients, recipes, and dishes as authentic by associating them with a particular geographic region, whether in the case of Tuscan wild boar stew, Vietnamese beef wraps, Maryland crab cakes, or Nashville hot chicken. (The specificity of place also serves as a marker of authenticity among consumers of globally popular music from Punjabi bhangra to Jamaican reggae.) Other culinary audiences legitimize food as authentic by emphasizing the rustic quality of homegrown or organic produce—heirloom tomatoes, baby kale, handpicked cilantro, shaved truffles—or else the modesty of handmade dishes such as black beans and rice or mint cucumber salad (Johnston and Baumann 2007).

Considering their invented quality, attributions of authenticity must often be passionately defended if they are to masquerade as actual facts, occasionally to ridiculous ends. Many locals insist that a truly authentic Philadelphia cheesesteak must be prepared with one of three kinds of cheese—American, provolone, or Cheez Whiz, even though the latter is perhaps the most artificial and synthetic of all foodstuffs, invented in a laboratory in 1952 (two decades after the introduction of the "original" Philly cheesesteak), and in Canada, no less. (When in 2003 U.S. presidential hopeful John Kerry accidentally ordered a cheesesteak in South Philadelphia with Swiss cheese, local reporters suggested that it may have marked the "unraveling" of his campaign.) Pabst Blue Ribbon beer is commonly hailed as a symbol of working-class authenticity by counter-culturally minded consumers presumably oblivious to the fact that the former Milwaukee brewer is now based in Los Angeles and owned by TSG Consumer Partners, a private-equity firm. Food companies liberally draw on ideologies surrounding authenticity to euphemize the use of flavor additives and extracts as "natural flavors" (Schlosser 2002). Meanwhile, national supermarket chains such as Whole Foods Market promote their most highly processed foods from frozen burritos and pizzas to TV dinners as "organic" as if such dishes were grown on small family farms rather than manufactured in industrial laboratories and packing plants (Pollan 2006).

Given that the authentic experiences American consumers value are inevitably rooted in stereotypical and fanciful images of reality rather than the messiness (and sometimes unpleasantness) of everyday life as it is actually lived, the search for authenticity can prove to be a risky balancing act. After all, few contemporary home buyers on the market for a "historically preserved" nineteenth-century Victorian carriage house are likely to desire one lacking indoor toilets. American diners at ethnic restaurants may crave exotic dishes from faraway lands, but not those foods so far removed from their customary palates that they deem them inedible, such as Swiss horsemeat, or Malaysian webbed duck feet, or *bosintang*, a Korean soup prepared with dog meat. In fact, the representation of cultural authenticity in dining and other entertainment settings almost always relies on a somewhat imaginary and aesthetically pleasing simulation of reality. In mainstream Chinese restaurants in the United States, dishes like Mongolian beef are prepared with lots of sugar to appeal to American tastes; soup is served as an appetizer course rather than at the end of the meal (as it would be in China); and traditional Chinese dishes such as beef tripe, ox's tail, and pig's tongue are excluded from most menus (Lu and Fine 1995). Feigning authenticity, Mexican restaurants in the United States serve tortilla chips before the meal and burritos as a main course—not because traditional Mexican folkways demand it (they do not), but because Anglo customers do (Gaytan 2008, pp. 325–26).

Within the media and culture industries, the production of popular music relies on similarly strategic methods of representing authenticity. In the early era of country-western music, record companies portrayed their actual artists as authentic old-timers, hillbillies, and cowboys (Peterson 1997). Contemporary recording labels rely on racially charged stock characters to market their male rap and hip-hop acts as gang-bangers, street thugs, pimps, convicted felons, ex-cons, and drug users. (Meanwhile, female rap and pop stars from Nicki Minaj to Iggy Azalea to Lana Del Ray are regularly accused of being inauthentic—of not writing their own raps, of not being able to sing, of pretending to be "street," of not keeping true to their roots.) Pop bands take their fashion cues from once-underground punk and skateboarding scenes to camouflage themselves in the symbolic authenticity of alienated youth and independent rock. Blues club owners in Chicago almost exclusively hire African American bandleaders for profitable weekend gigs in response to audience demand for the authenticity that affluent white consumers usually attribute to black blues performers (Grazian 2003). According to one local guitarist:

It's because white audiences and owners are ignorant. The owners know that tourists will ask at the door, "Well, is the band playing tonight a *black*

Tenry Johns Blues Band with Claudette playing at Blue Chicago, one of the city's most popular downtown blues venues. Why do blues clubs in Chicago almost exclusively hire African American bandleaders?

band, or is it a *white* band?" Because the tourists only want to hear black bands, because they want to see an authentic Chicago blues band, and they think a black band is more *real*, more *authentic*. When they come to Chicago, it's like they want to go to the "Disneyland of the Blues." You know, it's like this: people want German cars, French chefs, and well, they want their bluesmen black. It's a designer label. (quoted in Grazian 2003, p. 36)

Adventures in the Quest for Meaning in Popular Culture

While the search for authenticity among consumers has perhaps never been stronger, others embrace an alternative set of pop cultural pursuits that devalue, deconstruct, or otherwise challenge such explorations as tradition-bound, humorless, or else pretentious. For example, in the quest for meaning in popular culture, many postmodern consumers seek out exemplars of *hybridity* in which otherwise disparate cultures are melded together in a self-conscious manner to generate new possibilities for creative expression. In many ways, the entire history of American popular music in the twentieth century was marked by attempts at synthesis and fusion. Blues and jazz developed as a mélange of African and European musical traditions, while early rock 'n' roll pioneers developed the genre by blending urban blues with country music. Such experiments in hybridity are also evident in the aforementioned Bob Dylan's mid-1960s development of electric folk-rock (which signaled his supposed *lack* of authenticity among more traditional folk music adherents, including the aforementioned Pete Seeger); Miles Davis's forays into free jazz, funk, and psychedelic rock on albums like *Bitches Brew* and *On the Corner*; the appropriation of classical music techniques in 1970s and 1980s progressive rock and heavy metal; and the emergence of rap rock, an amalgam of punk, hard rock, and hip-hop music exemplified by 1980s and 1990s acts such as the Beastie Boys, the Red Hot Chili Peppers, and Rage Against the Machine.

Like the pursuit of authenticity, adventures in cultural hybridity are popular among foodies, as evidenced by the pervasiveness of global fusion cooking in fine-dining establishments worldwide. In New York, San Francisco, Chicago, and other cosmopolitan cities, three- and four-star restaurants prepare fashionable exemplars of hybrid cuisine that combine French cooking with a mixture of ingredients from Japan, Italy, Cuba, Mexico, and Morocco, among other locales. In downtown Philadelphia restaurants, fusion dishes include seared Kobe beef carpaccio, truffle-scented edamame ravioli, and chocolate mousse with fresh grated wasabi (Grazian 2003, p. 233). By playfully combining culinary traditions common to regional cuisines, chefs and dining patrons alike reject the social construction of authenticity in favor of global fusion.

If the pursuit of hybridity represents a challenge to cultural traditions, so do adventures in *irony*. We experience irony when we invert aesthetic and taste conventions to humorous effect, particularly when cultural creators and consumers playfully mock what they regard as the self-importance of authenticity displays. The self-consciously campy performances of gay drag queens call attention to the stylized artifice and theatricality of celebrity culture, as do pop music divas from Madonna to Lady Gaga and Katy Perry. The same can be said about the dead-on song parodies and music videos of Weird Al Yankovic, who has sold more than 12 million albums (more than any other comedy act ever) by sending up superstars such as Michael Jackson, Taylor Swift, Miley Cyrus, Pharrell Williams, and, yes, Madonna, Lady Gaga, and Katy Perry.

We also experience ironic detachment (and not a little nostalgia) when consuming outdated pop cultural fads and fashions as cheesy kitsch, whether 1970s disco music from the Bee Gees or the Village People or 1980s hair-metal rock bands such as Mötley Crüe or Guns N' Roses. Cult movies with demonstrable camp appeal among winking audiences include Ed Wood's 1959 film *Plan 9 from Outer Space*, widely considered the worst movie ever made (which ironically makes it one of the most *important* movies ever made), and

In his performances, Weird Al Yankovic, who specializes in parodies of songs by the biggest names in pop culture, emphasizes the artificiality of celebrity culture.

The Rocky Horror Picture Show (1975), a low-budget musical parody that today boasts the longest theatrical run in motion picture history. Since the 1970s, Troma Entertainment has produced and distributed gross-out science-fiction horror films that harken back to the alien and monster B-movies of the 1950s, including *The Toxic Avenger* (1985) and *Class of Nuke'Em High* (1986). More recent cult films include *Showgirls* (1995), an exploitive Las Vegas—based morality tale and box-office bomb that went on to earn $100 million in the home video rental market, and *Wet Hot American Summer* (2001), a sweaty summer-camp movie that later gained a following among pop culture fans when a number of its relatively unknown cast members became famous, including Elizabeth Banks, Bradley Cooper, Amy Poehler, and Paul Rudd. (In 2015, Netflix released a short TV series as a "prequel" to the film, starring much of the original cast.) Even certifiably awful films and other pop cultural duds can entertain audiences, and in doing so can be made meaningful, and even significant.

Why are urban centers such as New York City
and Los Angeles incubators for creative culture?

uptown funk

POPULAR CULTURE

AND URBAN LIFE IN THE CITY

FOR THE LAST 100 YEARS OR SO, NEW YORK CITY HAS BEEN an incubator for some of the nation's greatest achievements in home-grown art and music. The Harlem Renaissance of the 1920s spawned a generation of African American writers, poets, artists, composers, and musicians from Langston Hughes to Duke Ellington. During the 1940s and 1950s, the Abstract Expressionist movement, as represented by innovative painters such as Jackson Pollock, Robert Rauschenberg, Jasper Johns, and Willem de Kooning, turned New York City into the art capital of the world. In the 1960s, singer-songwriter Bob Dylan rose to prominence in the streets and cafés of Greenwich Village. Farther uptown, Andy Warhol created his iconic Pop Art lithographs and silkscreen paintings at his famous studio, the Factory, where he also made experimental films and managed the art-rock band the Velvet Underground. In the 1970s and 1980s, the downtown scene featured the punk and new wave music of the Ramones, Television, Blondie, and Talking Heads, and the spirited painting of Jean-Michel Basquiat. Meanwhile, in black neighborhoods in Queens and the South Bronx, 1980s rap artists from Run-D.M.C. to Grandmaster Flash and the Furious Five helped to popularize the hip-hop sounds of the city.

Across the globe, cities remain vital to the production and consumption of mass media and popular culture. The entertainment and culture industries in music, film, television, advertising, fashion, architecture, and book and magazine publishing are headquartered in the nation's two largest cities, New York and Los Angeles, with outposts in Chicago, Nashville, and other metropolitan areas throughout the country. In today's Internet age, we have grown accustomed to emphasizing the fluid networks of cultural production and consumption existing in cyberspace, easily accessed from wherever one finds a wireless hotspot. Yet the centrality of cities for the creation and experience of mass media and popular culture remains strong—even among digital workers themselves, many of whom congregate in urban technology centers such as New York's Silicon Alley, San Francisco's South of Market (SoMa) neighborhood, and northwest Austin in Texas. In this chapter we will discuss the importance of cities as centers of creativity and urban entertainment.

Creativity and Culture in the City

Cities have historically served as the birthplace for ideas and creativity, from ancient city-states such as Athens and Rome to the Italian cities of the Renaissance to today's global cities—New York, London, Paris, Tokyo, Shanghai. In his great book *The Culture of Cities*, Lewis Mumford (1938) explains the centrality of the city in the cultural and intellectual life of a civilized society:

> The city, as one finds it in history, is the point of maximum concentra-
> tion for the power and culture of a community. It is the place where the

diffused rays of many separate beams of life fall into focus, with gains in both social effectiveness and significance. The city is the form and symbol of an integrated social relationship: it is the seat of the temple, the market, the hall of justice, the academy of learning. Here in the city the goods of civilization are multiplied and manifolded; here is where human experience is transformed into viable signs, symbols, patterns of conduct, systems of order. Here is where the issues of civilization are focused: here, too, ritual passes on occasion into the active drama of a fully differentiated and self-conscious society. (p. 3)

What makes cities so special? According to the most basic tenets of urban sociology, cities share a unique set of properties (Wirth 1938). First and foremost, they have very large populations. In the United States, the most populous city is New York, with 8.5 million people living in its five boroughs, followed by Los Angeles, Chicago, Houston, and Philadelphia. Second, the people who live in cities often reside in close proximity to one another in dense concentrations as measured by population density, or number of residents per square mile. This density is best expressed by the high-rise residential towers where urban dwellers cluster together in downtown and waterfront areas of major U.S. cities. Third, urban populations are known for their human diversity, attracting immigrants of different national, ethnic, and religious backgrounds from all over the world. Again, take New York: Its population is 29 percent Latino, 26 percent black, 13 percent Asian, and 4 percent multiracial.

These three characteristics (population size, density, and diversity) make cities vital engines for the production of creativity and its byproducts—art, music, entertainment, knowledge, technology—and for a number of reasons. Dense cities with a diverse population of largely anonymous residents tend to invite high levels of unconventional behavior. The German sociological thinker Georg Simmel (1903/1971, pp. 336–38) argues that the anonymity of cities encourages "the elaboration of personal peculiarities" and "the strangest eccentricities" among urban dwellers, simply as a means of expression for individuals living among the crowded masses. (Think of what street musicians and other public performers do for attention on city sidewalks and subway platforms.)

The size, density, and diversity of cities also encourage the formation of urban communities and other subcultures. As we discussed in Chapter 4, *subcultures* are collective social worlds that stand apart from the larger society in some distinctively patterned way, often by investing in alternative symbolic identities and styles of living. According to Claude S. Fischer (1975), a sociology professor at Berkeley, the massive and anonymous crowds of residents, commuters, and visitors that flood city centers give urban dwellers the incentive to pull together into social groups that serve as protective pockets of intimacy and camaraderie. The sheer population size of the city ensures that it will generate a large number or *multiplicity* of subcultures, and the diversity of cities promises an excessive *variety* among those subcultures. Meanwhile, the human density of heterogeneous residents tightly sequestered in local neighborhoods bolsters the *intensity* of such subcultures, as groups increasingly define themselves in relation to one another.

The large populations of cities also supply subcultures with a critical mass of participants necessary for their *vitality* and *longevity* over time. For example, Philadelphia, the fifth-largest city in the country, also has a significant African American population (44 percent), and perhaps for this reason it has given birth to three distinct traditions in black popular music: the hard bop jazz of the 1950s and 1960s (locals included John Coltrane, Hank Mobley, Jimmy Smith, and Clifford Brown); the 1970s soul music known as the "Philadelphia Sound" (exemplified by songs like Joe Simon's "Drowning in the Sea of Love," the O'Jays' "Backstabbers" and "For the Love of Money," and the theme song from the TV show *Soul Train*); and the 1990s neo-soul movement, an alternative hip-hop/rhythm-and-blues (R&B) hybrid genre that includes the Roots, Jill Scott, and others. Meanwhile, the white teen pop music of the 1950s was popularized by Dick Clark on *American Bandstand*, which was taped in a TV studio at 46th and Market streets in West Philadelphia, and many of its signature performers—Bobby Rydell, Fabian, Frankie Avalon—grew up in the same working-class Italian American neighborhoods of South Philadelphia (Hodos and Grazian 2005).

Cities also have the urban infrastructure necessary for cultural creativity to thrive. Cities have a high concentration of universities, art colleges, music conservatories, and other institutions of higher education and fine arts training. New York not only hosts two of the nation's great universities, Columbia University and NYU, but also esteemed theater and music conservatories (the Juilliard School, Manhattan School of Music, New York Conservatory of Dramatic Arts), schools of art (Pratt Institute, Parsons School of Design, the Cooper Union, School of Visual Arts), and even fashion schools (Fashion Institute of Technology, LIM College). New York also has an extensive community college and city- and state-funded university system, which connects creative young people of all class and ethnic backgrounds with the worlds of art, culture, and media in the city, including both immigrants and first-generation college students.

These schools attract musicians, actors, artists, writers, and other aspiring cultural creators from all over the world, many of whom remain in the city long after graduation. In search of affordable rents, they tend to cluster in peripheral inner-city areas, whether former manufacturing zones or working-class ethnic communities located near accessible subway lines. In New York, these once marginal neighborhoods have played an outsized role as both temporary enclaves for cash-poor artists and as sites for cultural rebellion, lifestyle experimentation, and the production and performance of alternative popular culture, art, music, and media. Since the 1970s and 1980s such hotspots in the city have included Manhattan's East Village and the Lower East Side (Smith 1996; Hoban 2004; Gendron 2006, pp. 51–55) and, more recently, Brooklyn neighborhoods like Williamsburg, Greenpoint, Dumbo, and Bushwick (Zukin 2010, pp. 35–61). The affordability of apartments and converted studio spaces in these mixed-income areas is matched by the glamour and authenticity that artistic scene-makers and young consumers attach to the grittiness of urban blight and decay on the fringes of the postindustrial city (Grazian 2003; Lloyd 2005; Zukin 2010). Like the city itself, these neighborhood

Street musicians perform in the middle of Bedford Avenue in Brooklyn's Williamsburg neighborhood, an ethnically diverse enclave known for its art shows, food festivals, and biergartens.

scenes are often prized for their tolerance of unconventional behavior, racial and sexual diversity, and late-night noise (Lena 2012, p. 36).

Given their high levels of cultural capital (Bourdieu 1984), creative young people subsequently make up a sizable proportion of the potential audience for the city's local subcultures and art worlds, and some of its creators as well. Along with tourists and other transplants to the city, they populate New York's many museums, art galleries, experimental theaters, concert halls, comedy clubs, and cultural festivals. Freelance workers and young professionals who work in media and other creative industries—advertising, architecture, graphic design, software development, publishing—similarly gravitate to cities like New York that feature a rich array of cultural and recreational amenities (Florida 2002). Media and culture-industry workers thrive in cities with a go-go 24/7 economy that never sleeps, and they draw energy from the eclecticism of street-level spaces of urban leisure and entertainment, including popular music venues, bustling coffee shops, local ethnic eateries, late-night cocktail bars, used bookstores, vintage clothing shops, crossfit gyms, and yoga studios.

This is not only the case for cultural capitals like New York, but more modest second-tier cities and college towns as well, such as Austin, Portland, Seattle, Denver, and Boulder. (Franklin & Marshall sociologist Jerome Hodos [2007] refers to these places as *second cities* to distinguish them from their more populous counterparts.) Again, Philadelphia provides an interesting example. Although not as culturally rich or economically wealthy as New York, Philadelphia's downtown Center City nevertheless boasts a young and educated population, with more than one-third (35 percent) of its residents between 25 and 34 years of age, 86 percent of whom are college graduates (Center City District and Central Philadelphia Development Corporation 2011, p. 5). Many of these young people intern or work in the city's growing media-intensive creative sector, and they make up an enthusiastic audience for Philadelphia's eclectic indie culture and entertainment offerings, especially given the city's abundance of funky gallery spaces, tiny music clubs, BYOB restaurants, art-house movie theaters, speakeasies, dive bars, and alternative or "fringe" performing arts festivals. They share their zeal with more than 120,000 college and university students who study in and around Center City, including students enrolled in local art colleges (Pennsylvania Academy of the Fine Arts, Moore College of Art and Design, University of the Arts, Temple University's Tyler School of Art) and music conservatories (Academy of Vocal Arts, Curtis Institute of Music).

Moreover, Philadelphia enjoys a significant advantage when it comes to retaining creative young people, many of whom are financially strapped musicians, artists, and graduate students who can ill afford New York's super-expensive rents. (The same could be said for San Francisco and the entire Silicon Valley area.) In fact, artists and other creative people living in New York frequently decamp for Philadelphia—not only to partake in its quirky cultural scenes but also to take advantage of its far less costly rents. For this reason, Philadelphia has been described as New York's "sixth borough," with a 37 percent lower cost of living (Pressler 2005, 2006). According to one Philly musician, a guitarist for an indie-rock band, "New York is mythologically all about vibrancy and creativity, but it's hard to work a 40-hour week and come home and be Jackson Pollack." In an interview with the *New York Times* he explained that "by living in Philadelphia he could support himself teaching public school and devote the rest of his time to his band" (Pressler 2005). The affordability of second cities like Philadelphia gives creative types the freedom to explore avant-garde and other experimental styles of art, media, and popular culture without worrying about going broke, at least not right away.

Collaboration and Creativity in Urban Life

Great cities from Rome to London to Chicago have always provided ample public spaces for friendly interaction and sociability among residents. In New York's Greenwich Village neighborhood, neighbors and tourists flock to Washington Square Park to enjoy its 9.75 acres of tree-lined walkways, comfortable benches, lawns, playgrounds, and central fountain. On weekends, street performers and characters entertain and amuse park dwellers. One musician plays classical compositions on the baby grand piano he regularly wheels out to the park for impromptu concerts. At the park's southeast corner, hustlers challenge passersby to low-stakes games of chess and give children quick lessons on the side. Small jazz combos and banjo players entertain curious listeners, while nearby a local man douses himself with birdseed to attract the dozens of pigeons constantly encircling his head and shoulders. Acrobatic dancers perform flips in the park's fountain for applause and spare change. These street characters encourage conversation and sociability among strangers and barely known acquaintances by providing what William H. Whyte (1980, p. 94) refers to as *triangulation* in urban public places—"that process by which some external stimulus provides a linkage between people and prompts strangers to talk to each other as though they were not." New York hosts countless numbers of small yet sociable public places like Washington Square Park, and so do other cities around the world.

In New York's Washington Square Park, dancers, musicians, hustlers, and colorful street characters of all stripes encourage sociability among strangers.

Not surprisingly, artists, novelists, and other creative people thrive in cities that afford such opportunities for sociability. During the 1920s a group of expatriate writers living in Paris, most notably Ernest Hemingway, Gertrude Stein, James Joyce, Ezra Pound, and F. Scott Fitzgerald, routinely shared ideas about writing while drinking carafes of wine in cafés, hotels, brasseries, and studio apartments. In his posthumously published memoir *A Moveable Feast*, Hemingway describes Paris as "the town best organized for a writer to write in that there is," in part because of its availability of book vendors, libraries, and quiet cafés convenient for writing, but also for the richly sociable spaces of the city where intellectual worlds flourish (1965, p. 180). Back in the United States, the poets, novelists, and storytellers of the 1940s and 1950s Beat Generation, including Allen Ginsberg, Jack Kerouac, William S. Burroughs, Herbert Huncke, and John Clellon Holmes, gathered at Columbia University, Times Square, and other sociable New York City outposts. Their experiments with marijuana and heroin, Eastern mysticism, jazz music, and sexuality found their way into their stunningly adventurous writing, particularly in works such as Ginsberg's *Howl*, Burroughs's *Naked Lunch* and *Junky*, and Kerouac's *On the Road*.

Like great literature, the production of popular culture also relies on the collective creativity generated by the social interaction and public life afforded by cities. In American jazz and blues music, the ritual of the jam session provides a fitting example. The jam session dates back to the 1920s when musicians would congregate in after-hours clubs in Chicago, New York, and other U.S. cities to practice their craft by improvising with fellow artists in noncommercial settings as an alternative to the concerts, dances, and other public appearances where they typically performed for paying audiences. Held in the backrooms and basements of intimate nightclubs and secret speakeasies, these jam sessions were gathering places for musicians where they played and experimented with new ideas, networked and talked shop with fellow performers, and competed for in-group status among their peers (DeVeaux 1997; Grazian 2008a). Its

Several Beat writers and artists at a diner in New York City in the late 1950s. Clockwise around the table, they are poet Gregory Corso (back of head to camera), painter and musician Larry Rivers, writer Jack Kerouac, musician David Amram, and poet Allen Ginsberg.

socializing function among artists led African American writer Ralph Ellison to celebrate the jam session in a 1959 essay for *Esquire* as the "jazzman's true academy." As he explains:

> It is here that he learns tradition, group techniques and style. For although since the twenties many jazzmen have had conservatory training and were well grounded in formal theory and instrumental technique, when we approach jazz we are entering quite a different sphere of training. Here it is more meaningful to speak, not of courses of study, of grades and degrees, but of apprenticeship, ordeals, initiation ceremonies, of rebirth. . . . His instructors are his fellow musicians, especially the acknowledged masters, and his recognition of manhood depends on their acceptance of his ability. . . . [The jam session is] a retreat, a homogeneous community where a collectivity of common experience could find continuity and meaningful expression. (1964/1995, pp. 208–9)

Elsewhere in his essay, Ellison pays tribute to the jazz greats of the 1940s who soloed and accompanied one another in the famous jam sessions at Minton's Playhouse on 118th Street in Harlem: Dizzy Gillespie, Charlie Parker, Thelonious Monk, Coleman Hawkins, Ben Webster, Roy Eldridge, Charlie Christian, and Lester Young. At New York jazz joints like Minton's, these legends collectively created the bebop sound more than 70 years ago. Even today, jazz and blues jam sessions provide opportunities for musicians to converge and perform together in an inviting environment that encourages risk-taking and experimentation.

This is especially the case in contemporary blues clubs in Chicago, where jam sessions continue to provide a collaborative context for musical creation among a racially diverse mix of strangers. In many ways, it is the cultural conventions of the blues genre itself—a reliance on traditional blues scales, chord progressions, harmonies, time signatures, stanza lengths, norms of improvisation, and a repertoire of standards—that reduce the potential for confusion that might otherwise arise among musicians playing together for the first time (Grazian 2008a, p. 53). In my book *Blue Chicago* I describe the collaborative and supportive nature of one such jam session held weekly at a local blues club where I occasionally sat in as a young saxophone player in my early 20s:

> Sequestered at bar stools near the right side of the stage, brass and woodwind players congregate, harmonize softly to accompany the band, and switch off taking solos at the horn microphone. Their interactions provide opportunities for the passage of advice among musicians of varying degrees of ability. I experience such an encounter one night when I assist James, a black semiprofessional trumpet player and regular at the jam, by helping provide harmonic accompaniment to the band's performance. At the stage James asks me to follow his lead and begins to play off the major third, which I simply imitate until the song's completion. . . . We begin chatting about music and harmony, and he suggests that we play the same rhythmic part to lend a strong accompanying base to the musicians onstage. He then runs down a chromatic scale of successive notes on his horn. (A typical chromatic scale consists of twelve tones played at half-step intervals in ascending or descending order. For example, the chromatic scale in C major includes the following notes: C-C♯-D-E♭-E-F-F♯-G-G♯-A-B♭-B.) As I echo James's trumpet by singing the notes aloud, he continues his impromptu lesson: "See, that's your best teacher, right there. You've got to sing it to yourself, and then you play it. . . ." We begin playing to the music, and suddenly he stops to implore: "Here, see, follow me. Listen!" and he holds the root note of the first chord of the progression, and then continues, "Then we just play down the chromatic scale, like this. . . . Yeah, that's it . . . you've got it!" (Grazian 2003, pp. 107–8)

A similar kind of collaborative scene exists among amateur rappers at an open-mic workshop called Project Blowed in South Central Los Angeles. According to University of Toronto sociologist Jooyoung Lee (2016, p. 56), the workshop serves as "a vehicle for friendships, creative collaboration, and mentoring," although it also challenges rappers to develop their songwriting and stagecraft skills, or else endure being publicly shamed by a more experienced performer. With the audience demanding an ill-prepared rapper to "Please pass the mic!", the event's host advised, "*Get your bars up*, homie! Get a beat, write some lyrics, and practice your hooks! . . . How do you expect to get better if nobody tells you that you wack?" (pp. 48–50).

Just as the cafés of Paris provided an arena for provocative debate among expatriate American writers such as Hemingway and Fitzgerald, today's urban nighttime hotspots from the Chicago blues jam to Project Blowed similarly serve as meeting grounds for cultural creators who live and work in cities. In *The Warhol Economy*, USC urban planning professor Elizabeth Currid-Halkett (2007) illustrates how New York artists, musicians, fashion designers, and other makers of pop culture interact with one another in Chelsea art galleries, Williamsburg rock clubs, and East Village cocktail lounges. Crowded DJ nights, art openings, and fashion show after-parties provide a dynamic backdrop where creative people discuss their work, share innovative ideas, and build trusting collaborative relationships. As Currid-Halkett reveals in a chapter fittingly titled "The Economics of a Dance Floor," urban nightlife scenes are also ideal contexts for developing contacts with cultural creators across social networks, particularly within industries that reward artistic workers who can successfully bridge otherwise divergent commercial fields, whether music composition, photography, acting, digital animation, new media production, book publishing, graphic arts, or film editing. Of course, these nightlife zones of creativity are not particular to New York but thrive in other urban centers of art and pop cultural production as well, including Los Angeles, Chicago, Miami, San Francisco, and many others.

Landscapes of Urban Entertainment

The last decades of the twentieth century marked a tremendous shift in the organization of urban life, particularly as cities formerly known for industrial manufacturing like Chicago and Philadelphia were transformed into centers of cultural consumption—retail, entertainment, tourism, and leisure. Downtown areas and their public spaces strongly reflect the urban renaissance experienced by many American cities during the 1990s, as illustrated by the rise of flagship stores, gaming arcades, multiplex theaters, and tourist attractions. The new urban landscape evokes a notable overindulgence in branding among franchised outposts—Nike, J Crew, Toys 'R' Us, Dave & Buster's, Banana Republic, Foot Locker, Old Navy, Williams-Sonoma. (In fact, many such outposts do little more than celebrate trademarked popular culture itself, including Disney's ESPN Zone and the Bubba Gump Shrimp Company, the latter inspired by Robert Zemeckis's 1994 Oscar-winning film *Forrest Gump*.)

These sites of popular cultural consumption often are clustered in *urban entertainment districts* developed as part of a larger strategy of city growth and renewal (Hannigan 1998). Perhaps the most famous urban entertainment district in the country, Times Square in Midtown Manhattan attracts 50 million visitors a year. Although once filled with seedy XXX theaters and peep shows, Times Square today features gigantic digital billboards, live Disney productions of *The Lion King* and *Aladdin*, and family-friendly retail including Hershey's Chocolate World, M&M World, Kellogg's NYC, and the Disney Store. Costumed characters dressed as Batman, Spider-Man, Elmo, Minnie Mouse, and Elsa pose for photographs for tips in designated areas along Broadway. A world-famous icon of urban culture, every New Year's Eve one million spectators crowd around

In Times Square in Midtown Manhattan, tourists can take in a Broadway show, visit branded restaurants like the Bubba Gump Shrimp Company, or just mill about among the towering digital billboards and take pictures with costumed characters from Elmo to Elsa.

One Times Square and its surrounding streets to behold its Waterford crystal ball's annual descent during the last moments of the year as more than a billion viewers watch on television.

Urban entertainment districts typically feature the same retail and restaurant chains in cities across the country, making such city spaces feel homogenous and cookie-cutter rather than locally distinctive. For example, Chicago's North Michigan Avenue, famously known as the city's "Magnificent Mile," today features many of the exact same stores—Brooks Brothers, the North Face, Uniqlo, Ann Taylor, Vince, True Religion, Under Armour, Gap—that appear along Walnut Street in Philadelphia's Center City shopping district. The same could be said of urban entertainment districts that emerge along waterfronts from Cleveland to California. The revitalization of the nation's once decrepit ports represents a major effort to sanitize the American city of its blue-collar past by replacing its now-defunct shipbuilding, fishing, and transport industries with shopping malls and pop-cultural amusements. Baltimore's Inner Harbor today features Oriole Park at Camden Yards, the National Aquarium, the American Visionary Art Museum, shopping at H&M and Urban Outfitters, and mass-produced dining at Johnny Rockets, Cheesecake Factory, Hooters, and the Bubba Gump Shrimp Company. Chicago's Navy Pier features the Chicago Shakespeare Theater, Chicago Children's Museum, a 150-foot-high Ferris wheel, an IMAX theater, a six-story indoor botanical garden, and a bevy of branded attractions: its Pepsi

Baltimore's Inner Harbor has been wiped clean of its blue-collar past and now offers attractions such as an aquarium, an art museum, shopping, and chain restaurants.

Skyline Stage, Miller Light Beer Garden, McDonald's, Starbucks, and, naturally, another Bubba Gump Shrimp Company. As a tourist attraction, San Francisco's Fisherman's Wharf relies on refurbished cobblestones and nautically themed details to accentuate its distinctive history as the primary hub for the city's still-active fishing industry. Still, its crowded walkways resemble almost any other waterfront shopping mall, with corporate tenants that include Macy's, Hard Rock Café, Rainforest Café, Applebee's, Ben & Jerry's, and—yes!—the Bubba Gump Shrimp Company.

Amid this consumerist landscape in cities across the globe lurks the spectacle of the new urban nightlife, a bonanza of gentrified entertainment zones, velvet-roped nightclubs, and high-concept restaurants. These places tend to be highly stylized, demonstrating a concern with aesthetic imagery and playful design, and the restaurants of Philadelphia's nightlife scene provide an excellent case study. The Old City section of downtown Philadelphia features a set of commercial blocks lined with hip restaurants and nightclubs. At the intersection of Second and Market Streets sits the neighborhood's crown jewel, the Continental Restaurant and Martini Bar, its interior lit by halogen lamps shaped like giant Spanish olives. At Continental, attractive female servers present guests with fusion dishes splashed with curry, lime, coconut, and soy, and a limitless array of designer cocktails, including the White Chocolate Martini sprinkled with white crème de cacao and a Hershey's Kiss, and the Dean Martini served with a Lucky Strikes cigarette and matchbook (Grazian 2008b, p. 11).

Many of Philadelphia's most glamorous restaurants evoke a theatrical spectacle of global cosmopolitanism and myth. Morimoto features a cavernous dining room that beckons all comers like an ethereal banquet hall, a palace of dreams. Named for its executive chef and part-owner Masaharu Morimoto—better known as one of the culinary stars of cable television's *Iron Chef*—the most renowned Japanese restaurant in the city is bathed in light, from its 3-D lenticular hologram that greets patrons at the door to the sprightly lit dining booths that turn various shades of Technicolor neon as the evening progresses (Grazian 2005). Conceived by industrial designer Karim Rashid, the interior décor features a rolling ceiling of compressed bamboo rods: a larger-than-life-sized sushi mat built from 70 tons of wood (Quinn 2002). At Buddakan, an extravagantly ornamented pan-Asian restaurant, a foreboding 16-foot gilded statue of the great Buddha himself overlooks all patrons, emphasizing the relationship between decadent gastronomy and dramatic style in the postmodern global city. Across town at Pod, a pan-Asian hideaway near the University of Pennsylvania campus, the space-age interior evokes the futuristic chill of Stanley Kubrick's *2001: A Space Odyssey* (1968) and *A Clockwork Orange* (1971). Mechanized conveyor belts transport sashimi and spring rolls around the bar while customers fiddle with the fluorescent lights in their groovy booths that recall the Orgasmatron from Woody Allen's *Sleeper* (1973).

The many allusions to pop culture, cinema, and the theater in these nightlife spaces are not accidental. A former nightclub owner and concert promoter, *Bon Appétit* magazine's 2005 Restaurateur of the Year Stephen Starr—the creator of Continental, Buddakan, Morimoto, and Pod—specializes in branding high-concept dining as a theatrical event to be enjoyed as a total experience, a heady concoction of sight and sound, buzz and light. In this regard, he is as much a showman and entertainer as a businessperson: In fact, he refers to his dining customers as his "audience." As he told *Philadelphia* magazine, "I want people to feel like they're not in Philadelphia or near their home . . . when they come to one of my places. Let's face it—life is pretty mundane. . . . So I want their night out to feel like they're getting away. I'm selling the experience" (Platt 2000). Built as elaborate stage sets, each of Starr's stylized restaurants conjures up an imaginative fantasy world of trendy eclecticism and exotic delight.

If Pod makes the diner feel enveloped by a Tokyo sci-fi dreamworld, then Cuba Libre Restaurant and Rum Bar evokes

Morimoto, a Japanese restaurant in downtown Philadelphia, emphasizes theatricality and imaginative style.

the sultry paradise of 1950s Havana and its beach resorts and sidewalk cafés—or at least the Havana longingly conjured up in nostalgic films like *The Godfather, Part II* (1974) and *Before Night Falls* (2000). The dining mezzanine is designed as a tiled rooftop garden overlooking a faux outdoor streetscape replete with hanging flora, stained-glass windows, iron railings, and terra-cotta balconies. According to Danny Lake, a local publicist for various nightspots around Philadelphia, the cinematic metaphor is more than fitting to describe Cuba Libre. Its fabricated interior was constructed by a movie set designer and inspired by stock images of Cuba culled from various websites. As Lake explains in my book on urban nightlife, *On the Make*:

> Cuba Libre decided to build their brand to look like buildings in Cuba, to look old. And, you know, we had really serious issues. . . . Do we want to disclose how we made this brand look aged when it was brand-new? Because we used some interesting building materials: *Styrofoam*. The destination's built by a guy who owns a company called Dynamic Imagineering, and he builds movie sets. And it looks like a movie set (especially if you go back in, and now that I have told you that, you can see how it does), or like, I hate to use this word, but maybe like something you'd see in Disney—the street scene, the images, the crumbling planters, and the lush palms. . . . We went to salvage yards to find the wrought-iron gates that we had used for both the railings and part of the décor. And we did it this way because our research primarily on the Internet showed us images that looked just like this. (Grazian 2008b, pp. 32—33)

It is no coincidence that Lake invokes the magic of Disney to describe Cuba Libre. Through its many famous themed environments (Magic Kingdom, Epcot's World Showcase, Disney's Hollywood Studios, Animal Kingdom, Celebration), the Disney Corporation has led the way in creating artificially produced entertainment landscapes that prioritize simulated realities over seemingly authentic experiences (Zukin 1991, 1995; Sorkin 1992). The high-concept interiors of exclusive restaurant and nightclub spaces like Morimoto and Cuba Libre are similarly shaped by the aesthetic theatricality of the stage and cinema. Complicated lighting schemes strategically create shadow and aura, making up the most significant décor component of urban nightlife establishments. The muted lighting of nightclubs and restaurants also hides the weaknesses inherent in aesthetically pleasing designs featuring low-grade materials such as Styrofoam. As Jason, a Philadelphia bartender, explains, "The bars, when you see them with the lights on, they are nothing special. You are seeing behind the curtain at that point, because nobody is spending a lot of money on real quality construction or anything. . . . It's exactly like a movie set; so when you dim the lights, you are also hiding some of the flaws."

He explains that flimsy construction materials are not the only imperfections that remain hidden in the dimmed glow of dance clubs and cocktail lounges:

> Well, you are hiding the flaws. That's why you don't do direct lighting in the first place. You don't want to show off flaws in the location *or the people who are there*. So bars are dark. You get an *impression* of someone; you don't

get an actual look at someone. That's why anybody who has been at a bar when they turn the lights on has seen that it is not as pretty as it was ten minutes ago. . . . You do it for effect. (p. 36)

Of course, the so-called flaws of an unattractive clientele pale in comparison to the unsanitary conditions concealed behind the façades of Philadelphia's hottest restaurants and nightclubs. As a rule, restaurants try to keep the messy work of food preparation out of their patrons' line of sight, and even dining establishments with exhibition-style kitchens keep their dry-goods closets, staff locker rooms, roach spray, and mousetraps out of view—and much more, as it turns out. According to the Philadelphia Department of Health, local restaurants and nightclubs that received "foodborne illness risk" health code violations in the last few years include both Cuba Libre and Continental.

Urban retailers adopt similarly tactical staging and lighting techniques, including a strategy of *adjacent attraction* in which dissimilar objects are placed next to each other so consumers might identify them as parts of a whole (Crawford 1992, p. 14). At Urban Outfitters, old-school Atari 2600 video game machines and cheap couches are placed next to skateboarding shoes, retro bell-bottom jeans, bike-messenger shoulder bags, and snarky T-shirts, conjuring up a stage set of a super-hip teenager's room. Starbucks surrounds its packages of coffee beans with posters of the African landscape and other exotic climes. Barnes and Noble relies on cappuccino bars and plush armchairs to add an ambience of luxury and sophistication to its bookstores. In many ways, the book-lined walls themselves serve as little more than a backdrop for the main attraction: the best-sellers promoted on tables placed prominently at the front of their stores. As for the great majority of titles on display (of which most superstores sell fewer than two copies a year), the book industry disparagingly refers to the bulk of its merchandise as "wallpaper," as mere scenery (Miller 2007, p. 78).

Retail chains also use in-store music soundtracks to associate their merchandise with hi-fidelity style. Brooks Brothers plays elegant jazz ballads by Billie Holiday, Ella Fitzgerald, Dinah Washington, and Sarah Vaughan to give customers the feel of a cocktail soirée where their new blazers and ties will be the hit of the party. The Gap in-store playlist includes songs by Ed Sheeran, Maroon 5, John Legend, Charli XCX, and Pharrell Williams. American Apparel has its own Internet radio station, Viva Radio, which provides all its in-house selections from indie rock to dance music.

Retailers additionally rely on an entire science of shopping and consumption that consultants like Paco Underhill have spent the last several years developing by drawing on intensive fieldwork and human observation in shopping environments all over the world. In his eye-opening book *Why We Buy*, Underhill (2009) reveals how retail districts can be engineered to deliver their optimum purchasing potential. It begins outside the store itself, where retailers hope to attract passersby. Pedestrians typically move at a quick clip down the street, and to stop they must downshift to a lower speed, much like a car does. Once a customer enters a store, it takes them a few seconds to slow down and become fully acclimated to the lighting, temperature, and scale of its interior, which means that anything on display in the area that Underhill calls the "decompression zone" immediately inside the front door usually goes completely unnoticed by the consumer. Also, in part because Americans drive on the right side of the road, we almost always reflexively turn to the right when we enter a place of business. Retailers familiar with these behavioral patterns typically organize their shop floors accordingly by placing their most important merchandise, or at least those goods that require "100 percent shopper exposure," just beyond the decompression zone, on the right-hand side of the doorway (p. 80).

Underhill also observes that the longer customers spend shopping, the greater their chances of making a purchase. As a result, retailers rely on all sorts of tricks to increase the duration of time consumers spend in their stores. Supermarkets keep their dairy cases against the back wall, which forces consumers to walk past aisles of groceries and back again during even quick trips to the store for milk (p. 85). For the same reason, chain drugstores place their pharmacy counters toward the back area of their stores. In the interests of pulling (or trapping) consumers deeper into their cavernous spaces packed with merchandise, urban department stores often hide their restrooms in isolated corners, away from entrances and exits, and ascending and descending escalators are frequently kept at opposite ends of shopping mall corridors—all to ensure ever more foot traffic past yet another Banana Republic, another Burberry, another Jamba Juice.

The Hidden Labor of Urban Entertainment

Among the staging techniques designed to woo cultural consumers in urban retail shops, department stores, restaurants, and nightclubs, none are nearly as problematic as those involving human labor. At retail stores, much of this work is handled backstage in stockrooms, sometimes until 2 a.m. Clothing retailers usually invite consumers to fondle their tactile fabrics because when they interact with merchandise in a sensuous manner, they are more likely to purchase it (Underhill 2009, p. 172). Consequently, store workers—typically young people in their teens or 20s—spend their days and often late nights painstakingly refolding, straightening, and stacking up brightly colored sweaters and T-shirts on easy-to-reach counters. Sociologist Sharon Zukin (2004, p. 202) compares these irresistibly attractive piles of pink, violet, and crimson cashmere and cotton to "gumdrops in a candy store"—they are the product of excessive and tedious workloads performed largely by adolescents for little pay. One strategy for easing the workload is to stack sweaters in darker shades on top of lighter ones, making it easier to mask their grubbiness after hours of customer abuse (Underhill 2009, p. 190). Still, these notoriously unstable retail jobs require employees to stand on their feet for entire shifts, all for low wages and limited work hours without benefits. In fact, most brand-name companies in the retail service sector pay only minimum wage or else slightly more (Klein 2002, p. 236). (As of October 2016, the U.S. federal minimum wage was $7.25 per hour, although some states and cities mandate a higher minimum wage.)

It is perhaps a cliché but nevertheless true that after moving to the city, many struggling actors, musicians, dancers, models, artists, and other cultural performers wind up working day jobs in service positions in retail, dining, and urban entertainment. It is therefore unsurprising that these jobs require workers to draw on their performance skills when dealing with customers. According to Jason, the aforementioned bartender, "You are acting. . . . If you are a server, you are acting. You are going up to a table and putting on a performance. You have a captive audience of six people or whatever, and they have all eyes on you. So you are onstage—your environment is the stage."

Indeed, the youthful employees of branded companies like Zara, American Eagle, Urban Outfitters, H&M, American Apparel, and Gap not only fold clothes and ring up packages: They are the embodied representatives of the brand itself. At Abercrombie & Fitch, the clothier has long required its workers to adhere to the guidelines catalogued in its employee style guide regarding personal appearance and assigned positions on the sales floor on the basis of attractiveness (Meyers 2008). In 2013, female employees were instructed to choose a "nude bra or white strappy tank" when selecting "the right underlayer" to wear at work, and to "unbutton the top three buttons" when wearing a collared denim shirt (Maheshwari 2013). The British magazine *New Statesman* confirms that many retail stores "only hire beautiful people." According to contributor Harriet Williamson (2014), "The likes of American Apparel and Abercrombie & Fitch expect their sales staff to conform to a narrow conception of beauty, sometimes even calling them 'models' so they can reject those whose faces don't fit." The Center for Popular Democracy reports that at Zara, "Lighter-skinned workers of color and white employees tend to have higher status assignments, more work hours, and a stronger likelihood of being promoted" (Feldman 2015).

The expectations of service personnel in nightlife settings are also prefigured within commonplace ideals of beauty and sexual magnetism, particularly among women. According to Allison, a hostess and cocktail waitress in Philadelphia, female job applicants are often immediately flagged by the staff on the basis of their attractiveness and on-the-spot demeanor. "As a hired hostess, if someone fills out an application, we are permitted to write 'NRL' on the top—*Not Right Look*," she reveals. "They have to have the right look, everything from what you wear when you walk in to how you approach" (Grazian 2008b, p. 54).

Abercrombie & Fitch has been accused of hiring its young job recruits on the basis of their looks.

The mandatory uniforms often worn by young cocktail waitresses emphasize their sexuality as well, even to the point of discomfort:

> We have tight, black, long-sleeved crewneck shirts. . . . You wear your own black skirt. It has to be a skirt, no pants. . . . At first, I just wore the short skirt like everyone else did, and opaque tights, and that was fine. In the lounge at [a downtown bar and restaurant], the tables are really low, like, less than two feet off the ground. And it gets really busy, like standing-room only almost, and you have to fight to get through the crowds with your tray of these martini glasses. I mean, you don't want to spill all over everybody, so what you have to do is either bend over and wear shorts underneath your skirt or just squat like a catcher, put your drinks down, and then pick them back up. . . .
>
> One of my biggest issues is having to squat down and serve someone, and there are some people that really eat it up. Like they just know you are serving them and they are in love with it. . . . So at first I started with the short skirt, and then I didn't like the way that people would look at me and watch. . . . I would see guys leering . . . or guys would, you know . . . you see people looking at you and talking. And guys would try and talk to me. . . . They were always asking if I had a boyfriend, and then you are trying to remain professional and keep walking. . . . I switched to a skirt that went below my knees, and I made a lot less money. (quoted in Grazian 2008b, pp. 48−49)

As Allison's experience makes clear, worker-unfriendly dress codes often place heavy burdens on female service personnel by pigeonholing them into sexualized roles that invite ogling and unwanted attention from boorish men.

As embodied brand representatives, both retail and nightlife workers also engage in what sociologist Arlie Russell Hochschild (1983) refers to as *emotional labor*, in which workers manage and manipulate the outward display of their feelings as a controlled performance, all for the benefit of paying customers or clients. In retail settings, emotional labor involves greeting shoppers with a cheerful smile, complimenting their selections with enthusiasm—"That looks *fabulous* on you!"—and begging for their quick return. In nightlife settings, the emotional labor required of typically female servers and hostesses includes handling rude and suggestive comments from slobbering male patrons with playful come-ons and tactful wit, all while balancing unwieldy cocktails on small trays for hours on end (Grazian 2008b, p. 86). As Jason recalls from his years of bartending, "I can't necessarily say everything that's popping into my head. . . . Like I could be pissed off at the bar back for not getting me beer, but that's not going to come out onstage—that's behind the stage." (Caitlin, a former restaurant server, shares Jason's experience: "The worst is people that tell really dumb jokes and you have to laugh.")

The emotional labor required of nightlife workers also includes adherence to scripted guidelines for interacting with customers. Some restaurants have a "two-foot rule" that requires all personnel to greet any patron within a two-foot perimeter, no matter how inconvenient it might be. According to the employee manual used by one Philadelphia restaurant, "Smile easy and often. Smiling is a very big part of our business. Be ready with that smile at all times. Smile whenever you make eye contact." "Do not discuss money or tips during service or in front of the kitchen." Workers are also reminded to "avoid the word 'I'—use words like 'Our,' 'We,' and 'Us,'" and to offer guests a "genuine" farewell upon their departure (p. 50).

The Celebrity City

The rise of urban entertainment districts reflects how urban areas attempt to position themselves favorably within the global tourism economy. This often requires cities to market themselves in ways that emphasize their singularity and thus attractiveness in the public imagination as places of cultural authenticity and prestige (Grazian 2003). Memphis promotes itself on the basis of its music legacy, which draws tourists to the former recording studios of Sun Records and Stax Records, Elvis Presley's Graceland estate, and the blues clubs that line the city's famous Beale Street. Nashville similarly draws on its pop cultural heritage as the nation's capital of country music production to attract tourists and their dollars—they flock to the Country Music Hall of Fame Museum, the record companies along Music Row, the Grand Ole Opry and the Ryman Auditorium, the CMA Music Festival Fan Fair, and rowdy honky-tonks like Tootsie's Orchid Lounge. Even post—Hurricane Katrina, New Orleans still draws visitors to its French Quarter and raucous Bourbon Street, Mardi Gras parades, and annual springtime Jazz and Heritage Festival.

Of course, the celebrity reputation of cities and their attractions also owes a great deal to their symbolic characterization in media and popular culture itself. Songs celebrate the exciting pulse of urban life in bustling metropolitan capitals. "Chicago is my kind of razzmatazz/And it has all that jazz," Frank Sinatra boasts in "My Kind of Town," and praises New York as "a city that never sleeps!" in "New York, New York"—just as Taylor Swift announces, "I could dance to this beat forever more!" in her 2014 hit "Welcome to New York." Movies that take place in New York often open with establishing aerial shots of the Manhattan skyline, just as films set in Los Angeles appropriate the city's famous Hollywood sign and palm tree—lined streets in Beverly Hills. These place markers operate as a kind of visual shorthand for audiences, just as B-roll footage of the Golden Gate Bridge demarcates San Francisco and the Gateway Arch identifies St. Louis in television and film (Wohl and Strauss 1958, pp. 525—6). Once established, these iconic images not only symbolize cities onscreen but also on T-shirts, baseball caps, postcards, bumper stickers, children's coloring books, souvenir coffee mugs, and all other pop artifacts of a city's local urban culture (Suttles 1984).

Iconic urban scenes from classic popular movies—King Kong climbing the Empire State Building, Audrey Hepburn's Holly Golightly window shopping on Fifth Avenue in the 1961 movie *Breakfast at Tiffany's*, Woody Allen and

Diane Keaton sitting on a park bench overlooking the Queensboro Bridge in the 1983 film *Manhattan*—also draw audiences to their real-life locations. Katz's Delicatessen on New York's Lower East Side owes its popularity among tourists in part to an infamous scene between Billy Crystal and Meg Ryan (in which Ryan's character simulates an orgasm over lunch) in Rob Reiner's 1989 film *When Harry Met Sally*. Although the NBC TV sitcoms *Friends* and *Seinfeld* were both directed on stage sets in Los Angeles, both take place in New York and rely on establishment shots filmed on location in Manhattan. *Friends* fans from around the world therefore take selfies in front of a six-story walk-up at the corner of Bedford and Grove in the West Village because it was used for the establishing shot representing Monica and Rachel's apartment building during the series' 10-year run. Further uptown, *Seinfeld* fans can pretend to eat at the fictional "Monk's Café," the coffee shop where Jerry and George while away the hours, week after week. The establishing shot of Monk's is the exterior of a real-life diner called Tom's Restaurant, located on Manhattan's Upper West Side at 112th Street and Broadway. (Weirdly, by the time *Seinfeld* premiered in 1989, Tom's Restaurant had already become famous, having been featured in the 1987 pop song "Tom's Diner" by Suzanne Vega a few years earlier.)

At times, the pop cultural iconography of an urban location can surpass the original significance of the site. Founded in 1877, the Philadelphia Museum of Art houses world-renowned paintings by Hieronymus Bosch, El Greco, Peter

Seinfeld fans trek to the Upper West Side of Manhattan to check out Tom's Restaurant, which served as the exterior of the fictional Monk's Café.

Paul Rubens, Claude Monet, Paul Cézanne, Vincent Van Gogh, Pablo Picasso, and Marcel Duchamp. Yet most visitors to the museum come not for the art but to sprint up its 72 steps in homage to the fictional boxer Rocky Balboa as played by Sylvester Stallone in the 1977 film *Rocky* (and its six sequels). Balboa ends his inspirational training runs by climbing the six-flight staircase of the museum and taking a congratulatory leap at its summit. The enthusiasm among tourists making the climb up what are colloquially called the "Rocky Steps" is palpable and infectious, as observed by Penn sociology graduate student Elizabeth Jacobs (2016) one autumn morning:

> A group of four women in their late twenties or early thirties, all wearing sunglasses, make their way up the steps. They stop on the third flight and start posing for pictures. (Most groups stop around this halfway point.) One woman then pulls out her selfie stick, and summons her three friends to get close. They take off again for the final three flights at a sprint, seemingly filming their run from the vantage point of the selfie stick. When they get to the top step they pause for a minute, and one woman breaks away from the group, pulling out her digital camera. As she moves to begin taking her own pictures, her friend with the selfie stick pokes her in the back and waves her in for *another* group shot with the selfie stick. The woman with the digital camera pauses for a second, hesitates, and then joins the group. They pose for pictures from every possible angle—facing the art museum, facing the skyline, some with their faces directed at the camera, and some with their backs to the camera. *Hands in the air, just like Rocky.* At this point, the woman with the digital camera walks away, about five paces, and begins to take her own pictures with her own camera. Her friend with the selfie stick quickly puts the device down, and asks the camera-holding woman to take a picture of her on her own. They take the same combination of angles and perspectives that the group took. The group stands around at the top of the steps for about ten more minutes (probably half an hour start to finish), chatting and drinking water, before walking down the steps, stopping for more pictures along the way.

This incessant desire to visually document our urban tourism experiences—in part to post the evidence of our adventures on social media—extends to many other cultural pursuits in the city, from "foodspotting" our restaurant dinner plates and gourmet food-truck photos on Facebook to chronicling our nightlife exploits on Instagram and Snapchat. In fact, digital social media platforms play a role in further extending the celebrity reputations of cities, especially global capitals like New York, Paris, London, and Singapore. (According to Synthesio, a technology firm specializing in Internet analytics, the city of Paris has four times as many Facebook fans as it does actual Parisian residents, and every six seconds someone tweets about the Statue of Liberty in New York Harbor.) In our final chapter, we turn to a more elaborate discussion of global cities and the globalization of media and popular culture.

The Dubai Mall, in the United Arab Emirates, boasts more than 1,200 retail stores and over 200 eateries, an aquarium, an indoor SEGA theme park, a 22-screen theater, an Olympic-sized ice-skating rink, and a five-star hotel.

pop goes the world

THE GLOBALIZATION OF MEDIA AND POPULAR CULTURE

AT 4.2 MILLION TOTAL SQUARE FEET, THE MALL OF AMERICA IN Bloomington, Minnesota, is a pop cultural marvel by any measure. The Mall attracts 40 million visitors a year; it boasts 520 stores, an indoor NASCAR motor speedway, and a four-story LEGO Imagination Center. Its Nickelodeon Universe, where kids can meet Dora the Explorer, SpongeBob SquarePants, and the Teenage Mutant Ninja Turtles, is a seven-acre theme park that features more than 27 rides, including five roller coasters. If that is not enough, there is also an A.C.E.S. Flight Simulation, an Underwater Adventures Aquarium stocked with 4,500 sharks and other sea creatures, a Moose Mountain 18-hole miniature golf course, and a 14-screen multiplex movie theater. The Mall's themed restaurants, which include Hard Rock Café, American Girl Bistro, Benihana, Rainforest Café, and Hooters, are as well-known as its four anchors: Bloomingdale's, Macy's, Nordstrom, and Sears.

It may seem like nothing could be more American than a suburban megamall loaded with department stores, novelty shops, theme parks, food courts, mass media amusements, and throngs of consumer shoppers. Yet not one of the 15 largest shopping malls in the world (based on gross leasable area) is located in the United States, or even North America. In fact, they are all located in Asia: China, the Philippines, Iran, Malaysia, Thailand, Bangladesh, and South Korea. The most capacious is the New South China Mall in Dongguan, China, which features more than 1,000 stores and 7.1 million square feet of leasable retail space. It has seven themed areas evoking Amsterdam, Paris, Rome, Venice, Egypt, the Caribbean, and California. It includes replicas of Paris's Arc de Triomph, a mile-long Venetian canal with gondolas, and a 1,800-foot roller coaster. (Meanwhile, the largest mall in the world by *total* area is also in Asia—the Dubai Mall in the United Arab Emirates. At 12.1 million square feet, the Dubai Mall boasts 1,200 shops, including the world's largest candy store. It also houses the Dubai Aquarium and Underwater Zoo, an ice rink, a SEGA Republic indoor theme park, a 250-room luxury hotel, 120 restaurants, and 14,000 parking spaces.)

Popular consumer culture in all its manifestations—gaudy shopping malls, themed entertainment, extreme branding—is truly a global phenomenon in the new millennium. In *The Global Soul*, the travel writer Pico Iyer (2001) describes the cosmopolitanism of a mall complex in Hong Kong:

> We could order room service, I was told, from a hotel with 565 rooms next door, or from one with 604 rooms next to it; we could order food from the other hotel in the complex, which had 512 rooms. . . . Beneath us, in the area known as Admiralty, were the trappings of the new Empire—a four-story shopping mall (called simply—definitely—the Mall), where shiny signs pointed towards the Atrium, The United Center, One Pacific Place and

Two. "The thing about this place," Richard said to me as I slipped in and out of time zones, "is that you've got a miniairport on the ground floor, where you can check in for all Cathay flights. There's a Seibu department store on Level Two, where you can buy everything you want. My bank's next to the elevator, and the Immigration Office is next to my office. You never really have to leave the building."

There were four cinemas in the Mall where we were sleeping, more than twenty places in which to eat, and fully ninety-seven boutiques (Gucci, Guess, Valentino, Vuitton; Boss, Hugo Boss, the Armani Exchange). There was access to the MTR subway, to the Far East Finance Center, and to a car park. There were the great department stores of Britain, Hong Kong, and Japan. "A world of delights," as the literature announced, "under one roof." (pp. 81–82, 85)

A world of delights, indeed. *Globalization* refers to today's heightened mobility of people, money, goods, culture, and media across international borders. There is nothing necessarily new about the concept of globalization—after all, the world has experienced international mercantilism and commerce for hundreds of years, along with mass human migrations, the slave trade and the imperial subjugation of colonized peoples, and two world wars. But globalization in the new millennium represents an intensification of worldwide networks, markets, and exchanges that have truly revolutionized the culture of everyday life around the globe and, as we will discuss at the conclusion of this chapter, the environmental future of the planet.

We might point to three dramatic changes that have brought about the current era of globalization. First, efficiencies in *transportation* have made international shipping, travel, and migration easier than ever, allowing manufacturers and merchants to exchange goods across oceans, families to lead transnational lives in two or more countries simultaneously, tourists to experience different cultures around the world, and scholars to attend universities and conferences abroad. Second, technological advances in *communication* allow friends and colleagues to forge personal connections over e-mail, text, and Skype within seconds, thus enabling us to maintain network ties and even intimate relationships once limited by geographic distance (Wellman 1979). Digital networks give consumers access to electronic media—in word, image, and sound—from all over the world, including news and entertainment. These networks also allow for new and efficient forms of online commerce and exchange between businesses and customers. (I am old enough to remember an age when airline tickets had to be purchased through travel agents; checking-account transfers had to be made in person with a bank teller; books, clothing, and groceries had to be purchased in a brick-and-mortar retail store; and apartment hunting required scouring through classified ads in a newspaper, to say nothing of searching for a job, used car, or a blind date.) These newer online forms of exchange also include the emergent "sharing" economy made possible by global Internet platforms such as Uber and Airbnb. (As of 2016, Uber was active in 527 cities in 77 countries.)

Finally, these technological changes have been strengthened by new *legalistic and organizational frameworks* that allow for trade, governance, and cooperation across international borders. They include multilateral trade partnerships such as the North American Free Trade Agreement (NAFTA) and the European Union (EU) and regulatory authorities such as the World Trade Organization (WTO). They also include multinational corporations such as Apple and McDonald's and nongovernmental organizations (NGOs) such as the World Wildlife Fund, Oxfam, Amnesty International, and Médecins Sans Frontièrers (Doctors Without Borders). Globalization has opened markets around the world and led to greater financial interdependence among nations. Unfortunately, it has also helped to exacerbate economic inequality around the globe, both among countries and within them (Piketty 2014).

These forces of globalization affect our social and cultural landscape in innumerable ways, from the production of our toys and clothes to the multicultural richness of American cuisine to the international spread of reality TV. In this chapter we will first discuss the culture and aesthetics of globalization and its influence on popular culture and everyday life. Second, we look at how globalization affects the production and consumption of media and pop culture around the world. Finally, we conduct an audit of the human and environmental costs of the globalization of popular culture.

Globalization and Global Culture

In many ways the culture of globalization is best represented by the cosmopolitanism of global cities such as New York, London, Paris, Tokyo, San Francisco, Montreal, Beijing, Singapore, and Hong Kong. Global cities around the world all seem to resemble one another, sharing more in common than they do with more peripheral towns and regions within their own countries. They have large, diverse populations of migrants from around the planet and feature among the world's highest disparities between rich and poor (Sassen 1994). They host fine arts institutions, fashion shows, architecture competitions, international film festivals, "idea" forums and conferences, and contemporary art auctions, fairs, and biennales supported lavishly by the top economic "1 percent" (Thornton 2008; Freeland 2011). Global cities also host the kinds of high-end urban nightlife and entertainment districts discussed in the previous chapter. As Boston University sociologist Ashley Mears (2014) explains, a global circuit of exclusive nightclubs stretching from New York City to Miami (as well as from the Hamptons to the French Riviera) caters to wealthy men who spend extravagantly on VIP bottle service and host young fashion models for weekend all-night parties, all to generate status and forge social connections with other wealthy men. In the Far East, nightclubs in Tokyo and Ho Chi Minh City that play host to powerful Asian businessmen also traffic in women, from Japanese hostesses to Vietnamese sex workers (Allison 1994; Hoang 2015).

Global cities also support media and culture-producing industries such as telecommunications, entertainment production, architecture and design, fashion, advertising, publishing, software development, and technology services. Their infrastructures of knowledge production and media technology transfer include some of the world's top universities. (Global outposts of American universities include the Penn Wharton China Center in Beijing, NYU's Abu Dhabi campus, and the Yale-NUS College in Singapore.) Global cities also maintain some of the world's fastest digital fiber-optic networks, innovative business incubators, and its busiest airports—O'Hare, Heathrow, LAX, Frankfurt, Shanghai, Atatürk, JFK—which, like global cities, also resemble one another (Table 10.1). As Pico Iyer (2001, p. 43) observes, "A modern airport is based on the assumption that everyone's from somewhere else, and so in need of something he can recognize to make him feel at home; it becomes, therefore, an anthology of generic spaces— the shopping mall, the food court, the hotel lobby—which bear the same relation to life, perhaps that Muzak does to music." To paraphrase the T. S. Eliot poem "The Hollow Men," this is the way the world ends—not with a bang but a Starbucks.

The culture of globalization is also marked by the triumph of style and the pro-liferation of aesthetics in everyday life. *Aesthetics* refers to how we communicate and express through the senses, through sight and sound, taste and touch. The sensations produced through aesthetics are immediate and emotional, much like the arousal we experience from beauty or sexual attraction. We also react strongly to novelty and the excitement of aesthetic change, which explains the success of business strategies such as planned obsolescence (as we discussed in Chapter 3), in which the introduction of freshly redesigned products such as automobiles, women's shoes, handbags, and other fashionable commodities generates sales while devaluing last season's styles. It also explains why people associate ultra-new design and hard-to-find global imports (or else refurbished vintage fashion so old that it's practically new again) with high status. As cultural critic Virginia Postrel (2004) argues in *The Substance of Style*, "Sensory pleasure works to commercial and personal advantage because aesthet-ics has intrinsic value" (p. 75).

Our global and technological age provides opportunities for individual expression through mass customization and the consumption of aesthetics, style, and taste unavailable at any other time in human history. (*Mass customization* refers to the inexpensive mass production of individually personalized goods from distressed skinny jeans to tall mocha skim lattes with extra foam.) Once upon a time, fashionable attire could only be

TABLE 10.1
World's 15 Busiest Airports

1.	Hartsfield-Jackson Atlanta International Airport (USA)
2.	Beijing Capital International Airport (China)
3.	Dubai International Airport (UAE)
4.	Chicago O'Hare International Airport (USA)
5.	Tokyo Haneda Airport (Japan)
6.	London Heathrow Airport (UK)
7.	Los Angeles International Airport (USA)
8.	Hong Kong International Airport (Hong Kong)
9.	Paris-Charles de Gaulle Airport (France)
10.	Dallas/Fort Worth International Airport (USA)
11.	Istanbul Atatürk Airport (Turkey)
12.	Frankfurt Airport (Germany)
13.	Shanghai Pudong International Airport (China)
14.	Amsterdam Airport Schiphol (The Netherlands)
15.	New York's John F. Kennedy International Airport (USA)

Source: Airports Council International (2015).

Consumers today, when shopping for everything from furnishings to fashion to Frappuccinos, are confronted with boundless opportunities for individual expression.

enjoyed by royalty and the aristocracy, whereas today almost anyone can afford inexpensive yet durable clothing in a brilliant range of bold colors, styles, fabrics, and textures, thanks to the efficiencies of global supply chains and cheap manufacturing labor in the developing world. In fact, global fast-fashion firms that can quickly and cheaply bring runway trends to everyday shopping-mall consumers, such as Zara (based in Spain) and H&M (headquartered in Stockholm), have seen tremendous growth in recent years (Kosmann 2016). Crate and Barrel (with stores in Singapore, Dubai, and Peru) and West Elm (with locations in Mexico, Lebanon, Saudi Arabia, Kuwait, and the United Arab Emirates) bring high-concept design to the global middle classes, and thanks to IKEA (headquartered in the Netherlands), even lower-end home furnishings come in a dizzying variety of fabulous styles from modernist to funky. As for the global mass customization of coffee beverages, Starbucks—which boasts more than 24,000 locations in 70 countries on its website—claims that it offers consumers 87,000 drink combinations (Bialik 2008).

Meanwhile, networked online technologies empower ordinary people to aesthetically express themselves by distributing visual images, homemade videos, and digital soundscapes electronically to all corners of the globe. On dating platforms such as OkCupid, it has become common for users to try to stand out from the crowd by posting travel photographs taken in far-flung vacation sites from Machu Picchu to the Egyptian pyramids (Solman 2015). Personalized ringtones allow smartphone users to have their calls announced by Japanese wind chimes, or the ethereal Icelandic music of Sigur Rós, or anything else. According to my iPhone, Siri can speak in Arabic, Danish, Finnish, Hebrew, Japanese, Korean, Malay, Norwegian, Brazilian Portuguese, Russian, Swedish, Thai, and Turkish, and multiple forms of Chinese, Dutch, English, French, German, Italian, and Spanish. Digital word-processing software allows writers from around the world to compose in virtually any language or typeface that graphic designers can create for the screen.

The global rise of mass customization even extends to the human form itself. According to the International Society of Aesthetic Plastic Surgery, the largest national markets for plastic surgery in the world based on total procedures performed in 2014 were (in descending order) the United States, Brazil, Japan, South Korea, Mexico, Germany, France, and Colombia. (South Korea is the world leader in cosmetic procedures per capita.) The surgical procedures most performed by plastic surgeons worldwide that year included eyelid surgery, liposuction, breast augmentation, fat grafting, and rhinoplasty (or nose surgery), although it differed by country. In Brazil, Colombia, and Mexico, liposuction and breast augmentation were the most popular, while in Japan and South Korea patients were more likely to undergo eyelid surgery and rhinoplasty. Indeed, in that year more nose jobs were performed in South Korea than in any other nation. Among nonsurgical procedures, the most common worldwide involved botulinum toxin (or Botox injections), hyaluronic acid (a dermal filler used for reducing facial wrinkles and lines), and hair removal. In 2014, nearly one-quarter of all hair removal procedures in the world were performed in Japan, more than in any other country.

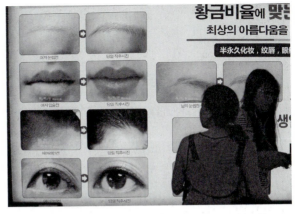

South Korea represents one of the largest national markets for plastic surgery, with the most cosmetic procedures per capita.

Mix It Up

In addition to mass customization, the aesthetics of globalization privilege hybridity and cross-cultural mashups, especially as artists, musicians, and filmmakers around the world become more familiar with each other's work. Throughout the 1980s American and British rock artists drew on elements of African and Latin polyrhythmic pop music (and partnered with artists such as South Africa's Ladysmith Black Mambazo and Senegal's Youssou N'Dour) to produce some of the most critically heralded albums of the decade, including Talking Heads' *Remain in Light* (1980) and *Stop Making Sense* (1984), Peter Gabriel's *Security* (1982) and *So* (1986), and Paul Simon's *Graceland* (1986) and *The Rhythm of the Saints* (1990). Wes Anderson's 2004 film *The Life Aquatic with Steve Zissou* features Brazilian singer Seu Jorge performing Portuguese covers of David Bowie songs, including "Ziggy Stardust," "Life on Mars?" "Changes," "Starman," and "Suffragette City." Quentin Tarantino's 2003–04 *Kill Bill* films pay homage both to Hong Kong martial arts pictures such as Lo Wei's *Fists of Fury* and Jeong Chang-hwa's *Five Fingers of Death* and Italian spaghetti Western films such as Sergio Leone's *The Good, the Bad, and the Ugly*—and to top it off, *Kill Bill, Vol. 1* includes a seven-and-a-half minute animated sequence directed by Japanese anime designer Kazuto Nakazawa. Today, black immigrants residing in low-income *banlieues* outside major cities in France perform politically charged hip-hop music that borrows from both American rap and African and Caribbean music traditions. In fact, France is the largest hip-hop market in the world outside the United States (Mitchell 2002, p. 11).

The aesthetics of globalization and hybridity also promote innovation in other areas of culture, notably cuisine that emphasizes unique pairings of different flavors, spices, and tastes. In Los Angeles and other global cities, food-truck vendors serve Korean-style tacos stuffed with kimchi and BBQ beef *bulgogi*;

Vietnamese hoagies made with pork belly, daikon, and spicy mayo on *bánh mì* baguettes; and Indian burritos stuffed with chicken vindaloo and basmati rice. One is reminded how earlier adventures in globalization such as the European conquest of the Americas led to the introduction of New World foods across the globe that today we take for granted—tomatoes on Italian pizza, hot chili peppers in Indonesian and Malaysian curry, papaya in Thai salads, chocolate and vanilla in Viennese pastry, and potatoes served as french fries (which may have actually originated in Belgium, not France).

At the same time, the commodified aesthetics of globalization can also promote a disingenuous sense of the world that blurs meaningful cultural distinctions among peoples and ethnicities, regions, and nations. In the United States and Europe, music labels and distributors lump together non-Western sounds as different as Latin salsa, West African rock, Moroccan chaabi, Brazilian samba, and Algerian rai into the generic category of "world music"—industry shorthand for "the music of everywhere else" (Brennan 2001, pp. 44–45). For this reason, Apple iTunes promotes its Latin jazz, Nigerian Afropop, and ambient Celtic tracks alongside one another as part of its catchall "world" collection, together with recordings by Jewish klezmer artists, Arabic pop stars from Lebanon, and Ghanaian highlife musicians. P. F. Chang's China Bistro international franchise specializes in a globalizing aesthetic that presents a mélange of different ethnic and regional offerings as if a unified (if thoroughly Americanized) "pan-Asian" cuisine consisting of Singapore Firecracker Chicken, Hong Kong Style Sea Bass, Korean BBQ Chicken Stir-Fry, Sichuan Style Asparagus, and Japanese sushi and tempura rolls.

Other global entertainment attractions promote the idea of an imaginary pan-Asian culture while trafficking in stereotypes of the Global South. As I discuss in my book *American Zoo* (Grazian 2015, pp. 161–62), the centerpiece of Disney's Animal Kingdom's generically labeled "Asia" pavilion is the make-believe township of Anandapur, which seems to evoke India, Nepal, Tibet, Indonesia, and Thailand all at once. Astride a lazy river, faux temple ruins and rickshaws loaded down with wooden crates line its winding paths. A souvenir shop sign warns, "No strollers, carts, motorized scooters or livestock allowed in building." High-speed amusement-park rides are similarly themed, including the Kali River Rapids and Expedition Everest—Legend of Forbidden Mountain. Live animals from distinct ecosystems cohabitate among ersatz relics along the theme-park's Maharajah Jungle Trek, a biogeographically jumbled, pan-Asian mutation of a forest preserve with Malayan tapirs, Indian pygmy geese, Argus pheasants, Rodrigues flying foxes, white-cheeked gibbons, and King parrots. (Unlike other accredited U.S. zoos, Disney also refers to all its tigers generically as *Asian* tigers, rather than by their specific, geographically informed subspecies, whether Bengal, Indochinese, or Siberian.)

Just as Anandapur does for Asia, Disney's Animal Kingdom similarly portrays all of Africa as yet another imaginary town called Harambe, which is Swahili for "working together in unity." The predistressed streets of pan-African Harambe overflow with stalls and souvenir shops brimming with trinkets for sale—Ghanaian percussion instruments, multicolored bead necklaces, rain sticks, drums with elephant carvings, thumb pianos. Outside the Mombasa Marketplace, a stenciled sign reads, "Please Respect Our Local Customs," apparently without any intended irony. Cultural "ambassadors" from a variety of sub-Saharan African nations (including South Africa, Zimbabwe, Namibia, Botswana, Uganda, and the Republic of the Congo) bang drums throughout the park (p. 163). Meanwhile, the nearby Animal Kingdom Lodge similarly manufactures an imaginary pan-Africanism that tends to blow aside differences among African countries, regions, and

In the imaginary pan-African village of Harambe in Disney's Animal Kingdom, visitors can enjoy boerewors sausage, shop for trinkets at the Mombasa marketplace, and listen to Wassoulou music.

cultures. At its main restaurant, Boma, the dinner buffet includes dishes such as fufu (West and Central African); peanut soup (West African); pap with chakalaka, sambal chili sauces, and bobotie (Southern African); couscous (West and North African); and falafel and yogurt (North African).

Lost and Found in Translation

As we are constantly reminded by television commercials for financial services, personal computers, and diet soda, everyday representations of globalization suggest that the international spread of consumer products around the world effectively erases age-old cultural differences among traditional nations and their peoples. This global village ethos was nicely expressed by Coca-Cola in 1971 when the ad agency McCann-Erickson introduced a 60-second spot that wrapped a message of cultural imperialism in a post-1960s hippie dreamscape: "I'd like to teach the world to sing in perfect harmony/I'd like to buy the world a Coke and keep it company." (Pop goes the world, indeed.)

This pro-globalization ethic reached its apogee when *New York Times* columnist Thomas L. Friedman presented his Golden Arches Theory of Conflict Prevention in his book *The Lexus and the Olive Tree* (2000, p. 248), in which he argued, "No two countries that both had McDonald's had fought a war against each other since each got its McDonald's." As it happens, the theory doesn't entirely hold for all cases—note the militarized conflicts between Chicken McNugget—loving countries like India and Pakistan, Israel and Lebanon, and Russia and Ukraine—but its point remains that countries participating in the global economy share interdependencies and a rising overall standard of living that ought to favor peace and stability over armed conflict. Perhaps as a consequence of rising conflagrations around the world in the wake of the 9/11 attacks and the subsequent U.S. "War on Terror," Friedman revised the theory for his 2005 book, *The World Is Flat*, in which he renamed the idea the Dell Theory of Conflict Prevention, which stipulates that "No two countries that are both part of a major global supply chain, like Dell's, will ever fight a war against each other as long as they are both part of the global supply chain" (Friedman, p. 421).

Politics aside, in recent decades we can see a global convergence of pop cultural tastes in a number of realms. In Chapter 6 we discussed how Hollywood films often find an international audience at the global box office. (In 2016, both *Captain America: Civil War* and *Zootopia* made over a billion dollars worldwide, each making over 60 percent of their respective gross revenues in non-U.S. markets.) The music industry's most successful pop singers are global celebrities who generate global hits. Adele's 2015 smash single "Hello" reached No. 1 on the *Billboard* pop chart in the United States in November of that year, where it remained for 10 weeks. The London-born singer's "Hello" also went to No. 1 in Australia, Austria, Belgium, Canada, Czech Republic, Denmark, Finland, France, Germany, Greece, Hungary, Ireland, Israel, Italy, Lebanon, Luxembourg, Mexico, the Netherlands, New Zealand, Norway, Poland, Scotland, Slovakia, Slovenia, South Africa, South Korea, Spain, Sweden, Switzerland, and the United Kingdom. In 2016 Drake's summer single "One Dance," featuring Wizkid and Kyla, hit No. 1 on the U.S. *Billboard* pop chart, and also made it to the top of the charts in more than 10 other countries, including his home nation of Canada. In that same year Justin Timberlake also hit No. 1 both in the United States and in multiple countries abroad, as did Barbados-born singer Rihanna, Australia's Sia, Drake's Canadian countryman Justin Bieber, and former One Direction member Zayn Malik, a British-born Sunni Muslim of Irish and Pakistani descent.

Despite the worldwide popularity of blockbuster films and pop music, in recent years sociologists and anthropologists have examined how the increased traffic of global media and culture breeds its own backlash as local communities grow even more protective of their regional customs, collective identities, and territorial attachments (Appadurai 1990). In popular culture this is perhaps best expressed by the increasingly dedicated fandom surrounding national Olympic teams and local sports franchises and clubs around the world, from the Jamaican track-and-field team to the New York Mets to Manchester United, although plenty of other examples abound. For instance, in reaction to the modern unification of continental Europe, countries such as Italy, France, Spain, Greece, Portugal, and Germany have successfully applied to the EU to have more than 700 foodstuffs assigned protective status on the basis of national identity and cultural patrimony. For example, Feta cheese and Kalamata olives are both marked with a "Protected Designation of Origin" label that gives Greece the exclusive right to sell them in Europe, just as only certain regional Italian pork producers can refer to their cured ham as authentically "Prosciutto di Parma." (However, protected foods may be sold by foreign purveyors both in the United States and elsewhere outside the EU, which is why one can buy cheese labeled "Bulgarian Feta" in New York but not in Bulgaria.) Sociologist Michaela DeSoucey (2010, p. 433) refers to this labeling practice as an example of *gastronationalism*, in which "food is a contested medium of cultural politics that demarcates national boundaries and identities" in the context of globalization.

Similarly, and perhaps ironically, the increased commodification of global popular culture creates an even stronger desire among many consumers for that which seems more *locally* grown, and thus resistant to the strong hand of Western cultural imperialism. Tourists seek out ethnic arts and crafts for purchase as exotic talismans of local authenticity, whether Mayan ceramics in Mexico, Lega masks in Zaire, or sacred Buddhist spirit houses in Thailand (Wherry 2006). In "fair trade" stores like Ten Thousand Villages, consumers purchase handicrafts such as jewelry, embroidery, woodcarvings, and handwoven baskets made by indigenous artisans working in Guatemala, India, Bangladesh, Niger, and elsewhere throughout the Global South (Brown 2013). Gourmet coffee stores and brand-name chains alike promote their sourcing of fair-trade and shade-grown coffee from small local

The "Protected Designation of Origin" label, which gives countries the exclusive right to sell certain regional food items, can be interpreted as a reaction to the unification of Europe.

producers in Nicaragua, Colombia, Papua New Guinea, and Ethiopia, sometimes with posters and brochures featuring "handsome, well-dressed peasants smiling and standing next to piles of beans" (Simon 2009, p. 206; Brown 2013).

Even American culture can be prized abroad for its local uniqueness, rather than for its global hegemonic popularity (as in the instance of Hollywood films or pop music). For example, when researching my book *Blue Chicago* (2003), I met devoted blues fans from Canada, England, Spain, Germany, Poland, Hungary, Australia, and Japan, all in search of a local and deeply authentic American blues experience. The blues evokes a profound sense of place among its fans, whether the sun-kissed stickiness of the Mississippi Delta or the honky-tonk burliness of the South Side of Chicago. One Canadian tourist told me during a local blues show, "There's great music in Toronto. But you know, this is Chicago, which has the history, and the culture, and so it's a special thing to come here to hear blues" (p. 68). Another global blues fan, a Polish student studying in the United States, gushed, "The one thing I love the most about Chicago . . . it's the blues. I love it! . . . Tonight, this is my first time hearing blues in Chicago. . . . I've always wanted to go, because the best place for blues is in Chicago, the blues originated in Chicago, so I've always wanted to go, and tonight I finally got to come. . . . It's probably the most important thing I've done since I've been here. It's amazing" (p. 67).

The global success of American exports has enriched our own culture immeasurably. Take American sports. During the 2015–16 season the National Basketball Association (NBA) rostered 100 international athletes from

30 countries and territories, including Argentina, Cameroon, Cape Verde, the Democratic Republic of the Congo, Germany, Israel, Italy, Latvia, Nigeria, Senegal, South Sudan, Tunisia, Ukraine, and Venezuela. Meanwhile, professional baseball has long been popular in Japan, where the sport is played with a smaller ball, on a smaller field with a smaller strike zone. (Here's another notable difference: In Japan's Nippon League, games are limited to 12 innings and permitted to end in a tie.) Moreover, since the 1990s American teams have regularly benefited from the talents of Japanese players recruited to play for Major League Baseball (MLB), especially pitchers. In the 2015–16 season, nine players from Japan played on MLB rosters, including six pitchers: Masahiro Tanaka, Hisashi Iwakuma, Yu Darvish, Kenta Maeda, Junichi Tazawa, and Koji Uehara. The league's remaining three Japanese players were outfielder Nori Aoki, shortstop and second-baseman Munenori Kawasaki, and outfielder and 10-time All-Star Ichiro Suzuki. (Ichiro was also the 2001 Rookie of the Year and American League MVP and the 2007 All-Star Game MVP, and he holds the MLB record for most hits in a single season.)

Of course, when popular culture migrates around the world, disseminators change certain elements to make them more legible to local audiences. Since its 1969 debut *Sesame Street* has been coproduced in more than 30 countries and territories around the world (including Afghanistan, Bangladesh, Egypt, and Northern Ireland), each with a different streetscape and unique cast of Muppets. South Africa's *Takalani Sesame* incorporates all 11 of the country's national languages and features Zuzu, Zikwe, and Kami—a non-symptomatic HIV-positive Muppet. Disney's live production of *The Lion King* has been translated into eight languages, including Japanese and Portuguese (Qin 2016). When a Mandarin-language production of *The Lion King* debuted at the $5.5 million Shanghai Disney Resort in 2016, it featured a brand-new character: the red-and-yellow-costumed Monkey Master, based on the mythical Monkey King figure from China's Song Dynasty. In an attempt to make the Shanghai theme park both "authentically Disney and distinctly Chinese" (Qin 2016), Disney and Pixar characters are reimagined as signs of the Chinese zodiac in an exhibit named "The Garden of the Twelve Friends," with Tigger (Year of the Tiger), Remy (Rat), Thumper (Rabbit), Kaa (Snake), and Pluto (Dog).

Similarly, the titles of feature films are often not merely translated when released abroad but actually altered for international audiences.

The German-language version of Sesame Street, *known as* Sesamstrasse, *debuted in 1973 and includes unique characters such as comic duo Pferd the horse and Wolle the sheep.*

In France, *Silver Linings Playbook* became *Happiness Therapy*, while *The Hangover* became *Very Bad Trip*, and *No Strings Attached* was changed to simply *Sex Friends*. Hollywood movies released in China have included *Wretch! Let Me Chop Off Your Finger* (*The Piano*), *I Will Marry a Prostitute to Save Money* (*Pretty Woman*), *His Great Device Makes Him Famous* (*Boogie Nights*), *Seabed General Mobilization* (*Finding Nemo*), *Touring Around on a Flying House* (*Up*), *One Night, Big Belly* (*Knocked Up*), *United States Cheat Bureau* (*American Hustle*), and *Interplanetary Unusual Attacking Team* (*Guardians of the Galaxy*).

In fact, the globalization of pop cultural platforms is often marked by variation in content across nations and regions. In India, McDonald's stores carry vegetarian substitutes for the beef burgers and Big Macs common in American fast-food res-taurants. Items include the McVeggie

Oftentimes feature film titles are reimagined for global audiences: In France, The Hangover *was renamed* Very Bad Trip.

(a batter-fried patty made with green peas, carrots, green beans, onions, pota-toes, rice, and spices), the McAloo Tikki (a potato and peas patty), the McSpicy Paneer (with tandoori mayonnaise), and the Veg Maharaja Mac (with cheese and corn double patties). In both *America's Next Top Model* (*ANTM*) and its Asian counterpart, *China's Next Top Model* (*CNTM*), aspiring fashion models are filmed engaging in emotive displays involving crying—indeed, the display of raw emotion is at the heart of the reality TV genre (Grindstaff 2002). However, as sociologist Junhow Wei (2014) argues, in the Chinese context these emotional displays are interpreted and framed differently than in the American case, given both the collectivist nature of traditional Chinese culture, which frowns on interpersonal conflict, and rigid state demands for cultural programming that reflects ideologies related to social harmony, rather than discord and strife. For example, although contestants cry during elimination rounds on both programs, on *ANTM* these out-bursts are often accompanied by accusations of unfairness, blame, and regret—"I really don't feel like the judges gave me the opportunity that I deserved"—while "crying at eliminations on *CNTM* is most often because of contestants' sympathy for friends or sadness that they must say goodbye" (Wei 2014, p. 208). On one episode of *China's Next Top Model*, an eliminated contestant explains during a

When visiting a McDonald's in India, where most of the population abstains from eating beef, diners can enjoy vegetarian options such as the McAloo Tikki and the McVeggie.

walk-off interview, "I'm crying not because of the competition, but because I cannot let go of them, cannot let go of my sisters. I want to thank them and everyone working on the show, because they were all so good to me" (p. 209).

There are also cultural exports with massive global popularity in various parts of the world that have not necessarily caught on in the United States. "Bollywood" movies from India provide an example. The Hindi-language Bollywood film industry based in Mumbai (formerly Bombay, hence the name "Bollywood") is the largest in the world, with 2.6 billion tickets sold globally in 2012, compared to only 1.36 billion tickets sold worldwide for Hollywood films. In that same year Bollywood produced 1,602 movies, or more than triple the number of U.S. films (McCarthy 2014). Since the plots of Bollywood films typically highlight clashes between the traditional world of the settled village and the temptations of the modern city and its marketplaces, they not only entice regional audiences from South Asia but also audiences from a vast array of developing countries that similarly experience this tension between tradition and modernity, including China, Nigeria, South Africa, Kenya, Colombia, Brazil, Peru, and parts of the former Soviet Union (Joshi 2009, 2015, p. 96). Meanwhile, Bollywood films are also popular among South Asian communities residing in the United States, which currently include more than three million Indian Americans. Yet despite the success of Danny Boyle's Bollywood-inspired 2008 film *Slumdog Millionaire*, which made over $140 million at the U.S. box office and won eight Academy Awards, including Best Picture, and a handful of Bollywood actors who have found fame in the United States such as Irrfan Khan (*The Amazing Spider-Man, Life of Pi, Jurassic World, Inferno*) and Priyanka Chopra (ABC TV's *Quantico*),

Bollywood is the largest film industry in the world and yet these films, which often highlight clashes between tradition and modernity and include elaborate song-and-dance numbers, have failed to catch on in the United States.

few Bollywood films have captured a substantial American audience the way that recent cinematic imports from Mexico, Spain, Hong Kong, and Taiwan have. (Indeed, think of how many current A-list Hollywood screenwriters and directors—Alfonso Cuarón, Guillermo del Toro, Alejandro González Iñárritu, Ang Lee, Steve McQueen—are foreign born.) The softness of the Indian film market in the United States may have to do with the degree to which the aesthetic conventions of Bollywood films—notably their length (typically three hours or longer) and heavy use of song-and-dance numbers—challenge American mainstream audiences, along with the tonal and rhythmic complexities of Hindi music styles.

Another example of an enormously popular cultural export lacking much of an audience in the United States is South Korean pop music, or K-pop. According to Jon Seabrook's *The Song Machine* (2015), K-pop groups like SHINee, Girls' Generation, TVXQ!, Wonder Girls, EXO, Super Junior, and BIGBANG are meticulously crafted by one of three major talent agencies based in Seoul: SM, JYP, and YG Entertainment. As pop idols-in-training, girls and boys are recruited on the basis of their attractiveness rather than their musical abilities, and many undergo plastic surgery to attain these looks—again, South Korea is the world leader in cosmetic procedures per capita. Young recruits undergo several years of media and performance coaching before they are organized into K-pop groups. (These are unusually large ensembles—for example, Girls' Generation has *nine* members.) They also learn to sing in Japanese, Chinese, and English (in addition to Korean, of course), and to modulate their performances when catering to audiences from different Asian countries. (The founder of SM Entertainment, Lee Soo-Man, refers to this meticulous system of artistic development as "cultural technology.") During their performances of commissioned songs and covers of

K-pop groups like Girls' Generation are meticulously crafted by talent agencies in Seoul.

American pop hits, K-pop bands stage elaborate shows, running through endless costume changes as they perform synchronized dances while wearing pounds of makeup.

Thanks to this formula, K-pop is huge throughout Asia—not only in South Korea but also in Taiwan, Singapore, the Philippines, Hong Kong, Thailand, Vietnam, Malaysia, and notably Japan, the world's biggest music market outside the United States. But K-pop can't seem to gain a foothold in the United States, for structural as well as more aesthetic reasons. K-pop groups like Girls' Generation emphasize eye-candy and attitude over musicianship, and so much of their revenue comes from Asian product endorsements. Meanwhile, they promote their records by appearing on Korean television every night, always competing against rival groups for public attention. Both endorsements and nightly TV appearances prevent K-pop groups from committing to extensive concert touring in the United States.

At the same time, K-pop's cultural aesthetics are perhaps simply too much for American audiences. How many singing groups in U.S. pop music history have had *nine* members? Plus, even the blandest of American and British pop stars have *some* edge, some claim to authenticity, however tenuous. As Seabrook (2015, p. 165) himself admits, "I found myself wondering why overproduced, derivative pop music, performed by second-tier singers, would appeal to a mass American audience, who can hear better performers doing more original material right here at home?" It is telling that the most famous Korean pop singer in the United States is the one-hit wonder Psy, whose record-breaking 2012 YouTube smash "Gangnam Style" pokes fun at the bombastic excesses of K-pop and Seoul's opulent Gangnam district where, perhaps not coincidentally, both SM and JYP Entertainment are headquartered.

Globalization and Its Discontents

Our discussion of globalization has emphasized the consumption of popular culture around the world, and how meanings and cultural conventions change as culture moves across borders. Yet these meanings cannot be disassociated from the global production of pop culture itself, and its overall impact on the planet in the long run. During the 1990s, advances in the three prime movers of globalization—transportation, communication, and new legal and organizational frameworks—allowed pop culture—producing firms from Nike and Levi's to Apple and IBM to segregate the *intellectual* labor of design, research and development, financing, branding, packaging, licensing, and marketing from the *industrial* labor required to source raw materials and manufacture khakis, sweaters, sneakers, toys, handbags, video game consoles, smartphones, and laptop computers assembled in factories. Container ships and next-day airshipping, digital networks and information systems, and the rise of trade agreements and regulatory bodies from NAFTA to the World Trade Organization all combined to allow multinational brands to efficiently outsource the material aspects of the production process to factories located overseas. While the strength of well-paying U.S. manufacturing jobs in northern cities from New York to Chicago to Detroit led to mid-century American prosperity and a growing middle class, by the end of the twentieth century companies were increasingly partnering with factories based in free-trade export processing zones in countries throughout the Global South, in Mexico, China, Thailand, Vietnam, Indonesia, the Philippines, Sri Lanka, and many others (Klein 2009). By doing so, companies lower their manufacturing costs considerably, since factories located offshore can often evade the power of unions, environmental regulations, and labor laws that typically protect U.S. workers from hazardous and unsafe working conditions, long hours with minimal breaks, on-the-job sexual harassment, and low hourly wages without benefits. This contributes to the downsizing of blue-collar manufacturing jobs in the United States and the increased exploitation of low-skilled workers overseas, including women and even children and adolescents (Broughton 2015).

By subcontracting their manufacturing operations to independent factories abroad, fast-fashion brands like H&M and Zara can more quickly respond to unpredictable cultural trends and market demands by relying on just-in-time production orders rather than endure the risks and overhead costs involved in running and maintaining their own factories. (This responsiveness to market conditions can prove especially advantageous during economic downturns, when sales may slacken due to drops in consumer spending.) For example, Liz Claiborne does not own any of the many factories that manufacture its fashion apparel—instead, it outsources its production orders to 256 facilities located across 32 countries around the globe (Collins 2003, pp. 104, 120). According to Liz Claiborne's vice president for manufacturing and sourcing, subcontracting with hundreds of global firms allows for an unusual degree of flexibility when working on specific orders in real time:

> Anything made of silk is made in China. . . . Otherwise, structured merchandise . . . we probably get the best ladies'-type suits out of Taiwan and places in China, but where we have to reach a price point and where those price points are combined with American fabric, we tend to do that in El Salvador. We tend to do our ongoing programs in cotton-type pants in the Dominican Republic, and our other-than-basic knits in Saipan. So we have developed our pockets—I don't suppose they are pockets of countries as much as they're pockets of manufacturers. (p. 115)

In fact, competing brands often subcontract with the very same factories, which is how one Mexican factory in Aguascalientes wound up manufacturing jeans for Liz Claiborne, Levi's, and Calvin Klein (p. 138).

Not only do middlebrow consumer brands such as H&M and Nike take advantage of this efficient production model by manufacturing their wares offshore in low-cost factories and sweatshops in places like China, but luxury designer brands like Prada and Céline do as well—although they don't like to admit it, given that their high-status value is dependent on their symbolic association with quality and Old World methods of handcraft production. Within the global industry surrounding the manufacture of luxury handbags—in which "hardware, like locks, come from Italy and China (primarily Guangzhou); the zipper comes from Japan; the lining comes from Korea; the embroidery is done in Italy, India, or northern China; the leather is from Korea or Italy; and the bag is assembled partly in China and partly in Italy"—status anxieties surrounding the production process even affect how high-end products are labeled, according to culture and fashion writer Dana Thomas (2007):

> Few bags actually carry the "Made in China" label. If they do, it is well hidden. For one bag, the tag was sewn into the bottom seam of the inside pocket. For another, it was stamped on the reverse side of a postage-stamp-size leather flap that bears the brand's logo. You need a magnifying glass to read it. The majority, however, carry a "Made in Italy," "Made in France," or "Made in the U.K." label. The brands have little tricks to get around the China label. One brand's "Made in China" label is actually a sticker affixed to the outer package. The luxury brand rips it off when the goods arrive in Italy and replaces it with a "Made in Italy" label. Another has the entire bag made in China except for the handle. The bag is shipped to Italy, where the Italian-made handle is attached. Some brands have the tops of shoes—the most labor-intensive part of the process—made in China and then attach the soles in Italy. These items can carry the "Made in Italy" label. (pp. 202–03)

By manufacturing their products abroad in free-trade export processing zones, brands such as Mattel and Apple are better able to concentrate their efforts on recruiting and retaining high-income, educated workers headquartered in the United States and Europe for their conceptual and technological skills. However, today many of these jobs are actually moving overseas as well, to rapidly growing economic powerhouses like India, Singapore, and the United Arab Emirates. Google has a South Asian campus in Hyderabad, where they have an indoor cricket pitch and chefs who prepare cuisines from all 28 Indian states. Twitter has offices in Dubai, Singapore, Hong Kong, and throughout India in Mumbai, Bangalore, and Gurugram. Apple has teams of software engineers working throughout Asia and the Middle East in New Dehli, Abu Dhabi, Beijing, Shanghai, Taipei, Seoul, Tokyo, and Hong Kong.

Despite its obvious tendencies as a destabilizing force that exacerbates social and economic inequality both within and among societies (including our own), there is no question that the globalization of cultural production from basketball shoes to video games has also provided a higher standard of living to millions of people living in India, China, and elsewhere around the world. Unfortunately, the same cannot be said for the environmental conditions of the Global South, or the West—or the planet itself, for that matter. Upon his initial arrival to Beijing and its dense brownish smog whose fumes burned the back of his throat, American journalist Tom Scocca (2011) reported:

> China's pollution problem was what an American would have expected to see. The pollution had deep, mythic resonance in our national consciousness. It was first of all a mark of China's sudden emergence as a rival economic power—both a metaphor and an actual problem, the smoke and dust and chemical vapor of a growing industrial monster (a dragon, if you must) gobbling down ever more of the world's raw materials at one end and squeezing out container ships full of finished goods at the other. The tainted air of China was blowing across the Pacific and into California, like a warning.
>
> Beneath that was the moral panic: the Chinese weren't afraid to poison their own country—even the capital—or the rest of the world, as long as they could keep expanding their factories. Still beneath that, if you cared to keep digging, was the awareness that, after all, these factories were making the iPods and DVDs and socket wrenches and flip-flops that Americans wanted to buy, so that we were maybe more directly implicated in this toxic manufacturing business than we would have liked to have been.
>
> Then, below even that, rarely more than half expressed at home, were the ideas that made up the commonplace Chinese view: that in the West's own pursuit of industrialization, London had buried itself in soot for decades, and the United States had poured waste into its waterways until the rivers caught on fire; and that the wealth we had now secured by plundering nature was what allowed us to now breathe clear air and drink clear water and sit in judgement on the environmental and social irresponsibility of countries that hadn't developed quite as early as ours had. And that what really might worry us was the notion that our Western standard of health and prosperity relied on the existence of places that were sickened and

People in Beijing, China, wear masks to protect themselves from the heavy smog produced by factories.

poor—that if we did cut the [1.3 billion] Chinese in on an even share (or a less-than-even share, former president Jiang Zemin's official goal for the People's Republic having been "moderate prosperity"), the planet and the economy and our own lifestyle couldn't take the shock. (pp. 10—11)

In fact, in today's throwaway society, the ecological costs of our consumption of popular culture—disposable Starbucks cups, Star Wars action figures, IKEA furniture, obsolete early-generation smartphones and computers—are almost too much to take. Scientists estimate that 5.25 trillion particles of plastic weighing nearly 269,000 tons float atop the world's oceans (Schwartz 2014). Much of that drifting debris concentrates around five major garbage patches, accumulations of consumer waste that oceanic winds, currents, and tides draw together in swirling masses of trash. The biggest is the Great Pacific Garbage Patch, a thickening ring of sludge and debris composed of, among other things, pop cultural detritus—children's toys, soda bottles, and polystyrene fast-food containers (Weisman 2008, pp. 140—61; Moore 2014).

—Meanwhile, Americans' addiction to fossil fuels—best symbolized by our love of automobiles (particularly fuel-inefficient sports cars and SUVs) but also by our insatiable desire for the newest clothes, toys, technologies, and other manufactured goods—contributes to greenhouse gas emissions and rising atmospheric concentrations of carbon dioxide, methane, and nitrous oxide. In its fifth assessment report released in 2013, the Nobel Peace Prize—winning Intergovernmental Panel on Climate Change (2013) conclusively identified these emissions as the primary contributor to environmental hazards that, like mass media and popular culture, are also global in scale—namely the warming of the Earth's surface, atmosphere, oceans, and climate system; increased ocean acidification; rapid polar ice loss and glacier melt; widespread species extinction; and global rising sea levels (McKibben 2006, 2011; Friedman 2009; Kolbert 2014, 2015). We have already begun to see how global climate change will affect human societies the world over and here in the United States: extreme storms, punishing droughts, heat waves, and other weather-related catastrophes; ruined agricultural harvests for a growing population; decreased access to water in unstable regions of the Global South; and the flooding of coastal cities from New York to Miami Beach to New Orleans. Unless we as a global society can figure out how to dramatically reduce our ecological footprint by taming the worst of our spendthrift impulses for the hottest and newest stuff, we will literally consume ourselves to death. Pop goes the world.

Bibliography

Absher, Amy. *The Black Musician and the White City: Race and Music in Chicago: 1900-1967* (Ann Arbor, MI: University of Michigan, Press, 2014).

Adorno, Theodor W. "On the Fetish-Character in Music and the Regression of Listening," in *The Essential Frankfurt School Reader,* Andrew Arato and Eike Gebhardt, eds. (New York: Continuum, 1997).

Adorno, Theodor W. "Perennial Fashion—Jazz," in *Critical Theory and Society,* Stephen Eric Bronner and Douglas MacKay Kellner, eds. (New York: Routledge, 1989).

Adorno, Theodor, and Max Horkheimer. "The Culture Industry: Enlightenment as Mass Deception," in *The Cultural Studies Reader,* Simon During, ed. (London: Routledge, 1993).

Allison, Anne. *Nightwork: Sexuality, Pleasure, and Corporate Masculinity in a Tokyo Hostess Club* (Chicago: University of Chicago Press, 1994).

Alterman, Eric. *It Ain't No Sin to Be Glad You're Alive: The Promise of Bruce Springsteen* (Boston: Back Bay, 2001).

Anderson, Benedict. *Imagined Communities: Reflections on the Origin and Spread of Nationalism* (London: Verso, 1991).

Anderson, Elijah. *Code of the Street: Decency, Violence, and the Moral Life of the Inner City* (New York: Norton, 1999).

Anderson, Elijah. *Streetwise: Race, Class, and Change in an Urban Community* (Chicago: University of Chicago Press, 1990).

Ansari, Aziz. "Aziz Ansari on Acting, Race, and Hollywood," *New York Times* 10 Nov. 2015.

Appadurai, Arjun. "Disjuncture and Difference in the Global Cultural Economy," *Public Culture* 2 (1990): 1-24.

Appelrouth, Scot. "Body and Soul: Jazz in the 1920s," *American Behavioral Scientist* 48 (2005): 1496–1509.

Appelrouth, Scot. "Constructing the Meaning of Early Jazz, 1917–1930," *Poetics* 31 (2003): 117–131.

Arndt, Johan. "Role of Product-Related Conversations in the Diffusion of a New Product," *Journal of Marketing Research* 4 (1967): 291–295.

Associated Press. "Final table set for World Series of Poker event in Las Vegas." (2016). Retrieved from http://www.bostonherald .com/news/national/2016/07/final_table_set _for_world_series_of_poker_event_in_las _vegas.

Atkins, E. Taylor. "Can Japanese Sing the Blues? 'Japanese Jazz' and the Problem of Authenticity," in *Japan Pop! Inside the World of Japanese Popular Culture*, Timothy J. Craig, ed. (Armonk, NY: M. E. Sharpe, 2000).

Ball, Philip. "The More, the Wikier." *Nature News* (2007).

Barnes, Brooks. "Making 'Suicide Squad' a Smash, Despite Withering Reviews," *New York Times* 7 Aug. 2016.

Baumann, Shyon. *Hollywood Highbrow: From Entertainment to Art* (Princeton, NJ: Princeton University Press, 2007).

Baxandall, Michael. *Painting and Experience in Fifteenth-Century Italy* (Oxford: Oxford University Press, 1972).

Bearman, Joshua. "The Perfect Game," *Harper's*, July 2008: 65-73.

Becker, Howard S. *Art Worlds* (Berkeley: University of California Press, 1982).

Becker, Howard S. *Outsiders: Studies in the Sociology of Deviance* (New York: Free Press, 1963).

Beisel, Nicola. "Morals versus Art: Censorship, the Politics of Interpretation, and the Victorian Nude," *American Sociological Review* 58 (1993):145-162.

Bennet, Andy. *Cultures of Popular Music* (Philadelphia: Open University Press, 2001).

Bennet, Andy. *Popular Music and Youth Culture: Music, Identity and Place* (New York: St. Martin's Press, 2000).

Bennet, Andy, and Richard A. Peterson, eds. *Music Scenes: Local, Trans-local, and Virtual* (Nashville, TN: Vanderbilt University Press, 2004).

Bialik, Carl. "Starbucks Stays Mum on Drink Math," *Wall Street Journal* 2 April 2008.

Bielby, William T., and Denise D. Bielby. "'All Hits Are Flukes': Institutional Decision-Making and the Rhetoric of Network Prime-Time Program Development," *American Journal of Sociology* 99 (1994): 1287-1313.

Binder, Amy. "Constructing Racial Rhetoric: Media Depictions of Harm in Heavy Metal and Rap Music," *American Sociological Review* 58 (1993): 753-767.

Bissinger, H. G. *Friday Night Lights: A Town, a Team, and a Dream* (Reading, MA: Addison-Wesley, 1990).

Bloom, Allan. *The Closing of the American Mind* (New York: Simon and Schuster, 1987).

Bloom, Harold. *The Western Canon: The Books and School of the Ages* (New York: Riverhead, 1994).

Boorstin, Daniel J. *The Image: A Guide to Pseudo-Events in America* (New York: Vintage, 1961).

Borer, Michael Ian. *Faithful to Fenway: Believing in Boston, Baseball, and America's Most Beloved Ballpark* (New York: NYU Press, 2008).

Bourdieu, Pierre. *Distinction: A Social Critique of the Judgment of Taste*, Richard Nice, trans. (Cambridge, MA: Harvard University Press, 1984).

Bourgois, Philippe. *In Search of Respect: Selling Crack in El Barrio*, 2nd ed. (Cambridge: Cambridge University Press, 2002).

Brennan, Timothy. "World Music Does Not Exist," *Discourse* 23 (2001): 44-62.

Brewster, Bill, and Frank Broughton. *Last Night a DJ Saved My Life: The History of the Disc Jockey* (New York: Grove, 2000).

Brodessor-Anker, Taffy. "Turning Microcelebrity Into a Big Business." *New York Times* 19 Sept. 2014.

Bromberg, Minna, and Gary Alan Fine. "Resurrecting the Red: Pete Seeger and the Purification of Difficult Reputations," *Social Forces* 80 (2002): 1135-1155.

Brooks, David. *Bobos in Paradise: The New Upper Class and How They Got There* (New York: Touchstone, 2001).

Broughton, Chad. *Boom, Bust, Exodus: The Rust Belt, the Maquilas, and a Tale of Two Cities* (New York: Oxford University Press, 2015).

Brown, Keith R. *Buying Into Fair Trade: Culture, Morality, and Consumption* (New York: NYU Press, 2013).

Bryson, Bethany. "Anything but Heavy Metal: Symbolic Exclusion and Musical Dislikes," *American Sociological Review* 61 (1996): 884-899.

Bumiller, Elisabeth. "White House Leter: When a Campaign Intrudes on Vacation," *New York Times* 19 July 2004: A12.

Byrne, David. *How Music Works* (San Francisco, CA: McSweeney's, 2012).

Cabral, Javier. "Why Do Mexican Americans Love Morrissey So Much?" *Washington Post* 8 Oct. 2014.

Calarco, Jessica McCrory. "'I Need Help!': Social Class and Children's Help-Seeking in Elementary School." *American Sociological Review* 76 (2011): 862–82.

Calarco, Jessica McCrory. "The Inconsistent Curriculum: Cultural Tool Kits and Student Interpretations of Ambiguous Expectations." *Social Psychology Quarterly* 77 (2014): 185–209.

Carter, Bill. "On TV, Timing Is Everything at the Olympics," *New York Times* 25 August 2008: C1.

Castronova, Edward. *Synthetic Worlds: The Business and Culture of Online Games* (Chicago: University of Chicago Press, 2005).

Caulfield, Keith. "Adele's '25' Rules as Nielsen Music's Top Album of 2015 in U.S.," *Billboard* 5 Jan. 2016.

Center City District and Central Philadelphia Development Corporation. "Leading the Way: Population Growth Downtown," *Center City Reports,* September 2011.

Champion, Sarah. "Fear and Loathing in Wisconsin," in Steve Redhead, ed., *The Clubcultures Reader: Readings in Popular Cultural Studies* (Oxford: Blackwell, 1997).

Chevalier, Judith A., and Dina Mayzlin. "The Effect of Word of Mouth on Sales: Online Book Reviews." Working Paper, National Bureau of Economic Research, 2003.

Christman, Ed. "U.S. Recording Industry 2015: Streaming Doubles, Adele Dominates," *Billboard* 5 Jan. 2016.

Cieply, Michael. "Thriller on Tour Lets Fans Decide on the Next Stop." *New York Times* 20 Sept. 2009.

Clifford, Stephanie. "A Product's Place Is on the Set," *New York Times* 22 July 2008, http://www.nytimes.com/2008/07/22/business/media/22adce.html.

Cohen, Lizabeth. *A Consumers' Republic: The Politics of Mass Consumption in Postwar America* (New York: Knopf, 2003).

Collins, Jane L. *Threads: Gender, Labor, and Power in the Global Apparel Industry* (Chicago: University of Chicago Press, 2003).

Collins, Patricia Hill. *Black Sexual Politics: African Americans, Gender, and the New Racism* (New York: Routledge, 2005).

Collins, Randall. *Interaction Ritual Chains* (Princeton, NJ: Princeton University Press, 2004a).

Collins, Randall. "Rituals of Solidarity and Security in the Wake of Terrorist Attack," *Sociological Theory* 22 (2004b): 53–87.

Collins, Randall. *The Sociology of Philosophies: A Global Theory of Intellectual Change* (Cambridge, MA: Belknap, 1998).

Cooley, Charles Horton. "The Social Self— the Meaning of 'I,' " in *On Self and Social Organization,* Hans-Joachim Schubert, ed. (Chicago: University of Chicago Press, [1902] 1998).

Crawford, Margaret. "The World in a Shopping Mall," in *Variations on a Theme Park: The New American City and the End of Public Space*, Michael Sorkin, ed. (New York: Hill and Wang, 1992).

Currid, Elizabeth. *The Warhol Economy: How Fashion, Art, and Music Drive New York City* (Princeton, NJ: Princeton University Press, 2007).

Dargis, Manohla. "Showdown in Gotham Town," *New York Times* 18 July 2008.

Davis, Michael. *Street Gang: The Complete History of Sesame Street* (New York: Viking, 2008).

"A Defense of Sugary Soda That Fizzled for Coke," *New York Times* 4 Dec. 2015.

DeSoucey, Michaela. "Gastronationalism: Food Traditions and Authenticity Politics in the European Union," *American Sociological Review* 75 (2010): 432–455.

DeVeaux, Scot . *The Birth of Bebop: A Social and Musical History* (Berkeley: University of California Press, 1997).

Dichter, Ernest. "How Word-of-Mouth Advertising Works," *Harvard Business Review* (1966): 147–166.

DiMaggio, Paul. "Cultural Entrepreneurship in Nineteenth-Century Boston: The Creation of an Organizational Base for High Culture in America," *Media, Culture & Society* 4 (1982): 33–50.

Douglas, Mary. *Purity and Danger: An Analysis of the Concepts of Pollution and Taboo* (London: Routledge, 1991).

Dowd, Maureen. "Waiting for the Green Light," *New York Times Magazine* 22 Nov. 2015.

Duhigg, Charles. "How Companies Learn Your Secrets," *New York Times Magazine* 16 Feb. 2012.

Durkay, Laura. "'Homeland' Is the Most Bigoted Show on Television," *Washington Post* 2 Oct. 2014.

Durkheim, Emile. *The Elementary Forms of Religious Life*. Karen E. Fields, trans. (New York: Free Press, [1912] 1995).

Dyson, Michael Eric. *Between God and Gangsta Rap: Bearing Witness to Black Culture* (New York: Oxford University Press, 1996).

Edin, Kathryn, and H. Luke Schaefer. *$2 a Day: Living on Almost Nothing in America* (New York: Houghton Mifflin Harcourt, 2015).

Egner, Jeremy. "Louis C.K. explains 'Horace and Pete,'" *New York Times* 4 Feb. 2016.

Ellison, Ralph. "The Golden Age, Time Past," in *Shadow and Act* (New York: Vintage, [1964] 1995).

English, James F. *The Economy of Prestige: Prizes, Awards, and the Circulation of Cultural Value* (Cambridge, MA: Harvard University Press, 2005).

Erickson, Bonnie. "Culture, Class, and Connections," *American Journal of Sociology* 102 (1996): 217–251.

Farrell, Michael P. *Collaborative Circles: Friendship Dynamics and Creative Work* (Chicago: University of Chicago Press, 2001).

Fatsis, Stefan. *Word Freak: Heartbreak, Triumph, Genius, and Obsession in the World of Competitive Scrabble Players* (New York: Penguin, 2001).

Faulkner, Robert R. *Hollywood Studio Musicians: Their Work and Careers in the Recording Industry* (Chicago: Aldine, 1971).

Faulkner, Robert R., and Andy B. Anderson. "Short-Term Projects and Emergent Careers: Evidence from Hollywood," *American Journal of Sociology* 92 (1987): 879–909.

Faulkner, Robert R., and Howard S. Becker. *"Do You Know . . . ?" The Jazz Repertoire in Action* (Chicago: University of Chicago Press, 2009).

Feick, Lawrence, and Linda L. Price. "The Market Maven: A Diffuser of Marketplace Information," *Journal of Marketing* 51 (1987): 83–97.

Feldman, Jamie. "Zara Accused of Demonstrating Racial Bias Toward Customers and Employees," *The Huffington Post* 25 July 2015.

Fine, Gary Alan. "Crafting Authenticity: The Validation of Identity in Self-Taught Art," *Theory and Society* 32 (2003): 153–180.

Fine, Gary Alan. "The Culture of Production: Aesthetic Choices and Constraints in Culinary Work," *American Journal of Sociology* 97 (1992): 1268–1294.

Fine, Gary Alan. *Players and Pawns: How Chess Builds Community and Culture* (University of Chicago Press, 2015).

Fischer, Claude S. "Toward a Subcultural Theory of Urbanism," *American Journal of Sociology* 80 (1975): 1319–1341.

Fischer, David Hacket . *Paul Revere's Ride* (New York: Oxford University Press, 1994).

Fish, Stanley. *Is There a Text in This Class? The Authority of Interpretive Communities* (Cambridge, MA: Harvard University Press, 1980).

Florida, Richard. *The Rise of the Creative Class* (New York: Basic, 2002).

Foer, Franklin. *How Soccer Explains the World: An Unlikely Theory of Globalization* (New York: Harper Perennial, 2004).

Fontevecchia, Agustino. "Christie's and Sotheby's Sold More Than $1.78B-Worth of Art in One Week," *Forbes* 13 Nov. 2014.

Fox, Emily Jane. "Halloween mask sales predict Obama win 60-40," *CNN Money* 23 Oct. 2012.

Frank, Robert H. and Philip J. Cook. *The Winner-Take-All Society* (New York: Free Press, 1995).

Frank, Thomas. "Why Johnny Can't Dissent," in *Commodify Your Dissent: Salvos from the Baffler,* Thomas Frank and Mat Weiland, eds. (New York: Norton, 1997).

Frederick, Jim. "The Intern Economy and the Culture Trust," in *Boob Jubilee: The Cultural Politics of the New Economy,* Thomas Frank and David Mulcahey, eds. (New York: Norton, 2003).

Freeland, Chrystia. "The Rise of the New Global Elite," *Atlantic* Jan./Feb. 2011.

Friedman, Hilary Levey. *Playing to Win: Raising Children in a Competitive Culture* (University of California Press, 2013).

Friedman, Thomas L. *Hot, Flat, and Crowded: Why We Need a Green Revolution—and How It Can Renew America,* 2nd ed. (New York: Picador, 2009).

Friedman, Thomas L. *The Lexus and the Olive Tree* (New York: Anchor, 2000).

Friedman, Thomas L. *The World Is Flat: A Brief History of the Twenty-First Century* (New York: Farrar, Straus and Giroux, 2005).

Gabler, Neal. *Life the Movie: How Entertainment Conquered Reality* (New York: Vintage, 2000).

Galanes, Philip. "It Takes Character," *New York Times* 13 Dec. 2015.

Gamson, Joshua. *Claims to Fame: Celebrity in Contemporary America* (Berkeley: University of California Press, 1994).

Gans, Herbert J. *The Urban Villagers: Group and Class in the Life of Italian-Americans* (New York: Free Press, 1962).

Gardner, Eriq. "Warner Music Group Settles Lawsuit Over Unpaid Interns," *Hollywood Reporter* 30 Jan. 2015.

Garner, Betsie, and David Grazian. "Naturalizing Gender through Childhood Socialization Messages in a Zoo," *Social Psychology Quarterly* 79 (2016): 181–98.

Gaytan, Marie Sarita. "From Sombreros to *Sincronizadas:* Authenticity, Ethnicity, and the Mexican Restaurant Industry," *Journal of Contemporary Sociology* 37 (2008): 314-341.

Geertz, Clifford. "Deep Play: Notes on the Balinese Cockfight," in *The Interpretation of Culture* (New York: Basic, 1973).

Gelder, Ken, and Sarah Thornton. *The Subcultures Reader* (London: Routledge, 1997).

Gendron, Bernard. "The Downtown Music Scene," in Marvin J. Taylor, ed. *The Downtown Book: The New York Art Scene, 1974-1984* (Princeton, NJ: Princeton University Press, 2006).

Gibbs, Nancy. "Lessons from the Spirit World," *Time* 21 August 2008, http://www .time.com/time/magazine /articles/0,9171,1834677,00.html.

Giles, Jim. "Internet Encyclopedias Go Head to Head." *Nature* 438 (2005): 900-1.

Gitlin, Todd. *The Sixties: Years of Hope, Days of Rage* (New York: Bantam, 1987).

Gladwell, Malcolm. *Blink: The Power of Thinking without Thinking* (New York: Little, Brown, 2005).

Gladwell, Malcolm. "The Coolhunt," *New Yorker* 17 March 1997: 78-88.

Gladwell, Malcolm. *The Tipping Point: How Lit le Things Can Make a Big Difference* (Boston: Back Bay, 2002).

Gluckman, Max. *Order and Rebellion in Tribal Africa* (New York: Free Press, 1963).

Godes, David, and Dina Mayzlin. "Using Online Conversations to Study Word-of-Mouth Communication," *Marketing Science* 23 (2004): 545-560.

Goel, Vindu. "Facebook Mirror's Tech Industry's Lack of Diversity," *New York Times* 25 June 2014.

Goel, Vindu. "With New Ad Platform, Facebook Opens Gates to Its Vault of User Data," *New York Times* 28 Sept. 2014.

Goffman, Erving. *The Presentation of Self in Everyday Life* (New York: Anchor, 1959).

Gramsci, Antonio. *Selections from the Prison Notebooks*, Quitin Hoare and Geoffrey Nowell Smith, eds. and trans. (New York: International Publishers, 1971).

Granoveter, Mark S. "The Strength of Weak Ties," *American Journal of Sociology* 78 (1973): 1360-1380.

Grazian, David. *American Zoo: A Sociological Safari* (Princeton, NJ: Princeton University Press, 2015).

Grazian, David. *Blue Chicago: The Search for Authenticity in Urban Blues Clubs* (Chicago: University of Chicago Press, 2003).

Grazian, David. "I'd Rather Be in Philadelphia," *Contexts* 4 (2005): 71-73.
Grazian, David. "The Jazzman's True Academy: Ethnography, Artistic Work and the Chicago Blues Scene," *Ethnologie française* 38 (2008a): 49-57.

Grazian, David. *On the Make: The Hustle of Urban Nightlife* (Chicago: University of Chicago Press, 2008b).

Grazian, David. "Opportunities for Ethnography in the Sociology of Music," *Poetics:* 32 (2004): 197-210.

Grindstaff, Laura. *The Money Shot: Trash, Class, and the Making of TV Talk Shows* (Chicago: University of Chicago Press, 2002).

Griswold, Wendy. "American Character and the American Novel: An Expansion of Reflection Theory in the Sociology of Literature," *American Journal of Sociology* 86 (1981): 740-765.

Griswold, Wendy. *Cultures and Societies in a Changing World*, 2nd ed. (Thousand Oaks, CA: Pine Forge, 2004).

Griswold, Wendy. "The Fabrication of Meaning: Literary Interpretation in the United States, Great Britain, and the West Indies," *American Journal of Sociology* 92 (1987): 1077–1117.

Griswold, Wendy. *Regionalism and the Reading Class* (Chicago: University of Chicago Press, 2008).

Griswold, Wendy. *Renaissance Revivals: City Comedy and Revenge Tragedy in the London Theatre, 1576–1980*

(Chicago: University of Chicago Press, 1986).

Grose, Jessica. "The $51 Billion Wedding Industry Toasts a Post-DOMA Bump," *Bloomberg* 28 Jun. 2013.

Gross, Daniel. "What's Wrong with Payola?" *Slate* 27 July 2005, http://www.slate.com /id/2123483.

Halle, David. *Inside Culture: Art and Class in the American Home* (Chicago: University of Chicago Press, 1993).

Hannigan, John. *Fantasy City: Pleasure and Profit in the Postmodern Metropolis* (New York: Routledge, 1998).

Hebdige, Dick. *Subculture: The Meaning of Style* (London: Routledge, 1979).

Hemingway, Ernest. *A Moveable Feast* (New York: Bantam, 1965).

Herszenhorn, David M. "Anti-Putin Stunt Earns Punk Band Two Years in Jail," *New York Times* 17 Aug. 2012

Hesse-Biber, Sharlene, Margaret Marino, and Diane Wats-Roy. "A Longitudinal Study of Eating Disorders among College Women," *Gender and Society* 13 (1999): 385–408.

Higie, Robin A., Lawrence F. Feick, and Linda L. Price. "Types and Amount of Word-of-Mouth Communications about Retailers," *Journal of Retailing* 63 (1987): 260–278.

Hirsch, Paul M. "Processing Fads and Fashions: An Organization-Set Analysis of Culture Industry Systems," *American Journal of Sociology* 77 (1972): 639–59.

Hoang, Kimberly Kay. *Dealing in Desire: Asian Ascendency, Western Decline, and the Hidden Currencies of Global Sex Work* (Berkeley, CA: University of California Press, 2015).

Hoban, Phoebe. *Basquait: A Quick Killing in Art* (New York: Penguin, 2004).

Hochschild, Arlie Russell. *The Managed Heart: Commercialization of Human Feeling* (Berkeley: University of California Press, 1983).

Hodos, Jerome. "Globalization and the Concept of the Second City," *City & Community* 6 (2007): 315–33.

Hodos, Jerome, and David Grazian. "The Philadelphia Sound," *Footnotes* July/ August 2005: 1, 7.

Hornaday, Ann. "The best movies of 2015: 'Spotlight,' "Love & Mercy,' 'Creed' make the top 10," *Washington Post* 9 Dec. 2015.

Huetteman, Emmarie. "Senate Report Says Pentagon Paid Sports Leagues for Patriotic Events," *New York Times* 4 Nov. 2015.

Hunter, James Davison. *Culture Wars: The Struggle to Define America* (New York: Basic, 1991).

Intergovernmental Panel on Climate Change. "IPCC, 2013: Summary for Policymakers," in *Climate Change 2013: The Physical Science Basis. Contribution of Working Group I to the Fifth Assessment Report of the Intergovernmental Panel on*

Climate Change (Cambridge: Cambridge University Press, 2013).

Iyer, Pico. The Global Soul: Jet Lag, Shopping Malls, and the Search for Home (New York: Vintage Departures, 2001).

Jacobs, Elizabeth. Unpublished field notes, University of Pennsylvania, 3 Oct. 2016.

James, Meg. "Viacom Agrees to Pay up to $7.2 Million to Settle Intern Lawsuit," Los Angeles Times 12 Mar. 2015.

Johnson, Steven. Everything Bad Is Good for You: How Today's Popular Culture Is Actually Making Us Smarter (New York: Riverhead Books, 2006).

Johnston, Josee, and Shyon Baumann. "Democracy versus Distinction: A Study of Omnivorousness in Gourmet Food Writing," American Journal of Sociology 113 (2007): 165–204.

Joshi, Priva. "Bollylite in America." Paper presented to the Penn Humanities Forum, University of Pennsylvania, 3 March 2009.

Joshi, Priva. Bollywood's India: A Public Fantasy (New York: Columbia University Press, 2015).

Kammen, Michael. American Culture, American Tastes: Social Change and the 20th Century (New York: Knopf, 1999).

Katz, Jack. How Emotions Work (Chicago: University of Chicago Press, 1999).

Kaufman, Jason, and Orlando Paterson. "Cross-National Cultural Diffusion: The Global Spread of Cricket," American Sociological Review 70 (2005): 82–110.

Kenney, William Howland. Chicago Jazz: A Cultural History, 1904-1930 (New York: Oxford, 1993).

Khan, Shamus R. Privilege: The Making of an Adolescent Elite at St. Paul's School (Princeton, NJ: Princeton University Press, 2011).

Klein, Bethany. As Heard on TV: Popular Music in Advertising (Surrey: Ashgate, 2009).

Klein, Naomi. No Logo: No Space, No Choice, No Jobs (New York: Picador, 2002).

Klinenberg, Eric. Fighting for Air: The Battle to Control America's Media (New York: Henry Holt, 2007).

Klosterman, Chuck. "Viva Morrissey!" in Chuck Klosterman IV: A Decade of Curious People and Dangerous Ideas (New York: Scribner, 2006).

Knopper, Steve. "Inside the Festival Economy," Rolling Stone 22 May 2014.

Kohn, Sally. "Stop Denying the Gender Pay Gap Exists. Even Jennifer Lawrence Was Shortchanged," Washington Post 17 Dec. 2014.

Kolbert, Elizabeth. Field Notes from a Catastrophe: Man, Nature, and Climate Change (New York: Bloomsbury, 2015).

Kolbert, Elizabeth. The Sixth Extinction: An Unnatural History (New York: Henry Holt, 2014).

Kosmann, Patricia. "Inditex's Unique Fast-Fashion Model Delivers More Breakneck Growth," Wall Street Journal 21 Sept. 2016.

Kozinn, Allan. "A Master's in Paul-Is-Definitely-Not-Dead," New York Times 8 March 2009: WK3.

Lachmann, Richard. "Graffiti as Career and Ideology," American Journal of Sociology 94 (1988): 229–250.

Lamont, Michele. Money, Morals, and Manners: The Culture of the French and the American Upper-Middle Class (Chicago: University of Chicago Press, 1992).

Lang, Kurt and Gladys Engel Lang. "The Unique Perspective of Television and Its Effect: A Pilot Study," American Sociological Review 18 (1953): 3–12.

Lapowsky, Issie. "Gender Bias Suit Will Soon Shine a Harsh Light on Microsoft," *Wired* 18 Sept. 2015.

Lareau, Annette. *Unequal Childhoods: Class, Race, and Family Life* (Berkeley, CA: University of California Press, 2003).

Lee, Jooyoung. *Blowin' Up: Rap Dreams in South Central* (Chicago: University of Chicago Press, 2016).

Lee, Steven S., and Richard A. Peterson. "Internet-based Virtual Music Scenes: The Case of P2 in Alt.Country Music," in *Music Scenes: Local, Trans-local, and Virtual*, Andy Bennet and Richard A. Peterson, eds. (Nashville, TN: Vanderbilt University Press, 2004).

Lehmann, Megan. "Battleship: Film Review," *The Hollywood Reporter* 11 Apr. 2012.

Leland, John. "For Rock Bands, Selling Out Isn't What It Used to Be," *New York Times Magazine* 11 March 2001, http://www.nytimes.com/2001/03/11/magazine/11SELLOUT.html?pagewanted=all.

Lena, Jennifer C. *Banding Together: How Communities Create Genres in Popular Music* (Princeton, NJ: Princeton University Press, 2012).

Levine, Lawrence W. "William Shakespeare and the American People: A Study in Cultural Transformation," in *Rethinking Popular Culture*, Chandra Mukerji and Michael Schudson, eds. (Berkeley: University of California Press, 1991).

Lieberson, Stanley. *A Matter of Taste: How Names, Fashions, and Culture Change* (New Haven, CN: Yale University Press, 2000).

Liu, Yong. "Word of Mouth for Movies: Its Dynamics and Impact on Box Office Revenue," *Journal of Marketing* 70 (2006): 74–89.

Lloyd, Richard. *Neo-bohemia: Art and Commerce in the Postindustrial City* (New York: Routledge, 2005).

Lofland, Lyn H. *A World of Strangers: Order and Action in Urban Public Space* (New York: Basic, 1973).

Long, Elizabeth. *Book Clubs: Women and the Uses of Reading in Everyday Life* (Chicago: University of Chicago Press, 2003).

Lopes, Paul D. "Innovation and Diversity in the Popular Music Industry, 1969 to 1990," *American Sociological Review* 57 (1992): 56–71.

Lu, Shun, and Gary Alan Fine. "The Presentation of Ethnic Authenticity: Chinese Food as a Social Accomplishment," *Sociological Quarterly* 36 (1995): 535–553.

MacCannell, Dean. *The Tourist: A New Theory of the Leisure Class* (New York: Schocken, 1976).

MacDonald, Dwight. "A Theory of Mass Culture," in *Mass Culture: The Popular Arts in America*, Bernard Rosenberg and David Manning White, eds. (New York: Free Press, 1957).

Maheshwari, Sapna. "Abercrombie's Preppy Police Enforce Rules for Staffers' Clothes, Internal Documents Show," *Buzzfeed* 2 May 2013.

Martin, Karin. "Becoming a Gendered Body: Practices of Preschools." *American Sociological Review* 63 (1998): 494–511.

Massey, Douglas, and Nancy Denton. *American Apartheid: Segregation and the Making of the Underclass* (Cambridge, MA: Harvard University Press, 1993).

McCarthy, Niall. "Bollywood: India's Film Industry by the Numbers," *Forbes* 3 Sept. 2014.

McCormick, Lisa. "New Fish on the Block," *Contexts* 8 (2009): 62–64.

McKibben, Bill. *Earth: Making a Life on a Tough New Planet* (New York: St. Martin's Griffin, 2011).

McKibben, Bill. *The End of Nature* (New York: Random House, 2006).

McLeod, Kembrew. "Authenticity within Hip-Hop and Other Cultures Threatened with Assimilation," *Journal of Communication* 49 (1999): 134–150.

Mead, George Herbert. *Mind, Self, and Society: From the Standpoint of a Social Behaviorist* (Chicago: University of Chicago Press, 1934).

Mead, Rebecca. *One Perfect Day: The Selling of the American Wedding* (New York: Penguin, 2007).

Mears, Ashley. "Working for Free in the VIP: Relational Work and the Production of Consent," *American Sociological Review* 80 (2015): 1099–1122.

Mears, Ashley. *Pricing Beauty: The Making of a Fashion Model* (Berkeley, CA: University of California Press, 2011).

Mendelson, Scott. "Box Office: 'Fifty Shades of Grey' Becomes 6th R-Rated Film to Top $500M," *Forbes* 5 Mar. 2015.

Meredith, Robyn. *The Elephant and the Dragon: The Rise of India and China and What It Means for All of Us* (New York: Norton, 2007).

Meyers, Jessica. "Employees: 'Hierarchy of Hotness' Rules at Abercrombie & Fitch," *Dallas Morning News*, 27 August 2008, http://www.dallasnews.com/sharedcontent /dws/dn/latestnews/stories/082708dnme tabercrombie.4027698.html.

Milgram, Stanley. *Obedience to Authority: An Experimental View* (New York: Harper & Row, 1975).

Miller, Daniel. "NBCUniversal to Settle Suit by Former Interns for $6.4 Million," *Los Angeles Times* 24 Oct. 2014.

Miller, Julie. "Hollywood Gender Discrimination Finally Receives Attention from Feds," *Vanity Fair* 6 Oct. 2015.

Miller, Laura J. *Reluctant Capitalists: Bookselling and the Culture of Consumption* (Chicago: University of Chicago Press, 2007).

Mishkind, Marc E., Judith Rodin, Lisa R. Silberstein, and Ruth H. Striegel-Moore. "The Embodiment of Masculinity: Culture, Psychological, and Behavioral Dimensions," *American Behavioral Scientist* 29 (1986): 545–562.

Mitchell, Tony. *Global Noise: Rap and Hip-Hop Outside the USA* (Middletown, CT: Wesleyan University Press, 2002).

Mooallem, Jon. "Raiders of the Lost R2," *Harper's* Mar. 2009: 62–69.

Moore, Charles J. "Choking the Oceans with Plastic," *New York Times* 26 Aug. 2014, A23.

Murphy, Cullen. "Lifosuction," *Atlantic* February 2002, http://www.theatlantic.com /doc/200202/murphy.

National Commission on Terrorist Attacks upon the United States. *The 9/11 Commission Report: Final Report of the National Commission on Terrorist Attacks upon the United States* (New York: Norton, 2004).

Neff, Gina, Elizabeth Wissinger, and Sharon Zukin. "Entrepreneurial Labor among Cultural Producers: 'Cool' Jobs in 'Hot' Industries," *Social Semiotics* 15 (2005): 307–334.

Negus, Keith. "Cultural Production and the Corporation: Musical Genres and the Strategic Management of Creativity in the US Recording Industry," *Media, Culture and Society* 20 (1998): 359–379.

O'Brien, Sara Ashley. "Twitter is Latest Tech Firm Sued for Sex Discrimination," *CNN Money* 24 Mar. 2015.

Ohmann, Richard, ed. *Making and Selling Culture* (Hanover, NH: University Press of New England, 1996).

"Olympics 2012: Your ultimate playlist," *Time Out: New York* 23 July 2012.

Orr, Christopher. "The Best Movies of 2015," *Atlantic* 18 Dec. 2015.

Pareles, Jon. "An Album Is Judged Obscene; Rap: Slick, Violent, Nasty and, Maybe Hopeful," *New York Times* 17 June 1990: sec. 4, p. 1.

Pareles, Jon. "Songs from the Heart of a Marketing Plan," *New York Times* 28 December 2008: AR1.

Parker, Ashley. "Donald Trump's Diet: He'll Have Fries with That," *New York Times* 8 Aug. 2016.

Peiss, Kathy. *Cheap Amusements: Working Women and Leisure in Turn-of-the-Century New York* (Philadelphia: Temple University Press, 1986).

Peterson, Richard A. *Creating Country Music: Fabricating Authenticity* (Chicago: University of Chicago Press, 1997).

Peterson, Richard A. "Understanding Audience Segmentation: From Elite and Mass to Omnivore and Univore," *Poetics* 21 (1992): 243–258.

Piketty, Thomas. *Capital in the Twenty-First Century*, Arthur Goldhammer, trans. (Cambridge, MA: Belknap, 2014).

Plat, Larry. "The Reincarnation of Stephen Starr," *Philadelphia Magazine* (September 2000): 82, 83.

Pollan, Michael. *The Omnivore's Dilemma: A Natural History of Four Meals* (New York: Penguin, 2006).

Postman, Neil. *Amusing Ourselves to Death: Public Discourse in the Age of Show Business* (New York: Viking, 1984).

Postrel, Virginia. *The Substance of Style: How the Rise of Aesthetic Value Is Remaking Commerce, Culture, and Consciousness* (New York: Perennial, 2004).

Pressler, Jessica. "Philadelphia Story: The Next Borough," *New York Times* 14 August 2005: Sunday Styles sec., p. 1.

Pressler, Jessica. "The Philly School," *Philadelphia Magazine*, May 2006.

Puig, Claudia. "'Fifty Shades' lacks gray matter, as well as heat," *USA Today* 12 Feb. 2015.

Putnam, Robert D. *Bowling Alone: The Collapse and Revival of American Community* (New York: Simon and Schuster, 2000).

Quinn, Jim. "The Making of Morimoto," *Philadelphia Magazine* January (2002): 72.

Qin, Amy. "Can You Say 'Hakuna Matata' in Mandarin?" *New York Times* 17 June 2016.

Radway, Janice A. *Reading the Romance: Women, Patriarchy, and Popular Literature* (Chapel Hill: University of North Carolina Press, 1991).

Rainey, Clint. "Coca-Cola Is Still Funding Pro-Soda 'Studies'," Grub Street 19 Jan. 2016.

Reed, Rex. "Rex Reed: The 10 Best Films of 2015," *Observer* 23 Dec. 2015.

Reynolds, Simon. *Generation Ecstasy: Into the World of Techno and Rave Culture* (New York: Routledge, 1999).

Rivera, Lauren A. *Pedigree: How Elite Students Get Elite Jobs* (Princeton, NJ: Princeton University Press, 2015).

Rooney, Ben. "iPhone is Back to Being the World's Top Selling Smartphone," CNN Money 3 Mar. 2015.

Rosenfeld, Michael. "Celebration, Politics, Selective Looting and Riots: A Micro Level

Study of the Bulls Riot of 1992 in Chicago," *Social Problems* 44 (1997): 482–502.

Ross, Edward. *Filmish: A Graphic Journey through Film* (London: Self Made Hero, 2015).

Roy, William G. "Aesthetic Identity, Race, and American Folk Music," *Qualitative Sociology* 25 (2002): 459–469.

Rucker, Philip, and Anne Gearan. "Hillary Clinton Talks Middle-Class Roots in Pitch to Iowa Small Business Owners," *Washington Post* 15 Apr. 2015.

Sacks, Oliver. *Musicophilia: Tales of Music and the Brain* (New York: Knopf, 2007).

Salganik, Matthew J., Peter Sheridan Dodds, and Duncan Watts. "Experimental Study of Inequality and Unpredictability in an Artificial Cultural Market," *Science* 311 (2006): 854–56.

Salganik, Matthew J., and Duncan Watts. "Leading the Herd Astray: An Experimental Study of Self-Fulfilling Prophecies in an Artificial Cultural Market," *Social Psychology Quarterly* 71 (2008): 338–55.

Sassen, Saskia. *Cities in a World Economy* (Thousand Oaks, CA: Pine Forge, 1994).

Schlosser, Eric. *Fast Food Nation: The Dark Side of the All-American Meal* (New York: Perennial, 2002).

Schor, Juliet B. *Born to Buy* (New York: Scribner, 2005).

Schor, Juliet B. *The Overspent American: Why We Want What We Don't Need* (New York: Harper Perennial, 1998).

Schuessler, Jennifer, and Dina Kraft. "Bob Dylan 101: A Harvard Professor Has the Coolest Class on Campus," *New York Times* 14 Oct. 2016.

Schwartz, Barry. "Memory as a Cultural System: Abraham Lincoln in World War II," *American Sociological Review* 61 (1996): 908–927.

Schwartz, Barry. *The Paradox of Choice: Why More Is Less* (New York: Ecco, 2004).

Schwartz, Barry. "Postmodernity and Historical Reputation: Abraham Lincoln in Late Twentieth-Century American Memory," *Social Forces* 77 (1998): 63–103.

Schwartz, Barry, and Howard Schuman. "History, Commemoration, and Belief: Abraham Lincoln in American Memory, 1945–2001," *American Sociological Review* 70 (2005): 183–203.

Schwartz, John. "Study Gauges Plastic Levels in Oceans," *New York Times*, 10 Dec. 2014.

Scocca, Tom. *Beijing Welcomes You: Unveiling the Capital City of the Future* (New York: Riverhead, 2011).

Scott, A. O. "Evil against Evil. Nobody Wins," *New York Times* 5 Aug. 2016.

Scott, A. O. "Review: In 'Fifty Shades of Grey' Movie, Sex Is a Knotty Business," *New York Times* 11 Feb. 2015.

Seabrook, John. *The Song Machine: Inside the Hit Factory* (New York: W.W. Norton, 2015).

Sey, Jennifer. *Chalked Up* (New York: William Morrow, 2008).

Shales, Tom, and James Andrew Miller. *Live from New York: An Uncensored History of Saturday Night Live* (Boston: Little, Brown, 2002).

Shenk, Joshua Wolf. *Powers of Two: How Relationships Drive Creativity* (Boston, MA: Mariner, 2015).

Shirky, Clay. *Here Comes Everybody: The Power of Organizing Without Organizations* (New York: Penguin, 2008).

Shively, JoEllen. "Cowboys and Indians: Perceptions of Western Films among American Indians and Anglos," *American Sociological Review* 57 (1992): 725–734.

Simmel, Georg. "The Metropolis and Mental Life," in *On Individuality and Social Forms*, Donald N. Levine, ed. (Chicago: University of Chicago Press, [1903] 1971).

Simon, Bryant. *Everything but the Coffee: Learning about America from Starbucks* (Berkeley, CA: University of California Press, 2009).

Simon, Richard Keller. *Trash Culture: Popular Culture and the Great Tradition* (Berkeley: University of California Press, 1999).

Smith, Lydia. "McDonald's 75th Anniversary: Top 10 Weirdest Restaurants from Windsor Castle to Guantanamo Bay," *International Business Times* 13 May 2015.

Smith, Neil. *The New Urban Frontier: Gentrification and the Revanchist City* (London: Routledge, 1996).

Solman, Paul. "How to Get What You Want from Online Dating," *PBS NewsHour* 13 Feb. 2015.

Sorkin, Michael. "See You in Disneyland," in *Variations on a Theme Park: The New American City and the End of Public Space*, Michael Sorkin, ed. (New York: Hill and Wang, 1992).

"Starbucks Wars," *Consumer Reports*, March 2007, http://www.consumerreports.org/cro/food/beverages/coffee-tea/coffee-taste-test-3-07/overview/0307_coffee_ov_1.htm.

Stempel, Jonathan. "U.S. Court approves Conde Nast $5.85 Million Intern Pay Settlement," *Reuters* 29 Dec. 2014.

Surowiecki, James. *The Wisdom of Crowds* (New York: Anchor, 2005).

Suttles, Gerald D. "The Cumulative Texture of Local Urban Culture," *American Journal of Sociology* 90 (1984): 283–304.

Taylor, John. "Word of Mouth Is Where It's At," *Brandweek*, 2 June 2003: 26.

Tepper, Taylor. "Americans Are Sinking Further Into Credit Card Debt," *Money* 9 Dec. 2015.

Thomas, Dana. *Deluxe: How Luxury Lost Its Luster* (New York: Penguin, 2007).

Thompson, Derek. "The Shazam Effect." *Atlantic* Dec. 2014.

Thompson, Derek. "Turning Customers Into Cultists." *Atlantic* Dec. 2014.

Thompson, Hunter S. *Hell's Angels: A Strange and Terrible Saga* (New York: Ballantine, 1967).

Thornton, Sarah. *Seven Days in the Art World* (New York: W.W. Norton, 2008).

Thorp, Brandon. "What's Valued in a Black Performance?" *New York Times* 21 Feb. 2016.

Tillet, Salamishah. "The Return of the Protest Song," *Atlantic* 20 Jan. 2015.

Tocqueville, Alexis de. *Democracy in America*, J. P. Mayer, ed., George Lawrence, trans. (New York: Harper Perennial, 1988).

Travers, Peter. "10 Best Movies of 2015," *Rolling Stone* 17 Dec. 2015.

Tucker, Robert C., ed., *The Marx-Engels Reader,* 2nd ed. (New York: Norton, 1978).

Underhill, Paco. *Why We Buy: The Science of Shopping* (New York: Simon and Schuster, 2009).

Veblen, Thorstein. *The Theory of the Leisure Class* (New York: Penguin, [1899] 1994).

Vega, Tanzina. "Shooting Spurs Hashtag Effort on Stereotypes," *New York Times* 12 Aug. 2014.

Virtual Worlds, Real Leaders: Online Games Put the Future of Business Leadership on Display. IBM Global Innovation Outlook 2.0 Report (2007).

Walker, Rob. *Buying In: The Secret Dialogue between What We Buy and Who We Are* (New York: Random House, 2008a).

Walker, Rob. "Enterprising," *New York Times Magazine* 28 December 2008b: 14.

Walser, Robert. "Highbrow, Lowbrow, Voodoo Aesthetics," in *Microphone Fiends: Youth Music and Youth Culture*, Andrew Ross and Tricia Rose, eds. (New York: Routledge, 1994).

Wareham, Dean. *Black Postcards: A Rock & Roll Romance* (New York: Penguin, 2008).

Wei, Junhow. "Mass Media and the Localization of Emotional Display: The Case of China's Next Top Model," *American Journal of Culture Sociology* 2 (2014): 197–220.

Weisman, Alan. *The World Without Us* (New York: Picador, 2008).

Wellman, Barry. "The Community Question: The Intimate Networks of East Yorkers," *American Journal of Sociology* 84 (1979): 1201–31.

Wherry, Frederick F. *Global Markets and Local Crafts: Thailand and Costa Rica Compared* (Baltimore, MD: Johns Hopkins University Press, 2008).

Wherry, Frederick F. "The Social Sources of Authenticity in Global Handicraft Markets: Evidence from Northern Thailand," *Journal of Consumer Culture* 6 (2006): 50–32.

Whyte, William. H. *The Social Life of Small Urban Spaces.* (New York: Project for Public Spaces, 1980).

Whyte, William Foote. *Street Corner Society: The Social Structure of an Italian Slum* (Chicago: University of Chicago Press, 1943).

Williams, Raymond. *Keywords: A Vocabulary of Culture and Society* (New York: Oxford University Press, 1983).

Williamson, Harriet. "Model Workers: The Clothes Shops That only Hire Beautiful People," *New Statesman* 18 July 2014.

Wilson, Christo. "If You Use a Mac or an Android, E-Commerce Sites May Be Charging You More," *Washington Post* 3 Nov. 2014.

Wirth, Louis. "Urbanism as a Way of Life," *American Journal of Sociology* 44 (1938): 1–24.

Witt, Susan. "Parental Influence on Children's Socialization to Gender Roles." *Adolescence* 32 (1997): 253–59.

Wohl, R. Richard, and Anselm L. Strauss. "Symbolic Representation and the Urban Milieu," *American Journal of Sociology* 63 (1958): 523–32.

Wong, Edward. "China Ranks Last of 65 Nations in Internet Freedom," *New York Times* 30 Oct. 2015.

Wright, Erik, and Joel Rogers. *American Society: How It Really Works* (New York: W.W. Norton, 2015).

X, Malcolm. *The Autobiography of Malcolm X* (New York: Ballantine, 1964).

Yuen, Nancy Wang. "Performing Authenticity: How Hollywood Working Actors Negotiate Identity." Unpublished dissertation, Department of Sociology, UCLA, 2008.

Zengerle, Jason. "The State of the George W. Bush Joke," *New York Times* 22 August 2004: sec. 2, p. 2.

Zillman, Claire. "McDonald's Wants to Open More Than 1,000 New Restaurants in China," *Fortune* 31 Mar. 2016.

Zolberg, Vera L. "Conflicting Visions in American Art Museums," *Theory and Society* 10 (1981): 103–125.

Zukin, Sharon. *The Cultures of Cities* (Cambridge, MA: Blackwell, 1995).

Zukin, Sharon. *Landscapes of Power: From Detroit to Disney World* (Berkeley: University of California Press, 1991).

Zukin, Sharon. *Naked City: The Death and Life of Authentic Urban Places* (New York: Oxford University Press, 2010).

Zukin, Sharon. *Point of Purchase: How Shopping Changed American Culture* (New York: Routledge, 2004).

Credits

Chapter 1

pp. 2-3, PeopleImages/Getty Images; **p. 5** (top left), Fin Costello/Redferns/Getty Images; **p. 5** (top right), Skip Bolen/WireImage/Getty Images; **p. 5** (middle), Estate Of Keith Morris/Redferns/Getty Images; **p. 5** (bottom left), Michael Ochs Archives/Getty Images; **p. 5** (bottom right), Archive Photos/Getty Images; **p. 7,** © Walt Disney Studios Motion Pictures/Lucasfilm Ltd./Courtesy Everett Collection; **p. 13** (left), Charles Trainor/The LIFE Images Collection/Getty Images; **p. 13** (right), Tom Copi/Michael Ochs Archives/Getty Images; **p. 14,** White Night Press/ullstein bild via Getty Images; **p. 15,** Bob Levey/WireImage/Getty Images; **p. 17,** Courtesy of the Everett Collection; **p. 18,** Kevork Djansezian/Getty Images; **p. 20,** Joe Amon/The Denver Post via Getty Images.

Chapter 2

pp. 22-23, Kevin Liles /Sports Illustrated/Getty Images; **p. 26** (left), ESB Professional/Shutterstock; **p. 26** (right), Hugh Sitton/Getty Images; **p. 28,** SUZY ALLMAN/ The New York Times/Redux; **p. 29,** "Statement by the Council of the American Sociological Association on Discontinuing the Use of Native American Nicknames, Logos and Mascots in Sport," March 6, 2007, http:// www.asanet.org/about-asa/how-asa-operates/council- statements/use-native-american-nicknames-logos-and -mascots. Reprinted with permission from the American Sociological Association. **p. 31,** John Sleezer/Kansas City Star/TNS via Getty Images; **p. 33,** Broadimage/ REX/Shutterstock; **p. 34,** A-Pix Entertainment/ Photofest; **p. 36,** JONATHAN NACKSTRAND/AFP/ Getty Images; **p. 37,** Alo Ceballos/GC Images/Getty Images; **p. 39,** Allan Grant/The LIFE Picture Collection/ Getty Images; **p. 42,** Dana Edelson/NBC/NBCU Photo Bank via Getty Images; **p. 43,** Joe McNally/Getty Images; **p. 44,** Courtesy Everett Collection.

Chapter 3

pp. 46-47, Courtesy of Adbusters, adbusters.org; **p. 49,** vario images GmbH & Co.KG/Alamy Stock Photo; **p. 50,** Contemporary Films Ltd./Photofest; **p. 52,** Warner Bros/REX/Shutterstock; **p. 53,** Adam Berry/Getty Images; **p. 56,** VCG/Getty Images; **p. 57,** Fox/Photofest; **p. 59,** G.M.B. Akash/Panos Pictures; **p. 61** (left), © Warner Bros./Courtesy Everett Collection; **p. 61** (right), © Showtime Network/Courtesy Everett Collection; **p. 64,** AP Photo; **p. 66,** John Warburton- Lee Photography/Alamy Stock Photo; **p. 67,** Everett Collection Inc/Alamy Stock Photo; **p. 68,** Irkin09/ Stockimo/Alamy Stock Photo; **p. 70,** Image Courtesy of The Advertising Archives.

Chapter 4

pp. 72-73, iStock/Getty Images Plus; **p. 76,** © Gramercy Pictures/Courtesy Everett Collection; **p. 82,** Bettmann/ Getty Images; **p. 84** (left), © Gramercy Pictures/ Courtesy Everett Collection; **p. 84** (right), Columbia Pictures/Photofest; **p. 92,** Photo by Jack Kurtz/Zuma Press; **p. 93,** John Lamparski/Getty Images; **p. 94,** REUTERS/Stephen Lam.

Chapter 5

pp. 96-97, TERRY O'NEILL/REX/Shutterstock; **p. 100,** AP Photo/Sal Veder; **p. 101,** David Dagley/REX/ Shutterstock; **p. 103,** Robert Smithson, Spiral Jetty, 1970, Great Salt Lake, Utah. Mud, salt crystals, rocks, water, 1500 feet long and 15 feet wide. Photo credit: Gianfranco Gorgoni. Collection: DIA Center for the Arts, New York. Courtesy of James Cohan Gallery, New York and Shanghai. Art © Holt-Smithson Foundation/ Licensed by VAGA, New York, NY; **p. 106,** Library of Congress; **p. 108,** Michael Putland/Getty Images; **p. 110,** Paul Hoeffler/Redferns/Getty Images; **p. 111,** Warner Brothers/Photofest; **p. 113,** JAN WOITAS/ EPA/Newscom; **p. 114,** The Advertising Archives/Alamy Stock Photo; **p. 115,** Jason Squires/WireImage/Getty Images.

Chapter 6

pp. 118-119, Walt Disney Studios Motion Pictures/ Photofest; **p. 121,** Twentieth Century Fox Film Corporation/Photofest; **p. 122,** Cindy Ord/Getty Images for Tory Burch; **p. 128** (left), Chen He/VCG via Getty Images; **p. 128** (right), Michael Tran/FilmMagic/Getty Images; **p. 130,** Frederick M. Brown/Getty Images; **p. 132,** ALY SONG/REUTERS/Newscom; **p. 134,** Photo by Hasbro, Inc. via Getty Images; **p. 135,** CBS/Photofest; **p. 138,** © Lifetime Television/Courtesy Everett Collection; **p. 140,** Scott Legato/Getty Images.

Chapter 7

pp. 142-143, Fox/Paramount/REX/Shutterstock; **p. 146,** Mark Gail/MCT via Getty Images; **p. 148,** Hulton Archive/Getty Images; **p. 151,** Paul Brown/Alamy Stock Photo; **p. 152,** JeffG/Alamy Stock Photo; **p. 154,** David Ramos/Getty Images; **p. 155,** Alberto E. Rodriguez/ WireImage/Getty Images; **p. 159,** Theo Wargo/ WireImage/Getty Images.

Chapter 8

pp. 160-161, FETHI BELAID/AFP/Getty Images; **p. 163,** Janet Ridley/Alamy Stock Photo; **p. 165,** Universal/Courtesy Everett Collection; **p. 170,** Courtesy Everett Collection; **p. 172,** Courtesy

Everett Collection; **p. 176**, TIMOTHY A. CLARY/AFP/ Getty Images; **p. 179**, Franz-Marc Frei/Getty Images; **p. 181**, Cassandra Hannagan/WireImage/Getty Images.

Chapter 9
pp. 182-183, LHB Photo/Alamy Stock Photo; **p. 187**, wendy connett/Alamy Stock Photo; **p. 189**, Richard Green/Alamy Stock Photo; **p. 190**, John Cohen/Getty Images; **p. 193**, REUTERS/Alamy Stock Photo; **p. 194**, ClassicStock/Alamy Stock Photo; **p. 195**, Courtesy of Morimoto; **p. 199**, AP Photo/Reed Saxon; **p. 202**, Jan Sandvik Editorial/Alamy Stock Photo.

Chapter 10
pp. 204-205, Shutterstock; **p. 210**, Ulrich Baumgarrten via Getty Images; **p. 211**, JEON HEON-KYUN/EPA/ Redux; **p. 213**, Andre Jenny/Alamy Stock Photo; **p. 215**, Geoffrey Kidd/Alamy Stock Photo; **p. 216**, Peter Bischoff/Getty Images; **p. 217**, © Warner Bros/Courtesy Everett Collection; **p. 218**, Indiaforte_Food/Alamy Stock Photo; **p. 219**, Collection Christophel/Alamy Stock Photo; **p. 220**, Han Myung-Gu/WireImage/Getty Images; **p. 224**, Shutterstock.

Index